ROMAN LONDON

A.D. 43–457

by

GORDON HOME

F.S.A. (Scot.)

1948
LONDON
EYRE AND SPOTTISWOODE

TO THE MEMORY OF

CHARLES ROACH SMITH

1807–1890

BY WHOSE ENLIGHTENED LABOURS, EX-
TENDED OVER MANY YEARS, DURING A
PERIOD OF PROFOUND INDIFFERENCE
TO THE ARCHAEOLOGY OF THE CAPITAL,
MUCH LIGHT WAS SHED ON LONDON
IN THE ROMAN PERIOD AND MANY
VALUABLE RELICS OF THAT AGE SAVED
FOR POSTERITY

THIS BOOK, FIRST PUBLISHED IN NOV. 1925 AND
REPRINTED IN JUNE 1926, IS NOW ISSUED IN A
COMPLETELY REVISED AND ENLARGED EDITION,
IN 1948, AND IS MADE AND PRINTED IN GREAT
BRITAIN FOR EYRE AND SPOTTISWOODE (PUB-
LISHERS) LIMITED, 15 BEDFORD STREET, LONDON,
W.C. 2, BY BILLING AND SONS LTD., GUILDFORD
AND ESHER

F3834

PREFACE TO THIS EDITION

LONDON having begun its existence as a Roman town just over nineteen centuries ago, the present time seems suitable for the production of a new and considerably revised edition of a book whose purpose is to reveal what is known of it in the four centuries when the British capital was a place of importance as the chief town of a province of the Roman Empire.

On the Continent cities of the size and consequence of Londinium have in the majority of cases preserved some relic of the Roman period above the existing ground level—an arena, a temple or a bath—whereas London can show little besides the remains of a few bastions of its town wall and two or three tessellated pavements.

Roman historians have made such scanty references to the London of their day and the inscriptions that have come to light up to the time of writing are so few, that those who endeavour to describe the chief city of Britain in the first four centuries of the Christian era are constantly obliged to restrict themselves to such cautious phraseology that the reader feels a wanderer in debatable ground with only a few distant landmarks to guide his steps. Yet it is this difficulty of seeing clearly in these dimly-lighted centuries that gives zest to the hunt for paths through the tangle of uncertainty.

Since this book was published twenty years have passed, during which there has been a fairly steady trickle of discovery brought about by the deepening of foundations when great blocks of offices have been rebuilt, and although this has added very little to the epigraphy of the Roman city, the cumulative effect of minor scraps of information has led in some instances to fairly obvious deductions. One of these, for example, is the suggestion made by the late Mr Quintin Waddington of the Guildhall Museum that about A.D. 130 there was a great fire in London. In addition, the scrappy plan of the chief basilica of the city has been completed, a second gateway in the town wall has been stumbled upon, and the position of an important thoroughfare adjacent to the basilica has been located. Another pottery site is now known and a great variety of small objects have been unearthed that throw light on the occupations and level of culture of the citizens of London.

In 1928 the Royal Historical Monuments Commission produced one of its fine quarto volumes devoted to all that has been discovered within and immediately without the city wall. Its publication was a notable landmark in the task of unveiling the earliest period of London. The committee of archaeologists that compiled this important work included the late Professor R. G. Collingwood, Dr R. E. Mortimer Wheeler, Keeper of the London Museum. Sir Alfred Clapham, Mr T. Davies Pryce, Mr Quintin Waddington, Miss M. V. Taylor, Mr William Page, Mr J. P. Bushe-Fox, and Dr Philip Norman.

In the light of the greatly extended knowledge of Romano-British archaeology that has been acquired since Professor Haverfield laid new foundations for its study some forty years ago, all available materials were searchingly re-examined by this committee. The conclusions arrived at were very lucidly discussed in sections devoted to each subject, and the volume was illustrated with ample and satisfactory thoroughness.

From these and other sources I have obtained materials for adding to and revising this book, and I am especially indebted to Mr Waddington not only for the information concerning recent finds that he has placed at my disposal, but for the suggestions he has made on reading the proofs of this new edition.

In the past there have been very few opportunities for the adequate examination of any site that has been opened down to the Roman levels of the city; in fact, nearly everything known of Roman London in the field of archaeology has been found in a haphazard manner during the laying of pipes and sewers, the boring of subways or the putting in of deeper foundations. It has therefore been impossible to obtain stratified results except in one or two instances when the Society of Antiquaries has seized a few opportunities of limited scope that have arisen. While the thousands of small objects and pottery fragments that are annually rescued from the barrows and skips of building contractors do provide a certain amount of information, their value is very much limited on account of the lack of anything better than the sketchiest chronology in regard to the layers in which they are found.

For archaeologists and historians this inability to apply modern methods to the Roman levels penetrated by the builder has resulted in a prolonged period of frustration. Site after site in the most important central area has been penetrated below the original surface of brick earth without the possibility of recording what has lain hidden in the "time-layers" that are destroyed. It appeared likely enough that this melancholy state of affairs would continue until the last square yard of the Roman nucleus of London had been broken up and lorried away, when suddenly the result of total war changed the whole outlook. Instead of piecemeal reconstruction extending over a long period, the great area north and east of St. Paul's extending almost to the Thames and the Walbrook that was burnt and shattered by German bombs will be rebuilt in one huge effort of reconstruction, for now the sirens have wailed for the last time and the great enterprise has begun, an opportunity for archaeological exploration hitherto undreamed of will present itself. Not only will the plan of a large proportion of London as it existed in the Roman period be recovered, but, in addition, a mass of other information showing the evolution of the city in the four centuries of its growth and decline will come to light through the careful examination of the contents of the successive occupation layers. That all this will be possible is due to the fact that in very few instances do the foundations of the buildings destroyed in 1941 go down more than 10 or 11 feet, which means that the strata accumulated during the Roman occupation of Britain lie undisturbed 5 or 6 feet beneath eighteenth- and nineteenth-century cellar floors. When these are broken up there must be provided for the exploratory work of archaeologists a suitable interval during which the rubble and soil accumulated in the Dark Ages can be examined before it is removed. In these upper layers are interred the secrets of more than six centuries of London's history and the solution of the long-discussed problem of continuity or destruction during the infiltration of the Anglo-Saxon conquerors of Britain.

At an average depth of 16 feet below the modern street level picks and shovels will begin to lay bare the top stratum of the Roman deposits, every foot of which will contain the long-sought-for materials that will, to expert watchers and recorders, spell out messages from the far-off years when London was the capital of a province that the central government could no longer defend. As each successive layer is uncovered and its contents examined, the pages of history will be turned backwards until the explorers in Time will stand on the soil of London's site as it was in the opening years of the Christian era.

All this is possible provided that the Government, in conjunction with the Corporation of the City of London, is prepared to discuss with the Archaeological Societies of London the ways and means for carrying out an obviously difficult but entirely possible operation. To miss the opportunity would be a disaster.

When this new source of light on the earliest centuries of London's history begins to illumine the horizon, this and all other books devoted to the subject will so quickly become out-of-date that unless fresh editions are soon forthcoming they will be as defunct as the periwig and the crinoline.

GORDON HOME.

GALASHIELS,
  November, 1947.

CONTENTS

LIST OF PLATES

LIST OF DRAWINGS, MAPS AND PLANS

Chapter I

THE BEGINNINGS OF LONDON

It is natural that Londoners and the British people generally should wish to know the age and origin of the capital city of the empire to which they belong, and it is equally natural that they should wish to be assured of its claims to a great antiquity. This desire to put the beginnings of London as far back as possible into the remote and shadowy ages, when ancestors of the British tribes described by Caesar were digging great hill-fortresses and erecting imposing stone temples, has hitherto led the majority of London's historians to lean as far as they dared towards the idea of a pre-Roman origin of the city whose dignity they desired to enhance.

Readers of these pages may therefore find it somewhat disconcerting to learn that the most recent examinations of the available evidence have produced little that points to the existence of a pre-Roman town on the site. In other words, London appears to date back no earlier than the decade preceding the occupation of Britain by the Roman legions of the Emperor Claudius in A.D. 43, and has therefore had a life extending to little more than nineteen centuries.

The site of London is, however, so pre-eminently suited to its purpose that it is difficult to explain how it could have avoided becoming at least a primitive landing-place and anchorage for the trading vessels of the first century B.C. It is certainly a fact that the conformation of Britain and the position of the Thames estuary in relation to the Continent were the governing influences that brought about the beginnings of London. There are, and have been, cities that have sprung into existence at the dictate of a single will, or of a powerful government, to achieve some special purpose. Such cities may flourish for a period, but, with the passing away of the temporary conditions that led to their establishment, they shrink, and have often disappeared from the map save as sites of antiquarian interest. Places of this type were represented in ancient Persia by Persepolis, that was simply an artificial royal centre created by Darius the Great. Alexander established numerous towns named after himself, but only one of them

13

grew to the stature of a city of the first rank. Notable examples
in Roman times are afforded by Caesarea in Palestine, and
Thamugadi (Timgad) and Volubilis in Africa. A good example in mediaeval times is Aigues-Mortes, the artificial
creation of St Louis of France. Coming to the eighteenth
century, another is found in Peter the Great's famous venture
of St Petersburg (Petrograd, now Leningrad), and in the
present century there is Canberra, the federal capital of
Australia.

Another and very common type of city is that which has
such great national importance that under civilised conditions
it endures, but hardly reaches a position of world-wide consequence. Examples of this class are Exeter, York, Bourges,
Burgos, Pavia, and Magdeburg.

The last and most important class of cities consists of those
that are so favoured by position and circumstances that so long
as commerce and industry endure they must continue to be
great centres of activity and trade. Of this type is London.

It is important, therefore, to look at its position on the map.
In the first place, it was at the point where a great estuary,
facing the Continent, narrowed to become a highway to the
interior, and it was thus inevitable that it should form the
gateway to that portion of Britain which, mainly through the
absence of mountains, was the most fertile, and was consequently the first to attain a fairly high level of civilisation.

The site thus favourably situated for commerce was likewise very happily placed centrally among three or probably
four areas of considerable fertility, viz., Essex, Hampshire,
Kent, and perhaps Hertfordshire and Buckinghamshire. The
climate has always been healthy in spite of a certain humidity,
and great extremes of temperature are rare. What is commonly accepted as the original site north of the Thames consists of twin hills well above high water mark, and formed of
deposits of terrace gravel and sand resting upon a foundation
of stiff blue clay. The gravel was covered with a layer of brick
earth, furnishing with the utmost facility the materials required
for building. The situation ensured a good water supply from
shallow wells.

The commercial and defensive advantages of the site are
very obvious, for the twin elevations lay commandingly above
the river, and, towards the land, were encircled with lower

ground, that may or may not have been water-logged in places, according to the season of the year, and was perhaps gradually changing to actual marsh as the result of slow earth movements that are referred to a little later.[1]

The two hills afforded an excellent habitable area, some 350 acres in extent. A natural wet ditch to the west was provided by the stream, later to be known as the Fleet—an English name properly applied only to the natural harbour formed by its estuary. Between the eastern and western hills ran another stream, afterwards called the Walbrook,[2] whose mouth, some fifty yards wide, provided a second and more central and protected harbour in the midst of the raised area. Yet another advantage enjoyed by the site was its command of the river over which its inhabitants could keep watch.

On the gentle slopes close to the twin hills there was ample opportunity for cultivation; beyond this arable belt the forests provided game of all descriptions, and the clearings gave pasturage for cattle and swine. In addition the river contained an abundant supply of fish, an advantage that continued down to the beginning of the eighteenth century.

These are natural conditions, but it should be pointed out that ultimately London occupied a remarkable position almost at the point where the boundaries joined of the four most important peoples of southern Britain. This also tended to foster the commercial growth of the town that became a gateway to all four regions. It would seem to furnish a parallel to the case of Rome itself, which grew up as a strategic and commercial centre at the point where Latins, Sabines, and Etruscans met.

All conceptions of pre-Roman London have been dominated by the idea of an elevated site girt about with marshes. From this impression has come the unquestionably erroneous suggestion that the original name was Llyn-din, meaning the lake fort. As long ago as 1885 Mr F. J. C. Spurrell[3] came to the conclusion, on both geological and archaeological evidence, that the land surface between London and the mouth

---

[1] Pp. 19 to 22 *infra.*

[2] Three or four of its feeders passed under the wall between Moorgate Street and Broad Street.

[3] *Archaeological Journal,* 1885, pp. 269-303; 1889, pp. 75-6; 1890, pp. 43-47 and 170. *Proc. Geol. Assoc.,* vol. xi., 1889-90, pp. 210-228.

of the Thames was several feet higher 2000 years ago. His opinions were generally endorsed by Mr William Whittaker, F.R.S.,[1] and much more strongly by Mr A. S. Kennard and Mr S. H. Warren.[2] The last two geologists considered that the London district was decidedly more elevated in pre-Roman times than it is at present. Mr Walter Johnson has, from his own observations, and a close study of his predecessors' work, decided that this difference in level was as much as from 10 to 12 feet. This important conclusion seems to be borne out by the fact that undoubted relics of the Roman period, notably in Southwark and at the Royal Albert Docks, have been discovered at places that would be 8 or 9 feet below normal high water level and sometimes even more. In Southwark, for example, Roman pottery was found just about the Ordnance datum line, that is, 12 feet 6 inches below high water mark; in some of these places the discoveries were more than 4 feet beneath this low level. As Mr Johnson very pertinently asks, can one imagine the intensely practical Romans preparing an area of forbidding bog for settlement by laboriously rearing high and massive embankments when there was plenty of good dry land available in the vicinity? In addition it has been maintained by Mr Spurrell and others that in the district below Purfleet there are no surviving banks of the Roman period, "while above that place none or but the slightest ones were needed, and no signs of any can be found."[3]

The geological evidence points to a slow, but long-continued subsidence with well-marked pauses, of which the closing stages were not attained until the Roman period was fairly well advanced. "Saxon relics," writes Mr Johnson,[4] "seem to be notably lacking where they might be expected to occur, and this absence must imply a change in the physical conditions unfavourable to human occupation."

If the level of the ground were different in the first century A.D., the tides cannot have reached so far up stream as at present. Of this Mr Johnson writes: "Since the fall from Teddington to London Bridge is fairly uniform, and averages about one foot per mile, the pre-Roman tides would be

---

[1] *Mem. Geol. Survey*, 1889, vol. i.

[2] W. Johnson, "Caesar's Ford," *Trans. Lond. and Middlesex Arch. Soc.*, 1917, p. 423.

[3] *Journ. Royal Arch. Inst.*, xlii. 269 ff.   [4] *Ibid.*, p. 426.

scarcely, if at all, felt in Chelsea Reach, and there would be virtually a non-tidal ford."[1]

This evidence seems to demolish the theory that the original site of London was in the midst of wide-spreading marshes that periodically assumed the character of a lagoon. It will doubtless take some time before the early impression, so repeatedly and often eloquently set forth by such conscientious writers as Dr Guest, J. R. Green, W. J. Loftie, and Sir Walter Besant, is entirely removed.

Given that the "lagoon" theory be untenable, then the suggested origin of the name just quoted must also be abandoned quite apart from the fact that *llyn*, as Dr Henry Bradley observes, is modern Welsh, and it is absurd to suppose that that language was spoken at London in A.D. 1. Further than this, he lays stress on the fact that a compound origin of the name Londinium (Old Celtic, Londinion) is impossible, for it has only one root and not two. This fact is quite familiar to all Celtic philologists, although it was overlooked by the

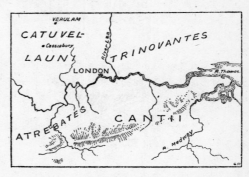

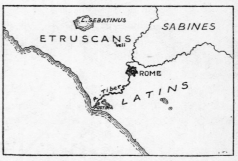

LONDON IN RELATION TO TRIBAL AREAS OF SOUTHERN BRITAIN COMPARED WITH THOSE OF ROME.

The similarity is notable.

group of writers on London just mentioned. According to Dr Bradley, the derivation is not quite certain, but three facts are beyond dispute:

1. The *Lon* is not *lindon* or *lindu* (Old Celtic =lake).
2. The *Lon* is not *longa* (O.C. =ship).
3. The *don* is not *dunon* (O.C. =fort).

[1] See *infra* in reference to Caesar's Crossing.

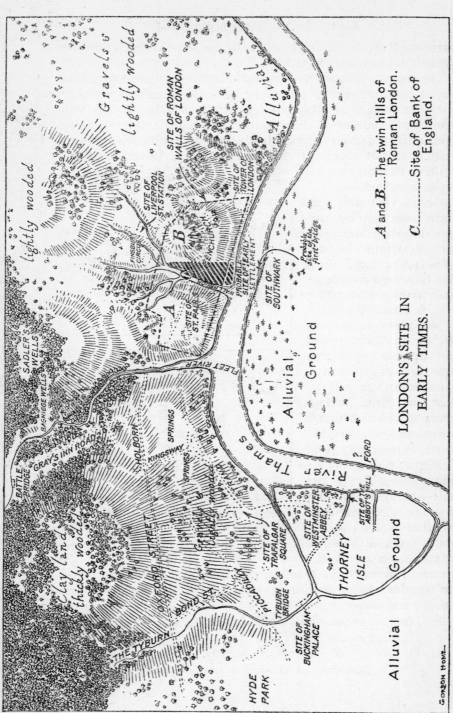

The map contains the following labels:

Gravels & lightly wooded

lightly wooded

Clay land thickly wooded

Alluvial

SADLER'S WELLS

BAGNIGGE WELLS

BATTLE BRIDGE

GRAYS INN ROAD

FLEET RIVER

FINSBURY CIRCUS

SITE OF LIVERPOOL ST. STATION

SITE OF ROMAN WALLS OF LONDON

SITE OF TOWER OF LONDON

FENCHURCH

B

A

SITE OF ST. PAUL'S

PROBABLE SITE OF EARLY SETTLEMENT

SITE OF SOUTHWARK

Probable site of the first bridge

HOLBORN

KINGSWAY

SPRINGS

SPRINGS

OXFORD STREET

STRAND

GRAY'S INN ROAD

River Thames

Alluvial Ground

FORD

?

SITE OF WESTMINSTER ABBEY

SITE OF THE ABBOT'S MILL

THORNEY ISLE

Alluvial Ground

THE TYBURN

PICCADILLY

BOND ST.

TYBURN BRIDGE

SITE OF TRAFALGAR SQUARE

SITE OF BUCKINGHAM PALACE

HYDE PARK

Alluvial

GORDON HOME

LONDON'S SITE IN EARLY TIMES.

A and B.—The twin hills of Roman London.

C ········ Site of Bank of England.

The Thames is given as it is to-day, but 2000 years ago its course must have varied considerably and its width was perhaps greater. Owing to the subsidence of the land which took place during and after the Roman period, many slight changes may have occurred. The tide may not have come higher than Westminster in the first century A.D.

He considers that Roman transcriptions of British names, whenever they can be tested, are very accurate, and if the Celtic name of London signified "lake-fort," the Romans would have rendered it Lindodunum. If, as has been suggested, it signified "ship-fort," its Roman name would have been Longodunum.

Having disposed of impossibilities, Dr Bradley comes to what he considers the only reasonable etymology. The name of London is a possessive formed from some such appellation as Londinos, derived from the Old Celtic adjective *londos*, probably meaning fierce. He carefully states that even this derivation is not absolutely certain owing to the imperfect knowledge so far acquired of Old Celtic, but that it is reasonable and the only one which is philologically possible.[1] This exposition points to the possibility that the twin hills beside the Thames formed, at some remote period, the possession and, perhaps, the stronghold of a person or family bearing the name Londinos.

The fact that London's name is a Celtic one has always been one of the most valuable weapons in the armoury of those who defend the idea of a pre-Roman origin of the place. Its value, however, is much discounted from the fact that although newly-founded Roman towns did have specially-made names given to them,[2] the Romans clearly showed an inclination towards names belonging to the locality.

The materials on which to base a decision in favour of a pre-Roman or a Roman beginning are still so scanty and there is so much to be said for either view that it is worth while to state both sides as fully as space will permit and leave the reader to form his own judgment.

Those who enjoy a hunt for the facts in such a presentation will find satisfaction in a study of the two pleadings, and those who do not can pass on to the Claudian invasion without delay. It may be here stated, however, that when, after the present war is concluded, the very extensive areas of the City are explored down to and through the Roman levels of occupation, the discoveries and revelations that are likely to be made will be of absorbing interest only to those who have

[1] *Morning Post*, Jan. 8, 1907, p. 4, col. 3. *Athenaeum*, March 7, 1908, p. 289.
[2] *Cf*. Forum Julii (Fréjus).

taken the trouble to ascertain what are the missing pieces in the puzzle that make a great search worth while.

Guest[1] held that there was no pre-Roman town on the site. He was followed and supported by J. R. Green[2] and by Loftie,[3] who cites the fourteenth-century chronicler Higden as saying that the old British road from Kent did not cross the Thames at London Bridge, but west of Westminster. The rise of Roman London was, therefore, according to these writers, due to a diversion of the road to the new bridge.

The danger of citing a mediaeval historian as an authority upon Roman conditions is self-apparent. Higden does not say that the road which touched the Thames west of Westminster was an old British track nor can he have been qualified to judge on such a point. In his day it was called Watling Street, and he is no doubt correct in saying that a branch of it crossed the Thames near Westminster. The late Professor Haverfield told Dr T. Rice Holmes that, in his opinion, there was no evidence that it existed before A.D. 43.

Dr Holmes sums up the evidence by declaring that "the notion that a British town stood on the site has the solid foundation of etymology."[4] He also observes that the advantages that attracted the traders of Rome would also have commended themselves to those of Britain.

The inhabitants of Britain at the time of Caesar's invasion were in many ways a civilised race—indeed, from the material point of view, in some respects highly civilised. This was seen by the famous Massiliot explorer, Pytheas, nearly three centuries before Caesar ran his transports ashore on the coast of Kent. He found the people of the remote promontory of Belerium (Cornwall) comparatively civilised, friendly, and ready to trade. In Kent and the neighbouring regions the inhabitants were busy agriculturists; corn was raised in abundance, and there were covered granaries in which it was thrashed and stored. The picture given by this early scientist and traveller is certainly not that of a wholly primitive people.

During the centuries which intervened between the visit of Pytheas and the invasion of Caesar there can be little doubt

---

[1] *Origines Celticae*, vol. ii. pp. 405-6.
[2] *The Making of England*, p. 117, note 1.
[3] *Archl. Journal*, vol. xxxiv. p. 165.
[4] T. Rice Holmes, *Ancient Britain*, pp. 704-5.

that some progress was made, for probably as early as two hundred years B.C. the Britons had definitely created their own coinage of gold, which must point to the existence of a relatively extensive commerce, each gold piece, with its weight ranging up to as much as 120 grains, representing a very large purchasing value, according to modern standards. The eminence to which the Britons had attained in decorative art is admirably instanced, not only in their beautiful spiral ornament, but also in the enamel with which they adorned the delicately conceived designs of their metal work. Caesar notes the solidity of their buildings, comparable with those of their kinsfolk across the Channel, and their chariots indicate that the science of the wheelwright's craft was well developed. Weaving and spinning were advanced to the point of producing tartan designs. The presence of clothing made of linen, wool, and leather properly sewn and fastened with buttons, is known from many discoveries in burials.

The Britons were experts in domestic woodwork in the form of tankards, bowls and cups, beautifully ornamented with bronze. Finally, the tribes on the coast must have developed a high level of skill in the construction of comparatively large ships, otherwise it is impossible to explain the facility of cross-channel transit noted by Caesar. It is hardly possible to conceive that an island people could fall behind the shipwrights of Armorica (Brittany), who were of the same race and spoke the same language.[1] That there was a regular sea-borne commerce carried on in these ships is testified by Caesar.[2]

Having taken this brief survey of the capacity of the Britons to establish permanent village settlements and ports, busy with the results of their industry, it is now necessary to consider the archaeological evidence that throws any light on the earliest settlements on the sites of London and Southwark.

In central London a number of pre-Roman objects have been brought to light, and in some cases their exact provenance is known, but too often there is no evidence forthcoming as to depth and relation to other datable deposits. There is thus nearly always a question of doubt as to whether an object is really pre-Roman or coeval with the early period of Roman occupation, when late Celtic implements, pottery, and ornaments would have still been in common use.

[1] Pp. 27 and 28 *infra*.   [2] *De Bello Gallico*, Book III. chap. viii.

The overlapping of archaeological periods complicates the problem and renders impossible any definite statements as to the size, importance or even the very existence of a pre-Roman London. At the same time, even making the widest possible allowance for this overlap, the number of late Celtic objects found actually within the walled Roman area is considerable. It is almost impossible to avoid the conclusion that some of this accumulation dates to the late Celtic period. It is also legitimate to make the conjecture that some, if not many, of the objects recognised as of Roman manufacture may have reached London some years before the Roman conquest, for there seem to be no legitimate grounds for rejecting Strabo's statement[1] that the Empire, as early as the reign of Augustus (43-31 B.C. to A.D. 14) was supplying Britain with small manufactured articles. He directly mentions glassware, but does not refer to pottery.

That Colchester existed at the time of the Claudian invasion has been revealed by the extensive excavations carried out in recent years. The pre-Roman site was W.N.W. of the Roman colonia, and the discoveries made in 1931[2] "showed intensive occupation for about half a century before the Roman conquest and a short time afterwards." Further digging (1938) yielded several habitation areas of the pre-Conquest period and signs of great destruction wrought by fire in Boadiccan times were particularly evident.

The paucity of relics of the Anglo-Saxon period so far found in the City area of London is very marked.[3] If archaeological discoveries have to be relied upon apart from history, it would be permissible to deduce that London was very slightly occupied by the English. Evidence of this character for the existence at London of a settlement in late Celtic times is perhaps greater than that for the unquestionable four centuries of Anglo-Saxon political domination.[4]

The case against the existence of a pre-Roman London was stated with great lucidity by Dr R. E. M. Wheeler in 1928 in

---

[1] Strabo, *Geographia*, Book IV. chap. v.
[2] *J.R.S.*, XXII, pt. 2, 1932, p. 211.
[3] *Victoria County History*, London, vol. i. p. 150, R. A. Smith, F.S.A.
[4] It is true that the Anglo-Saxon levels of London have been subjected to very much disturbance, and yet the same might be said of the pre-Roman surface of the city's site.

his introduction to the volume on Roman London compiled by the Royal Commission on Historical Monuments. It may be summarised as follows:

Of structural evidence no discoveries have so far been made. The piles that have been found embedded in the steep banks of the Walbrook were at one time attributed to a pre-Roman age, but General Pitt-Rivers, who was swayed towards the view that they had supported human habitations in prehistoric times, admitted that "Roman remains were interspersed at different levels from top to bottom throughout the peat."[1] In spite of this statement his conclusion was as follows: "Upon the whole, therefore, it appears not unlikely these piles may be the remains of the British capital of Cassibelaunus, situated in the marshes, and of necessity built on piles." The growth of this legend was arrested by the subsequent reports of Mr F. W. Reader,[2] whose evidence was entirely in favour of the Roman origin of the piles, and all excavations along the sides of the Walbrook that have since been watched have emphasised his opinion. That they are nothing more than the surviving relics of wharves and camp-sheathing built along the sides of the stream during the Roman period is sufficiently clear. Dr Wheeler disposes of the matter in his gently humorous manner in one crisp sentence:[3] "How unworthy these piles were to carry so imposing a historical superstructure has been amply demonstrated not only by Pitt-Rivers' own record, but by the consistent evidence of similar discoveries elsewhere in London."

London having so far yielded no relics of structural remains earlier than the Roman period, smaller survivals of the prehistoric periods must be examined. The pre-Roman objects of metal that have come to light are not numerous, and the fact that they are from scattered sites suggests that they may prove nothing in the nature of permanent habitation of the site in the Bronze and Early Iron Ages. There remains the evidence provided by pottery fragments.

It was considered that the only examples of London's "coarse" pottery that could with profit be brought into the discussion of the age of the site belonged to a type that is

[1] *Journal Anthropological Soc.*, V. lxxi.
[2] *Journal Royal Arch. Inst.*, LX. 137.
[3] *Royal Hist. Mons. Comm.*, vol. iii. *Roman London*, p. 20.

distinguished by a slender pedestal-base. Thirteen of this class were reviewed and the open verdict arrived at was as follows: (1) In no case could a pre-Claudian origin be considered certain. (2) In most cases there were features that definitely distinguished the group from the known prehistoric series. (3) The examples suggested "an old and native tradition in a new environment." Dr Wheeler then adds, "and to adopt the obvious course of attributing that new environment to the dominating historical event of the period (*i.e.* the Claudian invasion) is in all probability correct."

Since 1928, when these conclusions were arrived at, a con-

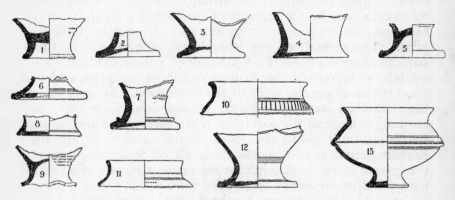

EXAMPLES OF THE BASES OF PEDESTAL-URNS DISCOVERED IN
LONDON.

Nos. 1, 2, 4 and 5 were found in 1925, 6 to 11 in 1926, 12 in 1924 and 13 in 1864.
These are examples of London's "coarse" pottery that are sufficiently datable to
assist in the discussion as to when the city was founded.

Reproduced by permission of the Royal Commission on Historical Monuments.

siderable number of fresh examples of the pedestal-urn has been found in various parts of the City; there are some forty specimens in the Guildhall Museum alone, and all have been discovered in circumstances suggesting that they were made after the Roman occupation. The conclusions arrived at by Dr Wheeler and his committee in this aspect of the discussion are thus confirmed.

From the very large quantities of fragments of red-glazed pottery known as "Samian" or "terra sigillata" that have been found in the Roman levels of the City and Southwark there are some fifteen or sixteen pieces that are classified as "Arretine" on account of their origin being traced to Arretium (the modern Arezzo) in Italy. Five of these bear the marks of potters who were producing in that town during the reign of Augustus (31 B.C. to A.D. 14), but some of these potteries continued their output for many years, long enough to bring them within two or three years of the invasion of Britain by Claudius. The pieces that are unsigned "cannot," in the opinion of Dr Pryce,[1] "be assigned to the flourishing period of the Italic industry. Typologically, they belong to the first four decades of the first century of our era. . . ."

"In summary," writes Dr Wheeler, "the geographical and archaeological evidence which can be brought to bear upon the possibility, or otherwise, of a pre-Roman London is as follows:

"(1) Occupation on a site such as this, hemmed in on three sides by forest and marsh at the head of a somewhat turbulent estuary, is unlikely to have developed far except under an influential and wealthy administration such as would attract regular overseas trade and could maintain costly communications with the hinterland. These conditions were fulfilled from the outset by the Roman régime, but in pre-Claudian times Cunobelin at Colchester could have found little use for a Thames-side port, and, if Verulam had been the deciding factor, the landing-stage and crossing would have been expected rather at Westminster than at London. Whatever influence Verulam may have had upon the early road-system, it may safely be assumed to have had little to do with the establishment of the Southwark crossing.

"(2) A small series of the earlier 'coarse' pottery from London is sufficiently reminiscent of distinctively pre-Roman type to demand special consideration. It has been found, however, that two of the fourteen or fifteen pieces in question were actually associated with Roman wares, whilst the remainder tend to suggest a Romanising tendency rather than a purely native origin. Until our knowledge of these wares becomes more exact, it is undesirable to exclude the possibility that some of the pieces may have been made rather before than after the Claudian invasion, although in every case a post-conquest date may be suspected.

"(3) The Arretine or Italic ware from London is mostly

[1] T. Davies Pryce in R.C.H.M. Roman London, p. 181.

late in type, and in quantity is at least markedly less than that recovered from the almost certainly pre-Roman but comparatively remote site of Silchester. Further, if A.D. 43 still be considered late for the importation of the Arretine, it must be remembered that soon after the conquest there was a great influx into London of traders, many of whom may be supposed to have come from districts where Arretine was still in common use, and vessels made in the previous decade or earlier would in all probability have been introduced into this country by them. Although, therefore, the Arretine pottery is at present the most admissible evidence in favour of some sort of occupation of the site of London prior to Claudius, it is far from conclusive.

"The evidence, therefore, has failed to prove the existence of a native London. But, if it has left a margin of doubt, it has at least set a limit to conjecture. It has shown clearly that we have in any case no reason for suspecting the existence of a settlement on the site more than a decade before the conquest. The whole of the 'border-line' evidence could be assigned comfortably to the latter part of the reign of Tiberius" [A.D. 14-37].

And Dr Wheeler inclines towards a final demolition of all but a small fragment of the picture of a pre-Roman London in his concluding statement on the matter. "On all grounds," he writes, "it must be admitted that, whilst the possibility of some pre-Claudian occupation of the site of London cannot yet be finally dismissed, there is at present no valid reason for supposing that London existed prior to A.D. 43."

From the foregoing discussion it is obvious that the fresh light that will be shed upon the problem when extensive uncovering of the virgin soil of London's "blitzed" areas takes place will be of absorbing interest.

Chapter II

LONDON FROM CAESAR'S INVASION TO THE CONQUEST OF BRITAIN
BY CLAUDIUS

It was midway in the last century of the pagan era that Britain came definitely into the ever-widening circle of Roman influence. By political and cultural ties, as well as racial kinship, the Britons—at least those of the south-east—were closely connected with the tribes of northern Gaul. There were Atrebates in Britain no less than in Gaul, and it is beyond question that the former were a division of the continental stock. The Belgic community in Hampshire and Wiltshire was obviously founded by a combined expedition sent from Gaul by the whole confederacy of the Belgae whom Caesar notes as being the most warlike and virile of the Celts of his time. The Atrebates in Berkshire, also of Belgic origin, appear to have separated themselves from the main body of adventurers, and established themselves quite independently on the southern confines of the Thames. There can be little doubt that the Catuvellauni, who created the only approach to a British Empire before the Roman Conquest, were an off-shoot of the Catalauni of the Marne (about Châlons). This tribe was probably not Belgic at all, neither were the Parisi, who located themselves on the Yorkshire coast, but they had nevertheless continental affinities, and probably belonged to an earlier wave of migration.

Political influence also was comparatively close, for Caesar[1] says that Diviciacus,[2] King of the Suessiones (about Soissons) had, at a slightly earlier period, established some sort of hegemony over part of Britain; it was probably limited to the tribes south of the Thames, and perhaps restricted to those of Belgic origin.

Elsewhere Caesar writes of the agricultural and pastoral wealth and the great fertility of south-eastern Britain. He also lays stress[3] upon the dense population, the thickly studded

[1] *De Bello Gallico*, Book II. chap. iv.

[2] This name has commonly been misspelt Divitiacus.

[3] *De Bello Gallico*, Book V. chap. xii. "Hominum est infinita multitudo creberrimaque aedificia fere Gallicis consimilia, pecoris magnus numerus" ="The population is extremely dense; buildings [farmsteads or villages] almost exactly like those of the Gauls are very frequent; livestock are very numerous."

settlements, and the quantities of cattle, and so far as can be judged by his laconic narrative, these conditions prevailed right up to the Thames and beyond.

Caesar therefore, very early in his operations in Gaul, discovered that the island across the Channel was an important factor in Gallic politics. It is not clear whether there were British auxiliaries in the Belgic armies that resisted the Romans in 57 B.C., but in Book IV. Caesar distinctly states that in almost all the campaigns that he had waged up to 55, the Gauls had received aid from their British friends[1] and trading associates.

It is worth while to mention here that this trade implied a very considerable number of vessels, and that some of them must have been of relatively large size—a condition entailed by the stormy and dangerous passages frequently made between the rocky coast of Brittany and the Solent or the Thames. Opinions must differ as to their precise dimensions, but Caesar states: 1. That their sides were of oak and a foot in thickness;[2] and 2. That they were too lofty to be boarded from the decks of the Roman war galleys; 3. He also lays stress upon their very solid construction and the extensive use of iron bolts and nails. Vessels of such a character could scarcely have been of less than 200 tons burden, and it should also be noted that to convey a force of about 10,000 men, only eighty of these ships were necessary, that is to say an average of over 120 per vessel, excluding the Gallic seamen.[3] Not only were the ships of relatively large dimensions and considerable draft, but they were also sufficiently numerous along the Gallic coast for Caesar to collect ninety-eight at very short notice. All this points to a notable volume of cross-channel commerce, Caesar definitely stating that the vessels were used in trade with Britain.[4] No difficulty in the way of transport would have

---

[1] *De Bello Gallico*, Book IV. chap. xx.

[2] *De Bello Gallico*, Book III. chaps. xiii and xiv.

[3] The Elizabethan war galleon carried one man to each 2 tons; *e.g.*, H.M.S. *Revenge* was a vessel of about 550 tons, and her crew was 260, excluding captain and servants. The standard of manning in Nelson's day was nearly the same. In regard to transports, it may be observed that after his victory at Oporto in 1809, Wellington wrote to the Admiralty for transport for 2000 prisoners of war, at the rate of 2 tons per man. The calculation given above shows only about 1⅓ tons per man. These Gallic vessels may have averaged considerably more than 200 tons.

[4] *De Bello Galico*, Book III. chap. viii.

been experienced in carrying ample assistance from one side of the Channel to the other.

It very quickly appeared to Caesar a matter of prime importance to cut off at its source this stream of reinforcement to his antagonists in Gaul. His first step was a reconnaissance in force in the summer of 55 B.C.,[1] with a view to discovering the nature of the coast and the quality of the resistance he was likely to encounter. Having obtained the necessary information, he withdrew, and at once proceeded to make preparation for an invasion on a large scale. This he carried out in the following year with a force of five legions, a proportion of light infantry, and at least 2000 cavalry, transported on a flotilla of some 800 vessels, of which 600 were shallow-draft barges specially built during the winter by the industrious legionaries, of course assisted by local labour.

On this occasion he was met by strenuous opposition; several of the tribes of the south-east being banded together under Cassivellaunus, King of the Catuvellauni. The landing-place, according to all probability, was between Deal and Sandwich, and the march westward, after the first local resistance had been overcome and the fleet secured, was almost certainly[2] via Canterbury and Rochester, or else along the Pilgrims' Way, that crossed the Medway below Aylesford. Caesar dismisses the story of this march of over 70 miles in a single sentence, and, although he must have passed over the Medway and the Darenth, and in spite of the fact that he emphasises the fertility and the dense population of the country, he mentions the name of no single village, stream, or locality.

At the end of this difficult march, during which it had been steadily harassed by the guerilla tactics of the Britons, the Roman army reached the Thames and forced a passage. The information given by Caesar is as follows:—

1. "The chief command and direction of the war was given by general vote to Cassivellaunus, whose territories the river Thames separates from the maritime tribes about 80 [Roman] miles from the sea."

[1] T. Rice Holmes, *Ancient Britain*, p. 496, refers to a slight but earlier reconnaissance that took place at Caesar's orders in 57-56 B.C. He writes: ". . . I can only suppose that Crassus, when he was in Brittany in 57-56 B.C., was directed by Caesar to visit and report on the tin-producing districts of the British Isles."

[2] *Ibid.*, p. 344, Rice Holmes thought that this was "morally certain."

2. "Having ascertained their plans, Caesar led his army to the river Thames into the territories of Cassivellaunus. This river can be forded at one place only and that with difficulty."

3. "On reaching the river, he [Caesar] observed the enemy drawn up in great force on the opposite bank. The bank was defended by pointed stakes planted along it, and stakes of the same description were fixed under water and covered by the flowing stream. Having ascertained these facts from prisoners and deserters, Caesar ordered forward his cavalry, and directed the legions to follow rapidly close in rear. But the troops rushed on with such speed and impetuosity, although only their heads showed above the water, that the enemy were quite unable to withstand the combined charge of the legions and horsemen. They abandoned the banks and took to flight."—Book V, chaps. ii and xviii.

This is the bare record of essential facts, in which all place-names are omitted, possibly on account of a certain desire on the part of Caesar to be brief in describing his British campaign. It appears to suggest the possibility of the Proconsul having realised that, notwithstanding the success obtained, there were few of the spectacular results that might have been anticipated in Roman society and official circles. The grey-green island of Britain produced little of real "colour" to appeal to the populace.[1] From wherever the Medway was crossed, Caesar would have been compelled to direct his march towards the Thames by some well-worn trade route, that would have existed in such a thickly populated and chariot-using part of the country. It is almost certain that he came by a track later converted into the arterial Roman road now called the "Watling Street." On the high ground west of the Medway there would be no difficulty in joining that route from the south, supposing that Caesar had been obliged to avoid the direct passage where Rochester now stands. Once upon the main track, the Thames became visible on the right

---

[1] Cassius Dio asserts that Caesar's invasion was neither an advantage to Rome nor to Caesar, but it must be remembered that, apart from his bitter bias, the earlier portions of his history (he wrote nearly three centuries after the events) may be classed as somewhat careless compilations.

flank fairly continuously all the way until it lay across the line of march. At high tide the aspect of the river would have been that of a wide estuary, even allowing for the subsequent subsidence of the ground noted by geologists, any marshy zones on either shore being partially submerged twice daily. Therefore, on coming over Shooter's Hill to Greenwich, Caesar saw the shimmering estuary, backed by the soft green hills of the country of the Trinovantes (now Essex), narrowing as it approached the high ground of London, and realised that he was nearing the point at which the British highway crossed the river.

If an infant London existed at this time he saw all there was to see of it. The gravelly bluffs backed by wooded hills would then have appeared broken by the shallow mouth of the stream afterwards called the Walbrook, with the western face protected as with a great wet ditch by the rapidly flowing stream subsequently dignified with the name Fleet River.

A small amount of shipping might have been lying in the Thames itself or in the convenient pocket formed by the Walbrook, for if the site of London had at this time developed primitive landing staithes for sea-borne trade there would have been some of the solidly-built Gallic type of merchant vessels anchored in the main stream or moored to the banks of the natural harbour. In any case it is possible to conceive the presence of fishing boats and coracles, for, as already mentioned, down to the Stuart period and later fish were plentiful in the Thames.

Along the east side of the Walbrook there may have been the most simple and rude types of wattle and daub dwellings, and even a few strongly built timber buildings, for such construction would have naturally come about as soon as the necessity arose for storing more fragile or perishable imports.

Whatever existed on the site at this time would have been seen by Caesar, but a small trading port, protected perhaps by little but a shallow ditch and the type of stockade that would provide protection against wild animals and pilferers, would be of very minor interest from a military standpoint, and he certainly made no reference to it in his account of the campaign. It has been suggested by General Pitt Rivers,[1] T.

[1] *Anthropological Review*, vol. v. p. lxxvii.

Lewin[1] and Sir Laurence Gomme[2] that the *oppidum* of Cassivellaunus was London and that it is inconceivable that a general of any capacity should have left in his rear an untaken stronghold. Sir Laurence Gomme even goes to the extent of saying that "it seems irresistible that London and not Verulam was the stronghold of Cassivellaunus."

Certainly Caesar's silence as to the reduction of London is a fact, but it is also a fact that, from his own description, he must have occupied or captured numerous British settlements on his way from the coast, yet still he is silent. As a trading centre it is more than likely that no attempt would have been made to defend it against the overwhelming force which its inhabitants could have seen with their own eyes approaching along the south bank of the Thames. Further than this, Caesar carefully states[3] that he strictly prohibited his soldiers from plundering and misconduct among the Trinovantes whose western boundary may have been the river Lea, that is, immediately east of London. The fact that he issued this special order suggests the possibility that he crossed that stream into the territory of these new allies.

A glance at the map will show that the large Roman army with its cavalry and its skilled intelligence officers had made practically a complete circle round the site of London at a very short distance from it. And yet Caesar had to be informed by the Trinovantes of the nature and position of the great stronghold of their enemy crowded with human beings and flocks and herds. To suggest that a great general, with able officers and a veteran army, had not by this time become aware of a very strongly fortified refuge within a mile or two of his outposts is a plain absurdity.

The refuge of the southern Catuvellauni, therefore, cannot have been London. A careful study of the statements made by Caesar and the topography of the country immediately north of the Thames lead to the conclusion that the neighbourhood of Verulam (St Albans) has the strongest claim to be the site. Sir Charles Oman considers that there is very little doubt on the subject.[4] Dr Rice Holmes is of the opinion that "more can be said for Verulam than for any other [place]

---

[1] *Archaeologia*, vol. xl. pp. 65-6.   [2] *London*, p. 23.
[3] *De Bello Gallico*, Book V. chap. xxi.
[4] *England before the Norman Conquest*, p. 48.

. . . but its identity with the *oppidum* in question has not been proved."[1]

The fog of uncertainty that formerly baffled historians in attempting to fix the scene of the defeat of Cassivellaunus has to a great extent disappeared since 1933, when Dr Wheeler published the results of his field-work carried out in the neighbourhood of St Albans. It is now possible to get a glimpse of what was happening in that part of Hertfordshire held by the Catuvellauni during the first century B.C. The provisional results of spade work between the rivers Lea and Ver have been illuminating and surprising. It appears that in the first half of the first century B.C. there was an important Belgic *oppidum* close to a ford a mile or two from Wheat-hampstead in the upper portion of the Lea Valley. "This," says Dr Wheeler, "is more likely than any other known site to have been the headquarters of Cassivellaunus at the time of the Caesarian invasion."[2] It was also found that at this time the country lying between the Lea and the Ver was to a considerable extent delimited by a valley-dyke of imposing dimensions that would provide a political boundary as well as a barrier to cattle driving. During the next half-century, a period of remarkable prosperity for the Belgic tribes of south-east Britain, two settlements were thrown out from the Wheat-hampstead city stronghold, one north-east to Welwyn and the other south-west to Verulam. There, on the hill site now known as Prae Wood, was established the *oppidum* that grew as its parent at Wheathampstead diminished. The new Belgic town on the Ver became the seat of tribal royalty for a time and then, a generation later, was transferred to the seaward end of the defensive line that led north-eastwards to Camulodunum (Colchester). There, in A.D. 43, the army of Claudius found it fully established. It was after the Roman invasion that the prehistoric hill-site was abandoned and Verulamium was established beside the Ver just below and there it grew so rapidly that it was honoured with the important Roman rank of *municipium*—perhaps the only town in Britain to gain that proud distinction.

Coming back to the moment when the army had reached the Thames, the position of the ford that it forced has to be

---

[1] T. Rice Holmes, *Ancient Britain*, p. 702.
[2] *Antiquity*, vol. vii. March, 1933, p. 32.

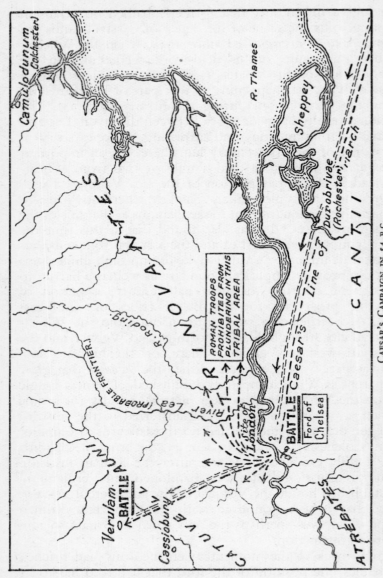

CAESAR'S CAMPAIGN IN 54 B.C.

His advance from the landing-place in Kent is shown by the dotted line. The battle at the crossing of the Thames, which Caesar describes, is shown as having occurred at Chelsea or Battersea, where large numbers of weapons and many British and Roman skulls have been found on the northern side of the river bed. The battle site indicated at Verulam appears from Dr Wheeler's discoveries five miles to the north-west to have been near Wheathampstead.

decided seeing that no place is mentioned by name. Caesar was definitely aiming at the territory of Cassivellaunus, and it is to be assumed that a fairly well-marked trackway led across the Thames into that part of the country. When Caesar says that the river could only be forded at one point, and that with difficulty, he doubtless intended to convey that there was only one ford available within his circumscribed scope of operations. That other fords existed higher up the course of the Thames must have been known or guessed, but to reach them would have involved the risk of entangling the army in marshy, wooded and intricate country that would have laid the marching columns open to the attacks of the light-armed Britons.

Where, therefore, was this one ford suitable for Caesar's purposes? The candidates are:

(1) Halliford (Cowey Stakes),[1] (2) Sunbury,[2] (3) Kingston,[3] (4) Petersham,[4] (5) Brentford,[5] (6) Chelsea,[6] and (7) Westminster.[7]

To reach the first two would have entailed a flank march through the low-lying riparian country that is more or less continuous as far as Staines, and would have furthermore involved the passage of at least four troublesome streams meandering through thickets and swamps. The same conditions apply more or less to Kingston and Petersham and even to Brentford, although the distance was shorter and the number of streams to negotiate fewer.

For Halliford and Sunbury there is no evidence at all except that for the first there is a shadowy tradition recorded or perhaps originated by Camden and the fact that its name does indicate a passage. Sunbury was a guess by Napoleon III. and his scientific assistant on "information" obtained from local boatmen. Kingston is also a guess, this time by a German.

---

[1] Camden's *Britannia*, vol. i. p. 168. Given as Coway. Guest, *Origines Celticae*, vol. ii. pp. 384-5, 388, 391-2.

[2] Napoleon III. (General Stoffel), *Hist. de Jules César*, ii. p. 191.

[3] Von Göler, *Caesars gall. Krieg*, p. 155. W. H. Black, *Archaeologia*, vol. xl. pp. 51-2.

[4] Manning and Bray's *Hist. of Surrey*, vol. ii. p. 760.

[5] Camden's *Britannia*, vol. i. p. 329. *Jour. of Brit. Arch. Assoc.* O.S., xvi. p. 135. Montagu Sharpe, *Bregant-forda and the Hanweal*, pp. 1, 22-7.

[6] "Caesar's Ford," Walter Johnson, F.G.S., 1917. Maitland's *Hist. of London*, vol. i. p. 8. *Jour. of Brit. Arch. Assoc.*, N.S., vol. iii. p. 102.

[7] *Gentleman's Magazine*, vol. xxvi. pp. 256-7.

Petersham may be set down as another English guess. The position is just below Ham House. Local inhabitants state that this ford could be used at the end of the last century and that at times the water only reached to the knees. This need not, however, be taken as a guide to conditions existing two thousand years ago.

Brentford is one of the places of passage for which some material evidence can apparently be produced. The remains of a line of stakes that once extended for about two miles between the mouth of the Brent and Isleworth were discovered by the Thames conservancy. These, it has been suggested, may be the stakes planted by Cassivellaunus that Bede[1] mentions (on hearsay naturally) as being "as thick as a man's thigh and cased with lead."[2] The last piece of information demonstrates clearly enough that such stakes were not planted for military purposes by the Catuvellaunian king. Can anyone imagine how, in an emergency, nearly two miles of thick stakes could have been protected with lead, the quantities required for the purpose being prodigious and the time and labour involved proportionately great? Further than this, no military advantage was to be gained by the leaden sheathing.

The presence of the lines of stakes at Brentford led Sir Montagu Sharpe to claim that point as the scene of Caesar's crossing, and he advanced various theories in support of his contention. One of these was "that the first practical means of crossing this barrier [the Thames] was by the ford at Brentford, the next being 50 miles up stream at Wallingford," but Sir Montagu ignored the fact that there are at least four fords between Brentford and Chertsey. Secondly, he stated that "on the Middlesex [=Brentford] ford converged therefore the principal chariot or trackways for miles around." In support of this statement there appears to be no evidence. On the south side of the river no early roads leading to Brentford have so far been discovered, and if the Watling Street represents the pre-Roman way to Verulamium, this is directed to a point between Chelsea and Westminster. Even the fact that the great Roman thoroughfare to the west passed through Brentford may be explained by the circumstance that in laying out a road from London that was to cross the river at Staines,

[1] *Hist. Ecclesiastica*, Liber I. cap. ii.
[2] One of the stakes is preserved in Ealing Public Library.

the Kew-Brentford bend must needs be touched. The loop comes sufficiently far to the north to force the Roman road to make an obtuse angle at this point. Three other contentions made by Sir Montagu seem to be without the support of any evidence. The presence of the stakes at Brentford appears to be explained by the necessity for protecting the banks that has existed for a very long time. On the north side where the piles are found, the bank being on the outer curve receives the impact of the current and is thus in need of artificial protection. But making allowance for this, and for the finding there of bronze or other weapons, it is difficult to set aside the fact of the obvious convergence of the known early roads upon the fordable points at Chelsea and Battersea. And, in addition, it should not be forgotten that two millenniums ago the land surface about Thorney Isle and the two places above it just mentioned was so much higher than it is to-day that these reaches of the Thames were either non-tidal or not far short of that condition.

In connection with the theory of the passage of the Thames at Brentford by Caesar's army it may be mentioned here that in 1929 the remains of a timber hut or pile dwelling of the Roman period were found on the Middlesex shore of the Thames at Brentford. They were discovered beneath an accumulation of mediaeval and later material.[1] The decayed stumps of piles upon which have been built theories of the defences put up by Cassivellaunus may have belonged to structures of the type found by the field-workers who explored the river bed under the directions of Dr Wheeler.

The last two fords on the list are those of Chelsea and Westminster, and as they are only a mile and a half apart they may be treated as one. Assuming that Verulamium and other places in that direction were of some importance and required a means of communication with the ports of East Kent, Chelsea or Westminster would be far more favourable points for the connecting road to pass the Thames than any other at a time when there was no bridge-building. That there was a ford or ferry somewhere between Chelsea and Westminster in mediaeval times is fairly well proved by the reference to the crossing of the Thames "west of Westminster" that is made

[1] Report by R. E. M. Wheeler in *Antiquity*, iii., 1929, pp. 20-32.

by Higden, the fourteenth century chronicler.[1] If this existed in Roman times it must mean that the course of the Watling Street from the north-west was continued in a fairly straight line to the river opposite the roadway known as Stangate. In this case the great pre-historic trunk route from Kent into the Midlands would have crossed the Thames to the west of London, necessitating a deflection of the route in Roman times in order to reach the bridge.

There is no doubt whatever as to the existence of fords in

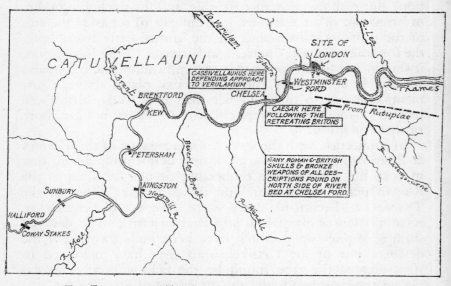

THE FORDS OF THE THAMES BY WHICH CAESAR MIGHT HAVE CROSSED.

Besides the seven indicated there may have been an eighth at London itself, just below the present London Bridge and, roughly, opposite the Customs House.

Chelsea reach, and there, as at Westminster, a stream flows in from the north. These are shown on the accompanying map. At Chelsea there have been at least two fords that exist in some form to-day in spite of the removal of much ballast from the bottom.

In the study of this problem, the physiographical changes in the valley of the lower Thames, already discussed, have much bearing on the subject. The salient point is that if these

[1] *Polychronicon*, Bk. II. cap. 46.

modifications took place—and there seems little reason to
doubt them—the tide would have almost, if not entirely, exhausted its force by the time it reached Chelsea, and such a
condition would no doubt increase the importance of a
ford at that spot. The same conditions would more or
less apply to Westminster, but the theory of a ford at that
place lacks adequate support.

Archaeological evidence is
almost entirely wanting at all
the fords that have been discussed with the exceptions of
Brentford and Chelsea. In
regard to the first, the age of
the stakes cannot be sufficient
to carry them back two thousand years. It is even possible
that they are not earlier than
the eighteenth century when
(in 1775) the Corporation of
London took measures to
protect the banks of the
Thames at such places as
Richmond and Teddington.
These, according to Sir M.
Sharpe, have already disappeared while those at Brentford are in excellent preservation, so that the natural inference is that they are of even
more recent date. In any case,
allowing that the Brentford
"palisading" was of considerable antiquity, it seems quite

BRONZE SHIELD OF THE IRON AGE
FOUND IN THE THAMES AT BATTERSEA
OR CHELSEA.

(*British Museum.*)

impossible that the portion not perpetually submerged could
have survived the destructive agencies operating throughout
twenty centuries.

Coming to the only remaining archaeological evidence,
there has been found at Chelsea ford testimony of a remarkable character. When the Chelsea Suspension Bridge was
being built in 1854-5 there were discovered in the river bed a
large quantity of British and Roman relics lying in utter con-

fusion in a manner indicating a desperate conflict. They included human skulls of two distinct types—British and Roman;[1] a number of British objects, including weapons, the sole of a Roman military boot, together with a spear-head and that of a javelin—both Roman. The beautiful enamelled bronze shield, that is one of the finest treasures of this period in the British Museum, was brought to light in the same place in the following year, and as all these finds were quite accidental, it might be reasonably inferred that the river bed at this point holds a great deal more than has been dredged up.

An interesting feature of this discovery was the fact that the bulk of the remains occurred from the Middlesex shore towards midstream — where one would expect to find them if there were a fight at this point in shallow water between one body of troops endeavouring to cross in face of opposition from another force defending the northern bank.

Reviewing the evidence with Caesar's account of his operations before one, there is nothing that militates against the suggestion that he crossed the Thames at Chelsea, while the whole of the archaeological evidence existing points to this place. The early roads, as far

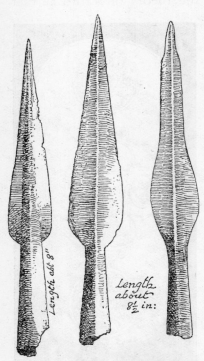

EXAMPLES OF IRON SPEAR-HEADS DISCOVERED IN THE THAMES AT BATTERSEA OR CHELSEA.

They were among many brought to light on the northern side of the bed of the Thames where large numbers of Roman and British skulls were found in great confusion, suggesting the results of a conflict.

as one can obtain any hints of their direction, would appear to point to a passage in this neighbourhood, but it might further be noted that if the land were higher and drier in 54 B.C. than it became some centuries later it is not

[1] *Jour. Brit. Arch. Assoc.*, 1857, vol. xiii. pp. 237-40.

necessary to suppose that Caesar was tied to any particular track.

In any case, wherever the ford may have been, Caesar safely negotiated the passage of the Thames. At this juncture he was met by envoys from the great tribe of the Trinovantes (Essex and part of Hertfordshire and Suffolk), who had been unwillingly brought into the defensive league by Cassivellaunus, after a war in which their king had fallen. His son Mandubracius had already taken refuge with Caesar, and the tribe now requested that their legitimate sovereign might be permitted to return. This request Caesar promptly granted, exacting in exchange supplies for his army. Hostages were given and his requisitions promptly fulfilled. A useful inference may be made as to the agricultural wealth of Essex two thousand years ago from the ease and rapidity of the execution of this condition, since at least 25,000 men and some 5000 horses had to be fed. Several small local tribes also submitted. They were the Cenimagni, the Segontiaci, the Ancalites, the Bibroci, and the Cassi. The last name is perhaps to be associated with Cashiobury Park close to Watford.

These deserters from the British cause informed the Roman general that a great tribal "oppidum" of Cassivellaunus,[1] crowded with human beings and livestock, was not far distant from his camp. This gave Caesar a welcome opportunity for dealing a decisive blow. He therefore immediately marched thither and stormed the fortified refuge, capturing the flocks and herds and a great number of prisoners.

The victory produced the desired effect, especially as the attack of the Cantii on his naval base in Kent had also been defeated. Cassivellaunus made overtures for submission and Caesar, who, as he himself says, was anxious to return to Gaul, imposed terms that he trusted would settle the British question for some time to come. The British king was to pay annual tribute to Rome, to keep the peace with the Trinovantes and give hostages.

During this last phase of his operations Caesar was, without doubt, within easy reach of whatever may have existed on the site of London. It is quite certain that he marched into Essex, for he mentions the issuing of an order to the army to refrain from all acts of indiscipline that might cause loss and resent-

[1] See p. 33 infra.

ment among the Trinovantes. A better site than London for an advanced base while operating north of the Thames could hardly be found, and although it may be thought a bold conjecture, it is at least possible that it was Caesar's engineers who built the first semi-permanent bridge over the river at this point. When one considers the prodigious rapidity with which he had bridged the Rhine[1] in the previous year, there can be no reasonable objection to his having done the same at London, where the conditions were very much easier, *i.e.* a river of less than half the width, with an infinitely smaller volume of water to encounter. The very expert engineers of the Roman army would not, with their ripe experience, have regarded the task as a really formidable one. While it is true that Caesar makes no reference to his bridging the Thames, such work must have been a commonplace of his campaigning. He only describes the building of his great Rhine bridge because it was an operation of unprecedented magnitude, carried out with great speed under exceptional difficulties.

The advantages of even the most temporary form of bridge as compared with a ford are so manifold and so obvious that it is unnecessary to dwell upon them. It might be urged that Caesar would not have undertaken any such semi-permanent construction for the needs of a brief campaign. Against such a contention, however, may be placed the fact that the great bridge over the Rhine, just mentioned, was built simply because, as Caesar says, it was not consonant with the dignity of the Roman nation[2] to pass its army across in boats, and having fulfilled its purpose, this remarkable example of Roman military engineering was destroyed after standing for only eighteen days.[3]

Summing up the probabilities it appears a reasonable suggestion that the first pile bridge erected in London was the work of Caesar, and if there were no particular reasons for its destruction on his leaving the country, it may well have been left standing. Far from there being such reasons for demolition, there suggest themselves grounds for its preservation.

---

[1] *De Bello Gallico*, Book IV. chap. xviii. Caesar states that the bridge over the Rhine was completed within ten days after the commencement of the preparation of materials.

[2] *De Bello Gallico*, Book IV. chap. xvii.

[3] *De Bello Gallico*, Book IV. chap. xix.

The advantage, from a military standpoint, of having a roadway across the Thames in case of the possibility of another campaign would have been apparent to a man of Caesar's farsighted vision. Who can say that, had he not been deterred by the uprising in Gaul that began in the ensuing winter, he would not have returned to complete the conquest of Southeast Britain? As regards the maintenance and protection of the structure he would have had an easy means at hand in the presence of the friendly Trinovantes whose territory practically touched London. It would be manifestly a case of shutting the eyes to probabilities to deny that Caesar made any such arrangement, for, as Mommsen[1] long ago pointed out, Caesar kept silence as to his political arrangements in Gaul and may well have done likewise in Britain. Secondly, a bridge would have appealed to the trading classes on both sides of the Channel, and it is quite likely that influential merchants would have appealed to Caesar to allow the preservation of a structure so useful for commercial operations. Lastly, a bridge flung across one of the greatest rivers of Britain would be a continual reminder in the absence of the Eagles of what Rome could do.

Having received the submission of Cassivellaunus, Caesar returned to the coast with his prisoners and spoil, and Britain saw him no more although his ten greatest years were yet to come. There has been much debate as to whether the tribute imposed upon the Britons was paid or not. It is customary to suggest that it was either immediately or fairly soon discontinued. Sir Charles Oman, who holds moderate views on the subject, inclines to think that no payments were made after 52 B.C. when all Gaul blazed into revolt under the leadership of Vercingetorix. Against this it should be remembered that the crisis quickly passed, and that Caesar still held the hostages, whose lives would have been in jeopardy had the stipulated *vectigal* not been forthcoming.

The use of this word *vectigal* raises a suspicion that the annual payment required by Caesar may have been calculated on the volume of trade between Britain and Gaul. It is noteworthy that he writes of it as levied on Britain as a whole and not upon the defeated Cassivellaunus. When, a little over half a century later, Strabo[2] refers to the island, he says that it paid

[1] *Hist. of Rome*, Book V. chap. vii., footnote 16.
[2] *Geographia*, Book IV. chap. v.

regular customs duties upon exports and imports at the ports of Gaul, and it seems reasonable, as Rice Holmes[1] has stated, that these duties were imposed as an easily collected substitute for the *vectigal* exacted by Caesar. The great geographer encourages this belief when he says that, in view of the substantial revenue that was flowing in, the Romans had no need to garrison the island. While the common-sense outlook of this statement doubtless reflects the reasoned policy of Augustus and his ministers, there is some reason to believe that in 27-26 B.C., when Caesar's successor was in Gaul, he momentarily contemplated following in the steps of his predecessor.[2]

The period of ninety-seven years between Caesar's departure and the great invasion by Claudius I. is not without a certain amount of historical illumination, enough to see a fairly distinct picture of Britain tending towards political unification in the south-east, a steadily increasing economic prosperity, and also comparatively rapid Romanisation in the same area.

To deal firstly with the development of political unity: soon after Caesar's death, that is to say about 40 B.C., there seem to have been three leading kingdoms in southern Britain, the Catuvellauni, still ruled by Cassivellaunus, the Trinovantes to the east, and, south of the Thames, a state consisting of the Atrebates and the Cantii under the rule of Caesar's formerly docile adherent, Commius, king of the Atrebates in Gaul, who later became Vercingetorix's colleague in the great revolt of 52 B.C., and afterwards fled to Britain, where he carved out for himself a new kingdom and remained in bitter hostility to Caesar.

Somewhere about 35 B.C. Cassivellaunus was succeeded[3] by his yet more energetic and warlike son, Tasciovanus, who conquered the Trinovantes and extended his kingdom to the north and west. After a reign of some forty years he was succeeded by his still greater son Cunobelinus, who destroyed the dominion of the sons of Commius and exercised a widespread hegemony. His reign was even longer than that of his father and he did not die until a year or two before the Claudian invasion of A.D. 43.

[1] *Ancient Britain*, p. 356.   [2] *Cassius Dio*, Book LIII. chap. xxv.
[3] Coins bearing the apparently abbreviated name "Andoco" indicate another chieftain before Tasciovanus.

It is clear that this unification must have tended to peaceful conditions, freer intercourse, both internal and external, and a consequent rapid increase in general prosperity. An impression of improved conditions is afforded by Strabo's list of British exports to the Continent. Skins, slaves, and hunting dogs might reasonably be expected, but corn and cattle suggest agricultural and pastoral development due, no doubt, to deeper ploughing applied to the heavier soils, probably in a certain degree a good deal of method and some beginnings of progress in stock breeding and grain production. When the list reaches the metals, iron, silver and gold, a certain feeling of surprise is inevitable. Strabo is so notoriously sceptical that it would appear that he obtained his information from traders or trade lists. His catalogue of imports into Britain is very much what may be expected: ivory, amber, jewellery, glassware and kindred merchandise which latter would naturally include pottery and better types of household articles than those which the Britons had hitherto been in the habit of manufacturing.

A ROMAN PEWTER BADGE SHOWING A GAULISH WARRIOR CARRYING A SHIELD OF THE TYPE IN USE DURING THE EARLY IRON AGE.

As the Southern Britons were to some extent of Gaulish blood and were closely in touch with their neighbours across the Channel, it is likely that this figure would bear a near resemblance to the Southern Briton in arms.

In view of this relatively important volume of trade with Britain, and having regard to the unique position of London, it has been thought possible that it was during the latter part of this period that a small river port at the head of the estuary of the Thames began to develop into the busy commercial centre which it is known to have been in the year 60. The archaeological evidence at present available is, however, incapable of supporting much in the nature of a settlement earlier than during the decade preceding the invasion of Claudius. If a bridge had not come into existence at the earlier date that has been suggested, now would have been the time when such a structure would have become a necessity. The question of the capacity of Britons, without the aid of Roman engineers, to construct a solid pile bridge is one requiring little discussion, for the driving of piles was an accomplishment infinitely older than the continental colonisation of Britain. Lake dwellings belonging to the Bronze Age were supported on piles sufficiently well-driven to make the superimposed structures safe places of residence. More than half a century before Cunobelinus had begun to reign in Britain, Caesar was recording the existence of permanent bridges over large rivers such as the Loire, and again and again he emphasises the skill of the Celts in engineering.

The testimony as to the advance of Romanisation throughout the south-east is strong. Strabo seems to make it clear that British princes—possibly Tasciovanus and his famous son —visited Rome and made offerings in the temple of Jupiter Capitolinus.[1] There is plenty of further evidence that the relations between Britain and the Roman Empire were close and friendly, but the strongest evidence is afforded by numismatics. Tasciovanus and Commius struck coins both in gold and silver with Latin inscriptions, and the far more abundant currency of Cunobelinus was remarkable for its excellent classical type, that may have been due to trained moneyers whom he had taken into his service.

[1] *Geographia*, Book IV. chap. 5.

Chapter III

FROM THE INVASION OF CLAUDIUS TO THE RESTORATION OF
LONDINIUM AFTER ITS DESTRUCTION BY BOUDICCA, A.D. 43 TO
CIRCA 70

TI·CLAVdio Drusi f CaeSARI
AVGVsto GermaniCO
PONTIFICi Maximo Trib PotesTAT · XI
COS · V · IMp XXI (?) patri pa TRIAI
SENATVS · POpulusque · ROmanus qUOD
REGES · BRITannaiai XI devictos sine
VLLA · IACTVRa in deditionem acceperit
GENTESQUE · Barbaras trans oceanum
PRIMVS · IN · DICI onem populi Romani redegerit[1]

*(To Tiberius Claudius Caesar Augustus Germanicus, the son of Drusus;
Pontifex Maximus; in the 11th year of his Tribunician power; his 5th consulate
and the 21st (?) occasion of his being saluted Imperator: Father of the State—
the Senate and the People of Rome, because without any mishap he received in
unconditional surrender eleven conquered British kings, and for the first time
reduced transoceanic barbarians under the power of the Roman people.)*

The first half-century of the Christian era was nearly spent
when Claudius I., the fifth Caesar, determined to transform
into direct dominion the vague suzerainty of Rome over the
southern parts of Britain still ruled by the descendants of
Cassivellaunus. Doubtless contemporary observers who had
watched or become aware of the process of Romanisation,
were convinced in their minds that sooner or later it would
become necessary to include southern Britain within the expanding frontiers of the Roman Empire. Tiberius had not
been an expansionist, but under his successor an obvious
forward policy set in, of which the most notable immediate
outcome was the definite annexation of Mauretania, conter-
minous with western Algeria and northern Morocco.

Claudius had undoubtedly personal reasons for desiring a
brilliant military achievement that should shed a halo of glory
upon his newly acquired imperial rank. He must have felt that
on account of his superficial weaknesses he was looked upon

---

[1] A record on the remains of a large marble slab discovered in Rome
and preserved there in the Palazzo Barberini. The words or parts of
words existing are in large capitals. The gaps have been conjecturally
supplied by Mommsen, but the general significance is unquestionable.

47

almost with contempt by the officials of the capital, and still more so by the rough legionaries, who had always been familiar with the presence of soldierly emperors in their midst —even the half-crazy Caligula had not failed to appear in camp in uniform. To this might be added the feelings of repulsion that Claudius held towards the mysterious cult and caste of the Druids with its stronghold in Britain, and still more or less alive in Gaul in spite of the strenuous attempts of Augustus and Tiberius to suppress it.

Statesmanlike reasons were not wanting. As in the days of Caesar, the virtually independent island was a safe refuge for the disaffected in Gaul, and in addition, it was a potential source of danger under certain circumstances, such as those that made Dacia soon afterwards so formidable an enemy to Rome. To these reasons must be added a somewhat inflated impression of Britain's wealth, especially in the precious metals. Strabo, as already mentioned, states that the island was exporting during the period not merely corn, cattle, dogs, and iron (the last from the Wealden region), but also gold and silver.[1] The provenance of the gold is something of a mystery, but the comparative abundance of British coins of this metal is undoubted evidence of some facility in procuring it. There is also no doubt that some of the princes and nobles were able to amass considerable wealth. Prasutagus, king of the Iceni, the husband of Boudicca, is a notable example of this type of high-born plutocrat. The powerful financial circles in which Claudius's Greek ministers, Pallas[2] and Narcissus, were prominent figures, doubtless brought their influence to bear, since the annexation of a new province would mean fresh fields for financial operations, legal or otherwise. Men, generally supposed to be of high character, such as the philosopher Seneca, were leagued with this moneyed circle, and a great part of Seneca's immense fortune[3] was acquired by loans issued at excessive interest to the British nobles after the conquest.

---

[1] Strabo, *Geographia*, Book IV. chap. v.

[2] Pallas was so wealthy, even from the modern standpoint, that Tacitus mentions his refusal of a gift of £150,000 (gold value).

[3] Seneca died worth 300,000,000 of sesterces, that is £3,000,000 in gold value, besides an enormous amount of personal property, including 500 ivory tables inlaid with citron wood. Cassius Dio, LXI. and LXII.

BRITISH COINS AND EXAMPLES OF THOSE STRUCK AT LONDINIUM.

1. Gold half-stater found in Surrey; *circa* 100-50 B.C. 2. Gold half-stater of Commius, King of the Atrebates, 50-25 B.C. 3. Silver coin of the Icini bearing the letter ECEN, *circa* A.D. 20. All three are attempted copies of one of the coins of Philip of Macedon. The monarch's head has become a meaningless pattern, and the chariot, driver and horses are very confused. 4. Gold coin of Tasciovanus, King of the Catuvellauni and Trinovantes, *circa* 35-5 B.C 5. Gold coin of Cunobelinus, King of South-east Britain, *circa* 5 B.C.-A.D. 40; on the reverse is an ear of corn and the mint-mark CAMV for Camulodunum. 6. Billon (= ⅓ silver, ⅔ copper) coin of Carausius struck for Legio II Augusta. ML=Moneta Londoniensis. 7. Carausius with Diocletian and Maximianus as brother emperors; mint-mark C, perhaps Camulodunum or Corinium. 8. Billon, Allectus, A.D. 293. ML. 9. Bronze, Diocletian, LON=Londinium. 10. Bronze Constantinus "the Great." PLN=Percussa (or pecunia) Londinio. 11. Aureus, Magnus Maximus, *circa* 383. AVGOB=pure gold of Augusta (Londonium).

VESPASIAN
In Britain A.D. 43.

CLAUDIUS I
In Britain A.D. 43.

HADRIAN
In Britain A.D. 120-1.

SEVERUS I
In Britain 208-211.

**ANTONINUS V
"CARACALLA"**
In Britain 208-211.

CARAUSIUS
Local Emperor
286-293.

**CONSTANTIUS I
" CHLORUS "**
In Britain 296 and 305-6.

ALLECTUS
Local Emperor
293-296.

**CONSTANTINE I
" THE GREAT."**
In Britain often,
306-312.

CONSTANS I
In Britain 343.

MAGNUS MAXIMUS.
In Britain 383.

CONSTANTINE III
In Britain 407.

ROMAN EMPERORS CLOSELY ASSOCIATED WITH BRITAIN

who are either known to have been in Londinium or whose presence in the capital on some occasions may be accepted as almost beyond doubt. To these twelve Geta, one of the sons of Severus I, may be added.

Both the great public services—civil and military—must have favoured the imperial project, the civil being attracted by the prospect of a fresh field of operations both as regards new appointments and new areas to tax. There was no lack of talented and ambitious officers for the high command; men such as Aulus Plautius, Ostorius Scapula, Corbulo, Suetonius Paulinus and Vespasian were only too ready to prove their mettle and win, if fortune favoured, the triumphal honours.

It should not be forgotten that Claudius's predecessor Caligula had four years earlier probably weakened Roman prestige in Britain by the ostentatious concentration of a great force on the coast of Gaul opposite Britain and subsequent abandonment of whatever enterprise he had had in view.[1] There was thus, from the point of view of the Roman statesman, a real reason for vindicating the dignity of the Empire, and, lastly, there existed the need, that was always present, of keeping the legions actively occupied in military operations. The extent to which troops stationed on a peaceful frontier became demoralised and unserviceable may be realised from Tacitus's account of the Syrian legions when taken over by Corbulo for the Parthian war.

Intervention was probably one of those happenings which may be termed inevitable, and it had been tending to become imminent since A.D. 39 to 40. For some forty years or more the greater part of South Britain had been united under the suzerainty of Cunobelinus, the grandson of Caesar's antagonist Cassivellaunus. Throughout his long reign he kept on friendly terms with Rome. About 39 or 40, when he had no doubt reached old age, one of his sons, Adminius, quarrelled with his father and fled to Caligula. This was the incident that incited the demented young Emperor to the display near Boulogne just mentioned, the futility of which is recorded. Shortly after the fiasco—but exactly when is not known—the aged *Rex Brittonum* passed away, leaving two sons, Caratacus[2] and Togodubnus, and possibly a third, Bericus. It appears that there was a civil war between the three, Caratacus and

[1] Suetonius, *Caligula*, cap. 44.
[2] Caratacus is the Romanised form of a Celtic name that, at various times, may have been Caratac, Ceretic, Corotic, Cerdic and Caradoc. It is usually assumed by philologists that Caradoc is the latest form, but it is quite probable that the pronunciation varied in different parts of

4

Togodubnus uniting against Bericus. This, however, is not quite certain, for the exact family affinity of Bericus is not known. It is, however, quite certain that he fled to Rome,[1] and that the two British kings demanded his extradition in undiplomatic if not violent terms.[2] It has been suggested that Bericus gave such information concerning the internal conditions of Britain that Claudius and his advisers were satisfied that a more favourable opportunity was unlikely to occur. This must have been at the very end of A.D. 42.

The fateful decision made, the organisation of the army of invasion was the next step. Four legions were selected, making with their accompanying auxiliaries and cavalry a total nominal strength commonly estimated to have been about 40,000 men,[3] but it might have been considerably more. The magnitude of the force is remarkable; it was not far short of that which under Caesar had conquered Gaul in eight campaigns. The conquest of Britain, up to the Tyne, was to take the greater part of this large army not eight years, but thirty-six—a proof that the Roman strategists had not overrated the warlike qualities of the tribes of Britain. The four legions chosen were taken from the finest armies of the Empire, those that defended the Rhine and the Danube against the fierce Germans and perhaps still more formidable Dacians. From the Army of the Rhine came the legions II "Augusta," XIV "Gemina Martia Victrix," and XX "Valeria Victrix"—the first and the last destined to remain in Britain until the fading shadow of Roman dominion had vanished from the island. The Army of the Danube, Legio IX "Hispana," provided one of the "unlucky" units of the Roman Army, that was to experience a more than usual proportion of disasters, and to meet annihilation in the sea-girt land it had come to conquer. As a reserve to this already formidable force Claudius himself brought from Rome part at least of the famous Praetorian Guard, and other troops, in-

---

Britain. The form Caractacus is a late corruption, having no foundation whatsoever. Some approximation to the original or Celtic form of British personal names can, as a rule, be obtained by dropping the Latin suffix *us* or *a*.

[1] Cassius Dio, LX. cap. 19.   [2] Suetonius, *Claudius*, 17.
[3] R. G. Collingwood, *Roman Britain*, p. 18; also R. G. C. and J. N. L. Myres, *Roman Britain and the English Settlements*, p. 78.

cluding a squadron of elephants. The chief command was given to Aulus Plautius—a veteran of long service, not only an able general, but very popular with the troops. Among the subordinate generals was the Sabine Titus Flavius Vespasianus, afterwards emperor, who was in command of Legio II at Strasburg.

A searching light is thrown upon the extent to which the Roman soldiers had come to regard themselves as fixtures in their frontier camps by the fact that all the four legions selected broke into something like mutiny when it became known that they were to be transported across the sea to unknown Britain. Claudius merely added fuel to the flames when, in order to soothe the discontent, he despatched as commissioner, of all people in the world, his minister Narcissus—a Greek, a civilian, and an ex-slave.

Eventually, by exercising the authority of the much-respected Aulus Plautius, these difficulties were overcome and the army sailed, landing in Britain without opposition.

It seems quite clear from the description, imperfect as it may be, given by Dio[1] that the march was direct from the coast (probably from Rutupiae) to Londinium, for the first resistance offered by the army of the British kings was behind a river that is called impassable, and, as from the context this could not have been the Thames, the alternative must be the Medway, there being no other river answering to the description between London and the Strait of Dover. Driven out of this position, mainly by the daring action of the North Gallic or German light infantry of the Roman army, "the Britons retired to the river Thames at a point near where it empties into the ocean and at flood-tide forms a lake. This they easily crossed because they knew where the firm ground and the easy passages in this region were to be found; but the Romans in attempting to follow them were not so successful."

Dio continues, "However, the Germans (*i.e.* the almost amphibious North Gallic light infantry just mentioned) swam across again and some others got over by a bridge a little way upstream (*i.e.* above the point which Dio considered the head of the estuary), after which they assailed the barbarians from several sides at once and cut down many of them."

The question now arises: "where exactly was this bridge

[1] Cassius Dio, Loeb Series VII.

situated ?" There can be no doubt at all that it crossed the Thames. Dio's words will bear no other interpretation. It is true that this historian is not always reliable and that he wrote more than a century and a half after the events, but it should not be overlooked he was an official of the highest standing, and would have had access to all records, public and otherwise. His description of this part of the campaign is comparatively clear and straightforward. In the first century of

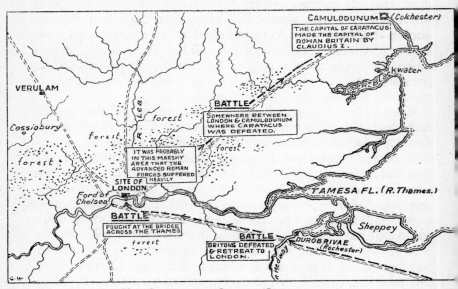

THE CAMPAIGN OF CLAUDIUS I. IN A.D. 43.

The advance from the landing-place on the Kentish coast (near Sandwich) is indicated by the broken line and arrows.

this era the head-waters of the estuary of the Thames at high water would have been just below the present London Bridge. The still surviving and famous term "The Pool" appears to point to the existence in early times of a very marked broadening of the river between the Isle of Dogs and London Bridge. In addition to this, the position provided by nature for bridging the river is obvious, namely where the gravel bluff of London's site provides an admirable approach from the north, facing the site of Southwark which was not at that time of a marshy character.[1] Sir Charles Oman endorsed this with

[1] See p. 16 *infra*.

emphasis when he wrote: "it is incredible that such a structure should have existed at any other point on the Thames estuary than that which was to bear the famous structure of later years."[1] In fact, with little fear of error, the second engagement of the campaign of Plautius might well be called the Battle of Londinium. It is true that Dio makes no reference to any town, and the book of Tacitus that deals with the campaign has yet to be found. Reasons for the existence of a river port of some description have been discussed in a previous chapter and the silence of the historian neither proves nor disproves anything. Dio is as parsimonious of names in describing the campaigns of Severus in Caledonia, although he wrote almost contemporaneously. It should be mentioned that he again omits all reference to Londinium in his account of the struggle with Boudicca in A.D. 60, although it is clear from Tacitus that it played a vital part in the operations.

When the bridge was rushed and the British front was threatened by the attack of the auxiliaries across the river the defence collapsed, but the Romans suffered severely through pursuing the fugitives too rashly into marshy country.[2] Presupposing that the centre of the British line of defence was the bridge, its flanks may have extended westward to the fords at Chelsea and Westminster and eastward to the site of the Tower beyond which lay the lower ground, perhaps marshy in places, of Barking and Limehouse. The direction of retreat was very likely eastward towards Caratacus's capital, Camulodunum (Colchester), and in that case it was in the marshes of the Lea, just mentioned, that the Roman advanced "foreriders" came to grief.

The occupation of the twin hills of Londinium, the site of Southwark, and the bridge gave the Roman army an excellent base of operations for the conquest of the northern part of the empire of the Catuvellauni. In the first stage of the campaign, Caratacus had lost his brother, Togodubnus, possibly in this very battle of the Thames crossing, and doubtless his incoherent forces had suffered heavily, but Dio says that the losses of the Roman army had been so severe that it was virtually immobilised until the arrival of Claudius with rein-

---

[1] *England before the Norman Conquest*, p. 53.
[2] Cassius Dio, Loeb Series vii. 419.

forcements. Although, again, there is no definite statement as
to the position at which the army rested, beyond the information that it was on the Thames, there seems every reason to
presume that it was at or near what was to become Londinium.
What had happened during the conflict is unknown; even if
a group of sheds and huts had remained intact it could not have
afforded shelter for more than a trifling fraction of the large
Roman army with its huge baggage train. According to the
castrametation rules given by Hyginus, a Roman imperial
army, nearly 50,000 strong, with at least 20,000 horses and as
many non-combatants, encamped for the night in a space of
eighty-six acres. For a residential camp or cantonment much
more space was naturally required, but even so, from fifty to
sixty acres was deemed sufficient for a legion of 7000 men
with its staff, servants, and stores. Therefore the 350 acres of
the twin hills, afterwards included within the Roman walls of
Londinium, were amply sufficient to accommodate the army
of Plautius for some weeks.

On the night of the battle, according to the invariable and
immemorial custom of the Romans, the camp would have
been fortified with a palisaded embankment and ditch. On
the hypothesis that the British settlement lay east of the
Walbrook in the angle between that stream and the Thames,
the most convenient camping-ground for a large army would
have been between the Walbrook and the Fleet river, the
centre of which would have been roughly the site of St Paul's
Cathedral. If Londinium at this time possessed any substantial buildings they would have doubtless been used as
store-houses, offices, or field hospitals. After the outpost
camps had been placed where necessary in the outskirts the
perimeter of the zone of effective occupation would in a day
or two have extended over many miles.

In due course the Emperor reached the Thames, and thus
the site of Celtic London witnessed the arrival of a Roman
Caesar. It would have been an occasion of considerable pomp
and circumstance, for Claudius was escorted by the Praetorian
Guard and other picked troops, while the presence of a
squadron of elephants would have added an unusual touch of
barbaric splendour to the scene. How these heavy quadrupeds
were conveyed across the river can only be conjectured. Had
the Roman engineers any doubts as to the advisability of

bringing them across the wooden bridge until it had been very much strengthened, there would have been the simple alternative of the ford situated at Chelsea or Westminster. Yet another method might be suggested, that of the raft as adopted by Hannibal when crossing the Rhône, but the shallow and meandering Thames of A.D. 43 was a vastly simpler obstacle to overcome than the broad, deep and impetuous Rhône, and one of the fords would have made the task an easy one.

Seeing that this military spectacle was the first of its kind that Londinium had witnessed, it is appropriate to make some attempt to picture the scene. As a guide there is the brief account given by Tacitus[1] of the triumphal entry of Vitellius in A.D. 69. In this case the procedure would be somewhat different seeing that it was the recepton of his Emperor by a victorious general. Claudius, in military attire of gold-plated cuirass, elaborately ornamented and cloaked in purple, on horseback, or perhaps in a chariot, followed by his brilliant assemblage of officials and officers and escorted by the gorgeously uniformed Praetorian Guard, would have been met presumably at the bridge-head by Plautius and his staff. Behind the commander-in-chief would

THE CAPRICORN BADGE OF LEGIO II AUGUSTA.

have marched the principal officers of the four legions, that is the *legati legionum* (=generals of legions); the *praefecti castrorum* (=quartermaster-generals); the *tribuni* (=colonels) and *primipili* or *primi pili centuriones* (=principal centurions, possibly equivalent to majors or senior captains). Behind each group of senior officers would be the eagle of the legion and the ten cohort standards. After the legionary officers and standards would come those of the cavalry regiments, and lastly, those of the numerous auxiliary cohorts. The eagles of the legions would have taken position in order of seniority, and in that case, at the head of the procession would have been the gilded capricorn of Legio II "Augusta." It has been conjectured that this curious compound of goat and fish might have been

[1] *Historia*, Book II. chap. lxxxix.

granted for its great services in the Alps and at Augustus's famous naval victories at Actium and on the coast of Sicily. Close to the eagle was to be seen the strongly-built sturdy figure of its commander, Titus Flavius Vespasianus, who, twenty-six years later, was to be Emperor of Rome. His features, familiar down the centuries from coins and marble busts, were those of the hardy Sabine farmer type, that must have been one of the strongest elements in the composition of the Roman race. Following Vespasian would come the staffs of two legions that dated back to the first and mightiest of the Caesars, the IXth "Hispana" and the XIVth "Gemina Martia Victrix," the latter destined seventeen years afterwards to win the proud title of "*Domitores Britanniae.*" Last, but not least, came the officers and standards of the XXth "Valeria Victrix," with its badge of the wild boar glittering on the shields of the escort. After the formal reception of the officers, the legions that had fought their way to the Thames would have been reviewed in gala uniform, those who had won decorations displaying them with pride.

THE WILD BOAR.
Badge of Legio XX Valeria Victrix.

This spectacle having been concluded the united army marched upon Camulodunum, where Caratacus was preparing to make his last stand as "*Rex Brittonum.*" The decisive battle was fought somewhere on the road between the two places, and the Britons being totally defeated and Camulodunum occupied, Claudius made preliminary arrangements for the constitution of South Britain as a new province of the Roman Empire with its capital at Camulodunum, and wasted no time in returning to the Continent. He spent only a short time in Britain and was back in Rome within six months of his departure.[1] It is possible that he sailed from the new capital, and in that case he saw no more of Londinium but merely passed across the mouth of the Thames. No doubt he took back with him many British captives, a necessary feature for the triumph that he forthwith celebrated with great splendour. On his palace, beside the civic crown, he placed a naval one to indicate that he had crossed and subdued the ocean. At this early stage of its history, therefore, Londinium, in spite

---

[1] Suetonius, *The Lives of the Caesars*, Book V. xvii.

of its very great geographical advantages, was evidently not yet of sufficient consequence to be chosen the capital of the new province. The reasons for its being passed over were obviously, first, that it possessed no royal associations such as those appertaining to Camulodunum, Verulam or Calleva, all of which had been the capitals of powerful British princes, and, second, that in all probability Camulodunum possessed buildings constructed by the wealthy Cunobelin, whose long rule and association with the Empire would have given both opportunity and incentive to house himself as befitted a king who had relations with Augustus. It should also be remembered that Claudius's hurried visit gave him time for only superficial considerations; he simply established the seat of government in the former royal capital.

Within a very short time, Camulodunum undoubtedly showed itself quite unsuitable, on account of its position, to be the capital of Roman Britain. Indeed, there is some reason for believing that it was very early superseded for all practical purposes. In A.D. 60, when Boudicca's revolt was imminent, it was obliged to send for military assistance to the Imperial Procurator, *i.e.* the Provincial Treasurer;[1] obviously, therefore, the actual administration had already been shifted elsewhere. It is not easy to think of any other town than Londinium as being this new centre, and it is almost as difficult to imagine under the Roman governmental system the separation of such a vitally important department from the centre of government.[2] Thus only seventeen years after the Claudian occupation of south-eastern Britain Londinium had assumed the position of capital; indeed, it may have been deliberately selected by the practically-minded officials on account of its manifold and obvious advantages of centrality and sea communications. After a very short acquaintance with the country these favourable circumstances must have urged themselves at every turn.

The immediate effects upon Londinium are told in a single laconic sentence from the pen of Tacitus.[3] It was, he writes, "not indeed distinguished by the title of 'colony' but

---

[1] Tacitus, Book XIV. chap. xxxii.　　　　[2] See p. 268 *infra*.

[3] *Annales*, Book XIV. chap. xxxiii.: "*Cognomento quidem coloniae non insigne, sed copia negotiatorum et commeatuum maxime celebre.*"

crowded with traders and a great centre of commerce." This brief but emphatic statement demonstrates very clearly the rapid progress made in less than two decades, during which Britain was still in process of subjugation, although the actual fighting front had been steadily advanced towards the north and west, and by this time had passed the Midlands. There had come not only the Roman troops, but in their wake followed numerous civilians who, during this early period, realising that southern Britain was now comparatively safe, entered the country, tempted by the prospect of forming profitable business connections. It is quite easy to picture the many openings for money-making in a fertile and largely undeveloped country that would quickly stimulate manufactures and certain forms of local enterprise. All mining operations were as usual the perquisite of the Emperor, but there was ample scope for private enterprise in dealings in corn, cattle, fisheries and other matters, including the importation of pottery, glass, and fine manufactured goods of all kinds. A dangerous branch of this immigrant activity was usury; Tacitus mentions it as distressing the "whole community."[1] A law had been made by Julius Caesar that settled the terms of lending money on the security of land.

It seems that Claudius had secured the allegiance of many British nobles by means of gifts, but besides this, certain prominent magnates, notably the philosopher Seneca, were immersed in usurious transactions. The somewhat careless and ostentatious British chiefs and landowners were an easy prey. All this multiplicity of enterprise would have brought in its wake much building activity, although it need not be inferred from this that the new dwellings and offices were constructed of stone or even brick, except for foundations. Brick and tile manufacturers may have found it difficult to keep pace with the early demand, and thus walls were more likely to have been of timber and rough cast with thatched roofs than of the more durable materials later to be employed in building the better class of houses and offices of Londinium. According to Mr F. Lambert,[2] who has watched many excavations, and collected records of earlier ones, in central London, the first Roman Londinium was for

---

[1] *Annals*, Book VI. 16.
[2] *Archæologia*, vol. lxxi. pp. 55 *sqq.*

the most part a town of half-timber and plaster buildings which a general conflagration presently reduced to red dust, mingled with burnt glass and pottery and coins fused by intense heat. It is interesting to note that a large majority of the coins were those of Claudius I.[1]

The question of the construction of defences at Londinium during this period now arises. In the first place it seems clear that immediately after the campaign of 43, Londinium ceased to be involved in military operations, although for a long time it must have been the principal military base in Britain. There is almost definite evidence for believing that Londinium was without permanent defences at this time; Camulodunum certainly did not possess any. The practice under the Roman Empire at this period seems never to have contemplated the walling of towns unless on the military frontier. There is no real evidence for the systematic fortification of towns in the interior of the Empire until the barbarian irruptions of the second century, when the frontier defences, hitherto regarded as an impregnable barrier, were penetrated. Certain places constructed as fortresses, such as Byzantium and Cremona, retained their ancient walls, but Londinium was not one of these, being an open and probably somewhat straggling commercial settlement that had grown up by the force of circumstances and the advantages of the situation.

The preconception that some form of elaborately constructed citadel existed in Roman London has led various modern writers on the subject to search for evidences in support of this theory. An area has been plotted out east of Walbrook.

Roach Smith, impressed by the massive character of the Roman walls discovered when Cannon Street station was being built, was inclined to assume the existence of an inner

---

[1] It is an important point that no coins later than Claudius have been found in this stratum of destruction, excepting one of Galba (A.D. 68), that may have worked itself down by some special chance—in the same manner as a nineteenth-century preserved meat tin was found at a lower level in the excavations of Stonehenge than the stone mauls with which the monoliths were dressed. It would therefore seem that the latest money in circulation in Londinium in the year 60 was that of an emperor who had been dead for six years. This may be partly explained by the fact that Nero struck no copper until 64, and thus there would be no coins of that metal in Londinium until after the Boudiccan revolt.

fortification of London. His suggested boundaries of this earlier enclosure were: on the west side from the Thames along Walbrook to the Mansion House where it turned eastward, roughly parallel with Cornhill and Leadenhall Street to Mark Lane that formed the eastern boundary of this purely theoretical enclosure. This conscientious and cautious investigator of Roman London was careful to state that his ideas were "almost wholly speculative."[1] Mr Arthur Taylor[2] seems to have been one of the first to develop the theory of quite a small enclosure at the head of London Bridge, bounded on the north by Cannon Street and Eastcheap, and his suggestion was more or less adopted by Loftie,[3] by Sir Laurence Gomme,[4] and by Mr F. W. Reader.[5] The area suggested by Roach Smith was the most reasonable in so far as it comprised a space large enough to contain a legion, but that indicated in a plan given by Sir Laurence Gomme's book is only sufficient to house about three cohorts. It should be emphasised that all this is theorising, built up on scarcely any archaeological evidence; in fact, all that has been brought to light in support of such an idea is limited to the foundations of walls under Cannon Street station, already mentioned, and portions of others in Cornhill, extending from the corner of Birchin Lane to Gracechurch Street. The massive Roman walls found at different times since 1891 near the Church of St Peter and under that of St Michael have, in recent years, been linked up with the extensive area of imposing foundations to the east belonging to the Basilica. The inference to be drawn from the portions of thick walls discovered in this part of the centre of the Roman city is that here, as at the present day, were grouped the most important structures of Londinium, and that such buildings, notably temples, government offices and treasuries, had substructures of great solidity. With the scanty evidence at present available it is still impossible to form any definite conclusion as to the existence of a citadel in Londinium, although it seems unlikely that such a structure ever existed. The lower portions of a fairly heavy wall, unearthed at the

---

[1] *Illustrations of Roman London*, p. 14.
[2] *Archaeologia*, vol. xxxiii, "The Original Site of Roman London."
[3] W. J. Loftie, *History of London*, chap. i. p. 31.
[4] *The Governance of London*, pp. 78 *sqq.*
[5] *Archaeological Jour.*, vol. lx. pp. 137-204 and 213-235.

rebuilding of the Guardian Assurance Company's offices at the foot of King William Street in 1921, pointed nearly north and south and gave no indications from which one could feel that it was associated with defensive works. The structures beneath Cannon Street station need have had no warlike purpose, for in such a position as the alluvial bank of the Walbrook, heavy substructures would have been a necessity before any large permanent buildings could have been erected close to the stream. Further than that it is quite possible that these were the quay walls.

From the evidence of Tacitus,[1] a nearly contemporary authority, who had access to the best sources of information, probably from his father-in-law, it is clear that there was no inner citadel at Londinium as early as A.D. 60. He writes of the sack by Boudicca of Camulodunum, Verulamium, and Londinium, and explains in the clearest terms why the three greatest cities of Roman Britain should thus have been destroyed; it was because the rebels deliberately avoided the Roman fortresses and garrisoned posts and fell upon defenceless places where they could obtain abundant plunder and gratify their desire for revenge. His words are: "for the rebels, avoiding fortifications and places under military protection, and eager for booty easily won, sought only what was most worth the plundering and was unguarded by defenders."[2]

Summing up the evidence, it seems fairly obvious that, admitting the probability that for some time in A.D. 43 and 44 there was at Londinium some form of entrenched camp, it cannot have been of a permanent nature. Professor Haverfield and others have suggested, without stressing the point, that the first Roman settlement may have been on the Southwark side of the Thames rather than on the higher ground on the opposite bank. Roman pottery of early dates as well as Roman buildings and burials of various periods have been discovered in Southwark. When the army moved on to fresh conquests and the town ceased to be a military headquarters, there can be little doubt that earthworks would have been an inconvenience in a rapidly growing commercial centre, and levelling would follow as a matter of course. It is hard to imagine that

---

[1] Tacitus, *Annales*, Book XIV. chap. xxxii. and xxxiii.

[2] *"Quia barbari omissis castellis praesidiisque militarium, quod uberrimum spolianti et defendentibus intutum, laeti praeda et laborum segnes petebant."*

any portions of them would survive except where they imposed no obstacle to the building and other activities of the new population. Finally, it is impossible to ignore the very precise testimony of Tacitus.

During the seventeen years following the conquest, Londinium grew and prospered, and those who had known it in 43 and revisited it after that interval of time would have doubtless rubbed their eyes with astonishment at the changes that had taken place. The population must have increased with remarkable rapidity, notwithstanding the fact that in the special circumstances a large proportion would have been floating or migratory. The number of ships entering and clearing "the Pool" would have been steadily increasing and the volume of trade could not have failed to grow by leaps and bounds, although exports would presumably have grown slowly in comparison with imports.

The presence of a number of officials and wealthy business men must have resulted in the development of a considerable degree of comfort in the houses and in some cases it may have reached the confines of luxury. At the same time the floating nature of a large proportion of the population would have tended to create a somewhat desultory and straggling fringe to the more dignified central portion near the Walbrook and the bridge-head.

This nascent prosperity was now to be checked by a really great disaster. In A.D. 60, when the bulk of the army was far away on the frontier between Lincoln, Anglesey, and Caerleon-on-Usk, a great deal of the supposedly subjugated region in its rear broke into open revolt. There were many reasons for the outbreak, and it must be admitted that both the Roman military and civil authorities were gravely at fault. Ostorius Scapula, the predecessor of the then Governor-General and Commander-in-Chief (Legatus Augusti pro-Praetore) Suetonius Paulinus, had founded a colony for time-expired veterans at Camulodunum.[1] To find lands for these military settlers, British farmers had been expropriated without compensation, while the personal conduct of the soldier colonists was licentious and oppressive in the highest degree.[2] Secondly, the Procurator, Decianus Catus, was demanding the repayment, no doubt at the demand of his extravagant master Nero,

---

[1] Colchester.   [2] Tacitus, *Annales*, Book XIV. chap. xxxi.

of the loans that had been made by Claudius, as already mentioned, to his British supporters. Thirdly, the "virtuous"
Seneca had chosen this moment to call in without warning
loans amounting to 10,000,000 sesterces (£100,000 gold
value); thus scores of British landowners were confronted
with ruin, if not actual slavery.[1] Finally, it should be added
that there is evidence that the discipline of the army was in
a most unsatisfactory state.

To all this mass of combustible material the torch was
set by the execrable behaviour of Roman officers towards
Boudicca,[2] the widow of Prasutagus, the late king of the
Iceni. This prince was renowned for his great wealth, that
he bequeathed by will in the proportion of one half to the
Emperor Nero, and the other half to his two daughters. The
Icenian territory included Norfolk and neighbouring parts and
occupied a semi-independent position analogous to that of
Cappadocia and Commagene under the Romans and that of
Kashmir under British rule. By his politic will Prasutagus
hoped to ensure an honourable security for his family, but the
very reverse was the case. In his brief account of what took
place, Tacitus states plainly enough that the terms of the will
were ignored, the dominions of Prasutagus being ravaged by
the centurions who had been sent to take over the Imperial
share. These officers showed themselves to be of a most
disreputable character; they literally despoiled the kingdom,
while the dead king's palace was sacked by their slaves.
Queen Boudicca was actually flogged, and her daughters were
violated. The result might have been foreseen. Rebellion was
imminent, and these outrages gave to it a leader of the highest
rank. Boudicca, maddened by this inhuman treatment, led
the revolt, and in a short time had achieved greater successes
than all the British leaders before her.

The rebels began by sacking the unfortified Camulodunum,
while Suetonius was isolated with two of his four legions far
away in Anglesey. Boudicca then turned to meet Petillius
Cerealis, who was advancing to attack her with Legio IX
from its station at Lindum (Lincoln), and inflicted upon him

[1] Xiphilinus, *Epitome of Cassius Dio*, IX. 2.
[2] This name appears to be the Celtic for Victoria. On an inscription
at Civitas Igaeditanorum in Spain it appears BOUDICA. *C.I.L. Hispaniae*,
Vol. 2, 455.

a crushing defeat. The infantry of his force was annihilated, and he only succeeded in escaping to Lindum with the survivors of his cavalry. These various operations, however, had occupied time, and when the news reached Suetonius he was able apparently to collect a strong enough force of cavalry to risk making his way through the midlands to Londinium before the victorious British tribesmen could interfere.

The fact that he aimed for Londinium after evacuating Anglesey proves very clearly that he regarded it as the strategic focus of Roman Britain. A glance at the map is sufficient to show that under the circumstances it was the natural place of assembly of the isolated portions of the army of occupation.

Although what actually happened at Londinium on the outbreak of the great rebellion is not fully known, one thing is certain: Catus, panic-stricken at the thought of what would befall him at the hands of the justly exasperated Britons, fled to Gaul,[1] leaving his colleague and his subordinates to extricate themselves as well as they could. By the time that Suetonius's force had completed its desperate race southwards, a distance of 230 miles, and its sweating horses were slowly entering the streets of the town, it was no doubt choked with panic-stricken refugees.

The Roman commander now found his position extremely precarious, for he had received the grim news of the disaster that had befallen the IXth Legion, while the IInd, for reasons not yet known, had failed to arrive from its station on the borders of South Wales. Tacitus[2] makes it clear that Suetonius had sent orders to this legion and states that Paenius Posthumus had disobeyed them and later committed suicide. Meanwhile, Boudicca's victory-intoxicated host was approaching and, worst of all, there was a shortage of provisions of an alarming character.

In this situation, so full of peril that the hold of Rome on the entire province was in jeopardy, Suetonius decided to sacrifice Londinium. He accordingly evacuated it, accompanied by all who were able or willing to follow his march, but a very large number stayed behind, some owing to age or physical inability, and others from an unwillingness to

---

[1] Tacitus, *Annales*, Book XIV. xxxii.
[2] *Ibid.*, Book XIV. xxxiii.

ROMAN TESSELLATED PAVEMENT FOUND IN 1803 IN FRONT OF EAST INDIA HOUSE IN
LEADENHALL STREET.

It is the finest mosaic pavement that has so far been found in London. In the centre Bacchus is shown riding on
a tiger with thyrsos and drinking cup. Surrounding this central medallion is a remarkable series of circular and
square borders.

(*British Museum.*)

PROVISIONAL RECONSTRUCTION IN THE BRITISH MUSEUM OF THE EARLIEST
MONUMENT LONDON POSSESSES

It belongs to the last half of the 1st century A.D. and is later than A.D. 61.

THE MONUMENT TO A PROCURATOR OF THE ROMAN PROVINCE OF BRITAIN.

Gaius Julius Alpinus Classicianus was appointed to take charge of the Imperial revenues of Britain
in A.D. 60, during the dangerous insurrection of Boudicca. The upper portion was found in 1852
and the lower, shown as it was discovered (upside down) in 1935, in a bastion of the town wall on
Tower Hill.

leave the spot.[1] All who decided to remain or were unable to follow the march of the retreating Roman forces were massacred by the oncoming forces of Boudicca.

In what direction Suetonius marched is not known, and Tacitus also omits to mention when and where the XIVth and XXth legions and their auxiliaries joined the commander-in-chief. By the actual order in which he mentions the arrival of these heavy reinforcements, Tacitus seems to infer that the linking up took place after the evacuation of Londinium. Had Suetonius marched northwards to meet his two legions coming from Anglesey he would have been going away from his supply areas into a heavily wooded country infested with an elusive enemy. His force was small, overworked, short of provisions, and encumbered with large numbers of non-combatants. There would have been the very serious risk of severing his communications with the Continent, and at the same time he would be abandoning all the south-eastern portion of the province to the mercy of Boudicca's primitive hordes.

It is unfortunate that neither of the Roman historians upon whom we depend for information concerning this extremely interesting campaign trouble themselves very much with the essential matters of time and place. Thus, the more their meagre statements are examined, the more convinced does one become that the scene of Boudicca's great defeat will remain a debatable matter, however ingenious may be the theories that point to one or another area. The consideration of the various problems that the situation presents is, however, sufficiently interesting to be examined with care, and thus what follows may help the reader to form his own opinion.

A suggestion which has been made, that he carried out a "flank march" to Camulodunum (Colchester), brings with it the necessity for plunging into a wasted country, fully in the occupation of the enemy with, as his objective, a deserted heap of ruins infected with putrefying corpses. The advantage from such a move would, of course, have been the proximity of sea communications for evacuation or the receiving of reinforcements.

The strategy now imposed upon Suetonius was that of sheer

[1] Tacitus, *Annales*, Book XIV. chap. xxxiii.

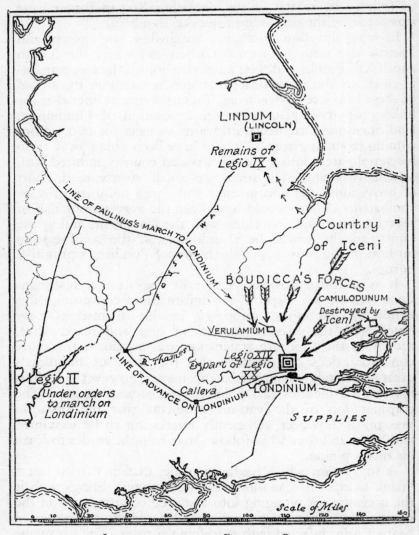

LONDINIUM DURING THE BOUDICCAN REVOLT.

Suetonius Paulinus hastened from Anglesey to Londinium to effect a concentration of his forces. He arrived, having passed through Verulamium (St Albans) just before the Britons swept down upon it and sacked the place. Londinium being unfortified and Legio II not having arrived, Paulinus abandoned the town, and it was consequently destroyed by Boudicca's followers.

necessity. Firstly, wherever he went and whatever he did, he was obliged to feed his army and those non-combatants with whom his humanity had encumbered it. Secondly, he must, as quickly as possible, obtain reinforcements in order that he might have a fair chance of giving battle with some success. Thirdly, he must maintain or re-open his communications with the Continent, since only thus could his depleted army be strengthened with men and military stores and disembarrass itself of its crowd of refugees. Supplies could undoubtedly be found either in fertile Kent, in Hampshire or, at the worst, in Gloucestershire.

Considering all these circumstances it is clear that the second could only be fulfilled by taking a westward direction towards the one complete strategic unit in the island over and above his own army. This was Legio II, stationed probably at Glevum (Gloucester), that by this time (if his orders, sent possibly nearly three weeks earlier, and doubtless reiterated, had been executed) must have been on its march to join him. That it really was on its way seems proved by the statement of Tacitus, to which reference has already been made, that the dilatory Praefectus Castrorum killed himself when he learnt that his delay had resulted in the loss by the IInd Legion of the glory reaped by the XIVth and XXth.

Communication with the Continent could be maintained either in Kent or Hampshire, but only by moving to the south-west could he fulfil all the requirements of the situation at one and the same time. His first objective would naturally be Calleva Atrebatum (Silchester in Hampshire), and it may be that the road north of the Thames leading to that place via Staines would have been avoided, since it would expose the right flank (north) to the attack of the British host, while on the left (south) lay the marsh-bordered Thames.

Presumably Suetonius had all these facts under consideration when he faced the situation on reaching Londinium. To obtain reinforcements and supplies it would seem that he had no choice other than to cross the Thames in order to gain the hills of Surrey and move westward, by whatever ridgeway existed, in the direction of the only region in which he would find at once what he so urgently required. It therefore seems reasonable to think that this was the course he adopted.

It should here be mentioned that it has often been suggested that the spot near King's Cross, known as Battle Bridge, was the scene of the famous victory that followed shortly after the evacuation of London. Apart from strategical conditions this site appears to be unlikely, for Tacitus mentions defiles enclosed in the rear by woods and such a conformation of land does not exist there. Further, in going out in this direction, far from evacuating Londinium, Suetonius would have been defending it, and in a far less favourable position than that of the town with its natural defensibility. In addition, there is the clear statement of Dio[1] that Suetonius wished to avoid a battle, and the same inference is to be made from Tacitus. A northward move was merely to hasten the conflict that the Roman general particularly desired to avoid.

Whether the advanced parties of Boudicca's forces engaged the Roman rearguard or not is purely a matter of conjecture, save for the indirect evidence afforded by the words put into the mouth of Suetonius by Dio when he reminded his men, just before the battle, that some of them had actually witnessed the atrocities perpetrated by the Britons on their conquered foes. This may be purely an invention on the part of Dio, but the practice of conveying information indirectly by means of imaginary harangues was common among the classical writers and the statement therefore need not be entirely disregarded. In that case it is perhaps permissible to picture rearguard cohorts making a final stand in the streets converging upon the bridge-head, while the last of the refugees were crowding across the narrow path to safety and the *fabri* were busy completing their preparations for destruction as soon as the last of the legionaries should have crossed. The usual method of destruction of wooden bridges under such circumstances was by fire—a method continued right down to the nineteenth century. A typical instance was at the two bridges of the Bérézina during Napoleon's retreat from Moscow. The ends on the Russian side of the river were fired simultaneously with perfect success.

By his evacuation of Londinium, Paulinus had saved his army, but the town was perforce left to its fate. Tacitus's description of what befell it is contained in four terribly emphatic words: *"Caedes, patibula, ignes, cruces"* = massacre, gibbets, fire, and crucifixion crosses. The number of persons

---

[1] Xiphilinus, *Epitome of Cassius Dio.*

massacred in the three places (Camulodunum, Verulamium, and Londinium) is given by Tacitus[1] at 70,000 Roman subjects and friendly Britons. The number is perhaps an exaggeration, but in view of the widespread nature of the revolt it may be not far from the truth.

The final phases of the campaign and the great victory of Suetonius do not concern the present narrative save that as an immediate result the burnt-out ruins of Londinium were re-occupied. Although the British warrior-queen had committed suicide and many thousands of Britons had fallen, the rebellion was far from being quelled; in fact, the failure of Suetonius as a governor was so obvious that in spite of his military ability he had to be recalled in the ensuing year, and Tacitus hints obscurely that the reason was a further disaster of some description.

Suetonius[2] states that Nero "even thought of withdrawing the army from Britain (presumably at this time) and only changed his purpose because he was ashamed to seem to belittle the glory of his father."[3]

Paulinus was superseded by Publius Petronius Turpilianus, a clement and tactful administrator who apparently, by conciliatory methods, re-established Roman authority on a sounder and more enduring basis than that afforded by martial law and occasional military and administrative licence.

There need be no doubt that under Petronius Londinium arose from its ashes, and with the restoration of peace it must quickly have recovered its former importance. It is quite possible that under this trained administrator, who had been consul in the previous year, Londinium officially reached the status of capital, a position it may have held previous to the disaster; in any case it is impossible to imagine a place more absolutely suited in every respect to be the headquarters of a man whose task it was to heal the wounds of war and bring contentment and loyalty out of smouldering hostility and dis-trust. It is recorded that offensive military operations were suspended for nearly ten years. A significant hint as to the policy of Petronius and his successor, Marcus Trebellius

[1] Tacitus, *Annales*, Book XIV. chap. xxxiii. "Ad septuaginta milia civium et sociorum iis quae memoravi locis cecedisse constitit."

[2] *Lives of the Caesars*, Book VI. xviii.

[3] Claudius was his adoptive father.

Maximus, is given by Tacitus, who says that the troops accused the latter of meanness and parsimony, a charge that clearly points to a policy of cautious economy. Evidently Britain was no longer under the flaying-knife. The historian further says that their administration was popular, and that the Britons, as he notes in his carping fashion, began to acquire a taste for the alluring vices of civilisation;[1] in other words, there was less military activity, and no doubt much road building, town planning, and the erection of comfortable houses.

It may be quite safely concluded that at the end of the ten peaceful years that followed Boudicca's defeat an excellent beginning had been made of transforming the desultorily-built trading centre into the dignified capital that Londinium was destined to become. Baths and porticoes and other signs of Romanisation were not, according to Tacitus, lacking under the rule of the brilliant Agricola, but while he gives the credit to Agricola, his father-in-law, the foundations of the new prosperity were laid by his immediate predecessors.

[1] Tacitus, *Agricola*, XVI.

Chapter IV

THE RISE OF LONDINIUM, FROM A.D. 60–286

THOSE who would trace the progress of Londinium after the year 60 are now confronted with a prolonged interval—a period of over two centuries, during which there is no mention of the city by any extant classical writer. This, however, will surprise no one who is acquainted with the indifference to topographical details shown by the historians of the time and even by Tacitus, who describes all his famous father-in-law's successive campaigns in Britain without mentioning a single town.[1]

It is proverbial that periods of great prosperity produce little in the way of picturesque events for the journalist to seize upon. Thus, without providing during this long period any large-scale events that were attractive to chroniclers, Londinium grew steadily in wealth and importance and towards its close ranked among the greater Roman cities of the Western Empire.

History being silent, one is thrown back on archaeology —its invaluable handmaid. Here, as has been emphasised already, the conditions are exceedingly difficult owing to the perennial disturbance of the site by the sinking of ever deeper foundations. But, mangled and distorted as this evidence may be, there emerges from it such clear indications of the existence of a really large and wealthy city that any reasonable doubt ceases to exist regarding what was in progress in these two pregnant centuries. And, at the very commencement of this period, the industrious handmaid has lately produced from building debris[2] the completion of the sepulchral inscription of Gaius Julius Alpinus Classicianus, procurator of Britain, sent in A.D. 61 to replace Decianus Catus, who had fled to Gaul during Boudicca's revolt and whose mistakes and mismanagement had in a great measure led to the rebellion. The task that faced Julius Classicianus was not easy, for in showing

---

[1] An apparent exception may be found in the reference to Portus Trutulensis, which *may* be Rutupiae; but that name was so well known that such a blundered rendering is scarcely likely. It might conceivably be some harbour in the south-west of Britain.

[2] See Appendix, pp. 247 and 254.

care for the welfare of the provincials he must have found himself opposed to Suetonius, the legate, upon whom it was his duty no doubt to act as a check. Professor Collingwood

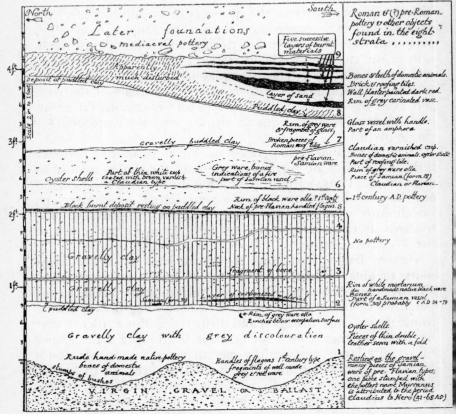

A SECTION OF ROMAN LEVELS OF LONDON EXPOSED AT No. 8 KING STREET, CHEAPSIDE.

Stratum No. 4 was covered with an even layer of carbonised material and immediately above it were shards of first century pottery.

It reveals an accumulation of over 2 feet of gravelly clay in the earliest years of the Roman period. A layer of burnt substances has been discovered in many parts of the city and it has been suggested that it dates from A.D. 60, the year of the burning of London by Boudicca.

thought that Classicianus did not obtain justice at the hands of Tacitus for his conciliatory efforts, the historian being more concerned to glorify Suetonius, who represented military power. The inscription proves that Classicianus died in office, and there is evidence that he did not survive his appointment to Britain for more than a few years.[1] His wife Julia Pacata, who erected the monument, was the daughter of Julius Indus, who can scarcely have been other than the Julius Indus who was on the Roman side in A.D. 21 during a revolt of the Treveri led by his compatriot and enemy Julius Florus.[2] Julia might have been born about this time, and Mr Hawkes makes the interesting suggestion that her second name, Pacata, may have been chosen in reference to the pacification of the Treveri in which her father took a prominent part. He commanded a regiment of cavalry that was without much doubt afterwards known as the *Ala Indiana*, and is known to have served in Britain.[3]

Until the very end of the period with which this chapter deals there were no threats of invasion from the Continent, and the peace of southern Britain was unbroken throughout. From the year 60 to about 125, when first the Welsh tribes, and then the Brigantes of the north, were slowly reduced to submission, Londinium, as the great arterial centre of Britain, could not avoid being affected in various ways. That it was the base depot for supplies and munitions was almost inevitable, and that the volume of its business transactions was greatly increased owing to this cause cannot be doubted.

In this early period of reconstruction and expansion, the forum of Londinium would become the great centre of news as to successes, checks, or reverses experienced in the North and West. It is easy to imagine the excitement and what would to-day be called "jingo" talk among the crowd of traders, brokers, and loungers when one of Agricola's couriers brought the news of another brilliant victory over the elusive Caledonians, or, conversely, there must have been black days of defeatism followed by calculations of bad debts, when in 119 the evil tidings filtered through that Legio IX had been annihilated in that still mysterious disaster in the North. Optimism and anticipation of an influx of profitable customers for a large variety of needs would have become widespread when, in the

---

[1] *Antiquaries' Journal*, vol. xvi., January, 1936, p. 6: "A procurator of Britain named Augustanus probably held office during the sixties (A.D.) and may therefore have succeeded Classicianus." F. Cottrill quoting E. B. Birley and C. F. C. Hawkes.

[2] Tacitus, *Annals*, iii. 42.   [3] *C.I.L.* vii. 66.

following year, it was announced that the Emperor Hadrian was on his way to Britain with reinforcements.

That the city was unwalled must have been a very disturbing fact in the minds of all Londoners at this time. The destruction of the famous Ninth Legion left the capital of the province open to attack from any armed forces of the Brigantes that cared to come so far south. If the Government did not decide very quickly on the construction of a strong defensive wall the disaster of only sixty years before might be repeated on a larger scale. The Emperor was a great builder; the danger ought to be pressed home upon him. What representations were made and on whom they were pressed are facts that may never be known, but that Londinium's first town wall was built at this time is becoming more and more an assured fact. The danger was not water-borne, and therefore the south side was sufficiently defended by the Thames, but the other three sides were threatened and were soon protected by a wall nearly 9 feet thick at its base with a suitable ditch outside it. The progress of this prodigious engineering effort would have been a major feature of town talk until its parapets and gates were completed, and reports of its huge cost and of delays and difficulties in getting the stone and other materials would have made much conversation, pessimistic and otherwise, wherever citizens met in forum, street or tavern.

This slight picture may be termed imagination, but it is of the type that Napoleon, who was accustomed to deal in realities, termed *imagination juste*, for the building of the wall is a fact and it has never been questioned that Londinium at this period was growing more rapidly than any town in Britain, and that its development was due to its favoured position. The port or "Pool" reflected this progress, and the number of ships entering and clearing could not have failed to be steadily increasing. To accommodate the influx, greater wharfage would have been required year by year, with a corresponding need for warehouses of a more substantial type than those hurriedly put up after the defeat of Boudicca.

An important feature of such a seafaring centre would have been the docks, although the only trace of them that has so far been recognised is at Queenhithe. None the less that they did exist may be taken to be as certain as the need of ropes and bollards. The heavy seagoing craft that came up the

Thames laden with Gallic pottery, wine, and olive oil in great jars (*amphorae*) from Italy; carpets and richly-coloured woven fabrics from Egypt; silk, perfumery, ivory and, above all, pepper and spices from the Far East, required "graving and tallowing" even as did their Elizabethan successors, and indeed all wooden ships before the days of copper-sheathing. Most probably these indispensable features of a port were below the bridge and, owing to the subsidence of the land to which reference has already been made,[1] may now be buried beneath many feet of Thames mud. No doubt, as is still the case with small vessels all over the world, repairs to hulls were effected by careening between tides where beaches were suitable, but in a city of the importance of Londinium docks and dockyard labour were part of the ordinary economy. That they were, for the most part, below the bridge is not improbable, but it is likely that there were building slips and repair yards at the mouths of the Walbrook and the Fleet, as well as on the Southwark shore. There is evidence for believing that the Walbrook was an open stream in the second century. Excavation under the Bank of England between 1928 and 1934 seemed to show an open waterway with houses containing tessellated pavements built on its banks, for sealed beneath these floors pottery was found that gave about A.D. 125 as their date. Mr Quintin Waddington also saw on this site evidence that suggested to him the existence of a boathouse.

There were occasions when, by bad seamanship or stress of weather, an incoming vessel met with disaster in the estuary. One such mishap is known to have occurred some time about A.D. 180, when Marcus Aurelius, the last of the "five good Emperors," lay dying in his camp on the Danube. A ship laden with Gallic pottery from the great Auvergnat centre of Lezoux was wrecked on the Pudding Pan Rock, four miles off the Kentish coast between Whitstable and Herne Bay. A number of perfect examples of this unlucky vessel's cargo, still bearing the marks of their seventeen hundred years' immersion, are preserved in the British Museum and in private collections in the locality of the wreck.

The earliest date for a bridge has already been discussed[2] but the question of the form that it took at this time remains to be considered. No foundations of a Roman bridge that

---

[1] P. 16 *supra.*   [2] P. 42 *supra.*

have been recognised as such have yet been found, and in default of such evidence, it may be assumed that the Roman Government did not care to go to the great expense of a stone structure, but was content with a *pons sublicius*, no doubt of very solid timber construction and not improbably having in its centre a drawbridge to allow the passage of vessels. It is just possible that the need for this opening was the reason for maintaining the original type of bridge. The same practice appears to have been followed in Gaul, for at places where one would have expected to find indications of stone bridges none have been discovered. It is questionable whether the economically-minded Romans ever felt disposed towards the construction of stone bridges over wide and deep rivers, where the expense incurred would be relatively enormous and the advantages from the point of view of navigation doubtful. There is what might be regarded as a notable exception to this rule at Mérida (Augusta Emerita) in Spain, where a bridge of 81 granite arches and 858 yards in length crossed the Guadiana. The exception is only apparent, however, for this river is wide, shallow and not navigable.

Evidences of the existence of a bridge throughout the whole of the Roman period of Londinium were discovered when the bottom of the river was being dredged in connection with the deepening of the channel after the removal of the mediaeval London Bridge. Extending across the Thames on the line of the old structure at a considerable depth in the gravel and silt[1] were found "many thousands of Roman coins with abundance of Roman pottery . . . and, beneath some of the central piles, brass medallions of Aurelius, Faustina, and Commodus."[2] The coins ranged from Julius Caesar and consuls of his era to Honorius (A.D. 423), and those particularly abundant were of Claudius, Nero, Vespasian, Titus, Domitian, Trajan, Hadrian, Tetricus, Claudius II. (Gothicus), Diocletian, Maximian, Carausius, Allectus, and the dynasty of Constantine. In addition to the coins, there were discovered on this same line numerous objects of art, mostly in bronze. They included the famous colossal head of Hadrian, statuettes of Apollo, Mercury, Jupiter, a hermaphrodite, a model of the bows of a Roman galley, and also the bronze forceps illustrated on page 204, besides numerous other small objects including rings,

[1] C. Roach Smith, *Roman London*, pp. 20-21.   [2] *Ibid., Archaeologia.*

spearheads and fibulæ. Roach Smith noted that the coins were dredged up in definite sequences as if they had been deposited as votary offerings when rebuilding or repairs were carried out upon the bridge, as well as on the accessions of new Emperors. He considered that his hypothesis was confirmed by the fact that very many of the coins were "as sharp as when issued from the mint." It is scarcely necessary to observe that with the Romans, as with practically all peoples down to the present day, the opening for use of a work of great public utility was marked by a religious ceremony of dedication. On these occasions newly-minted money was thrown into the river in accordance with a usage which is as ancient as religion itself. The motive was the propitiation of the river deity.

This archaeological evidence, collected by a skilful and cautious observer, seems to be decisive as to the existence and periodic repair or rebuilding of a bridge maintained throughout the Roman period only a few yards below the position occupied by its mediaeval successors. It should be noted that at four of the five places in Britain where the Roman name indicates a bridge, *i.e.* Pontes, Durolipons, Tripontium, Ad Pontem, and Pons Aelii,[1] no indications of any such structure have been found. Among the remains of Roman bridges known to have existed are the stone abutments of those that spanned the Tyne at Corbridge, the North Tyne at Chollerford and the Irthing at Willowford.

Throughout this period it would seem that the sides of the Walbrook experienced much embanking and the erection of massive substructures for large buildings close to the river front. The very thick walls found beneath Cannon Street station were probably connected with these works. Possibly, judging from its position, it may have been a great quay and the principal scene of activity of the water front; certainly the position was at the very hub of Londinium at the time of its greatest expansion.

That building activity on a large scale developed fairly soon after the reoccupation of A.D. 61 is tolerably certain. Before the Boudiccan disaster the dwelling houses, stores and shops were

---

[1] Some indications of the bridge at Pons Aelii (Newcastle-on-Tyne) were found in 1775. Wooden piles and the "framework of the foundation of one at least of the Roman piers were met with and removed." (*J. C. Bruce's Handbook to the Roman Wall*, p. 43.)

not as a rule built in a very solid or permanent manner. The evidence points to the use of timber and wattle, lath, daub and thatch. When the reconstruction took place there was no doubt a considerable amount of replanning and the use of brick, stone and rubble coated with cement within and sometimes without seems, from the evidence available, to have become common. As late as the reign of Hadrian the use of timber covered with wattle and daub was widespread.

The comparatively rare occurrence of fragments of roofing tiles has particularly impressed Mr Waddington during the whole time that he has been watching excavations in the City. This has led him to think that wooden shingles or thatch must have been the rule for the roofing of domestic, as contrasted with public, buildings throughout the whole of the Roman period. In an age when transport was slow, expensive, and difficult, the building of a city depended very largely on local materials. At Aquae Sulis (Bath) and Corstopitum (Corbridge) stone was largely used for the construction of walls on account of its abundance in the localities concerned, but the neighbourhood of Londinium was lacking in anything of that nature, the nearest quarries being those not far from Merstham, some twenty miles to the south in the wooded uplands of the Wealden forest. The Kentish ragstone district (near Maidstone) was still farther off, although easily accessible by water. It is nevertheless clear that stone was brought to Roman London in prodigious quantities for the town wall, and that the lower portions of the walls of buildings that have been discovered are not infrequently of stone with brick bonding-courses. The frontage of a shop or house found in Lombard Street[1] suggests that it may have been entirely of brick. For foundations and the more solid buildings that were immediately necessary concrete was employed, and for its composition the Thames could furnish an inexhaustible supply of ballast. The other necessaries of building, namely, lime and sand, were obtainable within a radius of half a dozen miles.

Londinium can, therefore, from this time onwards be pictured as a city containing a fair proportion of stone and brick structures, with public buildings of stone relieved with bands of brick-coursing rising massively above them. But this does not complete the scene, for interspersed along the

[1] See p. 181.

quaysides and in all the less important streets there would be timber-built houses of all sizes and condition, thatched and with wattle and daub walls. It is just possible that, owing to the climate and the dearth of good building stone in the vicinity, the growing seaport possessed comparatively few pillared porticoes and courtyards.

In plann.ng the essential features of the new city, one of the first considerations would have been the provision of a forum and the necessary public buildings. There is now ample archaeological evidence for placing the basilica on the site of Leadenhall Market, where its extensive foundations have gradually been discovered. This building has been found to be one of very large dimensions, but whether it was the first built or a later reconstruction is not yet known. The chief forum would have normally occupied a considerable space on the south side of the basilica; it is there that one looks for a parallelogram without foundations. Excavations on both sides of Gracechurch Street in 1934 have, however, confirmed previous reports of buildings in this area. The lengths of wall exposed were very massive and must have been associated with imposing structures of approximately the same age as the basilica itself. They occupied a central position in the western half of the presumed forum space and it may be that they are all that survives of the substructures of more than one temple that stood there.[1]

That a Capitoline temple arose within the area of the city during this period of growing prosperity is very probable, but no temple sites have yet been identified. It is possible that the pagan fanes were demolished for the purpose of building Christian churches in later ages. There is some reason for thinking that a Mithraeum stood near the Walbrook and five or six other temples have been inferred. Public baths, an invariable adjunct to Roman cities, must have existed, and after the Great Fire of London what appeared to be the remains of one of these came to light. Places of amusement have left no trace, and yet there is no doubt at all that they existed in the city—to cite one piece of evidence, the memorial to a gladiator is sufficient to point to the prevalence in Londinium of the sanguinary displays that made a Roman holiday.

[1] See the conjectural view of Londinium c. A.D. 130 between pp. 144 and 145.

In casting a comprehensive glance over this period of un-interrupted growth it may be that at its end Londinium was nearing its maximum expansion. It should be remembered that there was, in addition, a considerable transriverine quarter at the southern end of the bridge, and certain evidence leads to the conclusion that to the west, at least along the banks of the Thames between the Fleet and the Tyburn brook, and even as far as Thorney Island, there were suburbs.

The space enclosed within the walls amounted to about 326 acres. The question of population depends very much on the density of occupation. To-day London has about 60 persons to the acre, but this proportion is greatly exceeded in the cases of Paris and Berlin, where the figures range to the neighbourhood of 150. A study of permanent Roman camps shows that the Romans considered that about 170 soldiers could live in health upon one acre of land. The relation of civil to military figures in this respect is not an easy calcula-tion, but there is a considerable amount of evidence for stating that the streets of an average Roman town were rather narrow, and that the houses generally were of two storeys above the ground floor, although it is known that in Rome it was not unusual to build a block of houses "high with many stories." There were also fewer open spaces than in modern times. It therefore seems reasonable, on a strictly conservative calcu-lation that takes into consideration the area occupied by the Walbrook and its tributaries and unoccupied patches within the town-wall, to infer a density of not less than 140 human beings per acre; and this would give the area already men-tioned a population of about 45,000. To this must be added the transriverine quarter and such suburbs as existed. Further, there should be included the considerable floating population due to the presence of visitors, ships' crews and perhaps small military details. On all these grounds, and assuming that the central area was not as yet built up to any exceptional height, the population of Londinium between A.D. 200 and 280 may be reckoned at not less than the figure stated; it may have been more, but can hardly have been less.

There is no doubt whatever of the pre-eminence of Lon-dinium among the cities of Roman Britain. The nearest in walled area (in the fourth century) was Corinium (Cirencester); that covered about 240 acres, and as it seems unlikely that in

MARBLE AND OTHER STATUARY FOUND IN ROMAN LONDON.

1. Decapitated marble figure (23 in. high) of a Genius or Bonus Eventus. From near Walbrook. 2. Head and shoulders of a marble representation of a river-god—a very fine piece of work showing Hellenistic influence, and must have been imported. (1 and 2, *London Museum*.) 3. Sculptured lion found in the core of the Camomile Street bastion (No. 10). It is on a very superior level to the crude lion found at Corbridge (*Guildhall Museum*). 4. Mutilated bronze statuette of a Mercury, or, according to Sir Richard Westmacott, a Jupiter. It was found in the Thames during the demolition of Old London Bridge (*British Museum*).

ROMAN GLASS VESSELS.

1. Neck and handle of a carafe found in London. When complete it would probably have been very similar to 5, found in East Kent. 2. A small globular two-handled bottle: second half of 2nd century and early 3rd century. 4. A bottle of serpentine glass, yellowish-green streaked with white. Found in Old Broad Street.

(British and London Museums.)

such a spot, in an open agricultural plain, there would have been any tendency to crowd together, the total might therefore be reckoned at roughly 30,000. Eboracum, with its military camp, may at times have had a similar population; and Verulamium, with an area of just over 200 acres, possibly housed from 20,000 to 25,000. Certainly no other cities in Roman Britain equalled these, for Viroconium (Wroxeter) covered not more than 170 acres, and Camulodunum and Calleva (Silchester) only 108 and 102 respectively.

In comparison with the great cities of the empire Londinium, even at its apogee, did not stand in the first rank. It could not compare with the group that included Rome, Antioch, Alexandria, Carthage, Mediolanum (Milan), Smyrna, Ephesus, Cappadocian Caesarea, and Thessalonica. Its area is very much less than those of Athens, Nimes, Trèves and Syracuse, and other instances might be enumerated, but on the other hand it probably stood high among the cities of the second rank such as Massilia (Marseilles), Patavium (Padua), and Colonia Agrippinensis (Cologne). It was certainly much larger than the last, the walled area of which was only 239 acres.

The establishment and development of industries in Londinium and the immediate surroundings would have synchronised with the growth of the city. A steady and increasing demand for bricks and tiles would have resulted in a number of busy brickyards; the household consumption of earthenware would lead to the establishment of potteries of which the site of one was discovered in 1936 under Copthall Close, Moorgate. This potter signed his mortaria "MAX," and towards the end of the first century was turning out in Londinium mica-dusted wares and black pottery decorated with incised lines and semicircles. Timber for houses implies large carpenters' yards; tools and implements of all descriptions as evidenced by the plough-share, and a variety of tools in the Guildhall Museum suggest small factories for their production; a great demand for household furniture required joiners' shops; footwear and clothing implied factories on some scale, and the warming of houses by means of hypocausts necessitated much charcoal-burning.

Mills for the grinding of corn would be needed by a large urban population, but in Londinium it would seem that the grinding of corn for bread-making was largely done in the

6

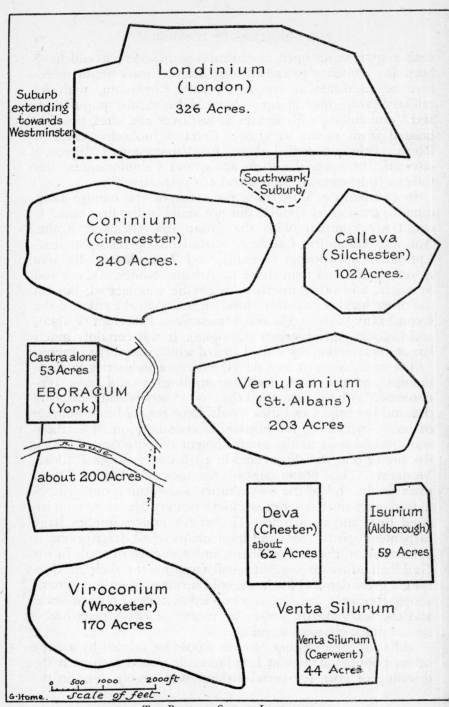

Londinium
(London)
326 Acres.

Suburb extending towards Westminster

Southwark Suburb

Corinium
(Cirencester)
240 Acres.

Calleva
(Silchester)
102 Acres.

Castra alone
53 Acres
EBORACUM
(York)

about 200 Acres

R. OUSE.

Verulamium
(St. Albans)
203 Acres

Deva
(Chester)
about
62 Acres

Isurium
(Aldborough)
59 Acres

Viroconium
(Wroxeter)
170 Acres

Venta Silurum

Venta Silurum
(Caerwent)
44 Acres

0   500   1000   2000ft

G. Home.   Scale of feet.

THE RELATIVE SIZE OF LONDINIUM.

Comparative plans of the chief Roman cities of Britain. Deva had suburbs outside the walled boundary of the camp, but their area is not known.

home. To what extent stone hand-mills for corn were employed in the individual households is not known. Those found in London excavations show that both the small hand-mill and the large variety worked by asses or mules were in use.[1]

Market gardening in the outskirts of the city must soon have become an extensive and flourishing industry, even if private gardens were usual in the suburbs and on the fringe of the more compactly-built centre within the town-wall.

Over and above the productions of British potteries, an enormous quantity of red glazed ware, the type known as Samian or *terra-sigillata*, was imported. Almost every site produces many fragments of this fine quality of earthenware.

Food supplies in large quantities had to be brought in daily to the markets of Londinium, and, apart from oil and wine, it may be taken that at first nearly all requirements were produced within a short radius. With growth of the population an increasingly large area would doubtless have been tapped. Good roads having come into existence, and with the useful waterway of the Thames in addition, the question of the transport of supplies presented no difficulties whatever. An appreciable portion of the city's food was obtained from the unpolluted Thames itself. The upper reaches still swarm with coarse fish, including pike, perch, roach, dace, and barbel. Of the more delicate kind trout are abundant, and salmon did not disappear until after 1812, while Southwark plaice were a delicacy until as late as the seventeenth century.

AN AMPHORA TYPICAL OF THOSE FOUND THROUGHOUT THE WALLED AREA OF LONDON. *2 ft. 11 ins. high.* (Guardian Assurance Company's Offices, King William Street.)

Throughout the first eighty years of the period under review it is probable that the city was unwalled. If the need for such a defence was felt after the catastrophe of A.D. 60 it does not appear to have been acted upon for nearly two generations. It may be that something in the way of gateways

[1] C. Roach Smith, *Roman London*, p. 147.

stood on the roads at certain points of entry into the city area
—bars as it were for administrative purposes, but this is only
a conjecture.

Londinium was in no sense a military station. It was the
great commercial centre and civil capital of the Province of
Britain. If any military units were stationed in the city they
would have been exceedingly small, and might merely have
been details to form the guard at the Treasury and the residence or offices of the administrative headquarters. Monuments of soldiers belonging to the legions on the frontiers
have been found in London, but this merely indicates that
retired soldiers came to live or happened to die in the capital.

Of the nature of the buildings in which the civil population

A FOURTH-CENTURY STREET FRONT IN ROME.
It is of brick and is probably typical of those built in Londinium at that time.

lived and carried on their business the discoveries that have
been made provide only the scantiest materials to work upon.
It would be unsafe, in endeavouring to envisage the type of
buildings occupied, to think only of such plans of structures
as those that have been conjecturally restored at the quiet little
country town of Calleva (Silchester). A better standard of
comparison is established by the brick-built continuous ranges
of houses found at Rome, Ostia, Pompeii and other Italian
towns. The single arch of the ground floor shop has perpetuated itself to-day in Italy and in certain parts of France—
notably Auvergne, that was the last fragment of Gaul to be
conquered by the Visigoths. Buildings of this type must have
been the rule all over the central part of Londinium. As to
the public offices, if they were built upon anything of the same
scale as that of the great basilica, they would have been imposing in architectural style. A certain amount of evidence

exists for believing that their embellishment was not unworthy of the city's rank.

In conjunction with the famous Bacchus mosaic pavement
found on the site of East India House were several pieces of
green porphyry (or *verde antique*), pointing to handsome
decorative effects in marble. The late Professor Lethaby[1]
thought that this building, close to the forum and the basilica,
may have been the Governor's palace, or, as it would be called
to-day, Government House. As the most important official
residence in Londinium, it would have received those
emperors who came to Britain. That the capital was honoured
when imperial visits took place may be regarded as inevitable,
for, owing to its position at the great road centre of the
province, Londinium could not be avoided, quite apart from
its political importance that would have made it the natural
objective in any case.

When, therefore, in 120, Hadrian hurried to Britain after
the disaster to Legio IX it may be taken as almost certain that
he came to Londinium in connection with that administrative
reorganisation to which Spartianus makes brief allusion.[2]

Not many years after this imperial visit to Britain a great
fire occurred in the city. The evidence that points to a date
between 125 and 130 for such a disaster was found in 1929
when foundations for Regis House between King William
Street and Fish Street Hill were being dug. Mr Quintin
Waddington records the uncovering of a layer of burnt
materials of great extent on this site, and he has also found
that it occurs on both sides of King William Street from
London Bridge to the southern side of the Bank of England,
and, still more significantly, on the west side of Walbrook
along the northern side of Cannon Street. That the fire was
widespread and in the heart of the business centre of the city
is thus obvious; now the Regis House site discoveries have
told something more. It was found that the burnt débris at
this place had been collected from a considerable area to
form ballast behind the massive timbering of the river embankment, for it had been rammed down, forming in places a
layer 7 feet thick. It consisted of what appeared to be crumbled
brick interspersed with particles of charcoal that were evidently the remains of wattle and daub, and embedded in it

---

[1] *Londinium*, p. 175.   [2] Spartianus, *Vita Hadriani*, chap. xi. p. 2.

BRONZE HEAD OF HADRIAN.

Found in the bed of the Thames at London Bridge. It is the only portrait bust of a Roman Emperor recorded to have been discovered in Britain.

The bronze hand unearthed in Lower Thames Street may or may not have any connection with the head. The scale of the two relics does not entirely rule out the possibility. To Hadrian, Roman Britain and its chief city owed a great debt, and if he had decreed the construction of the defensive wall, London would have wished to possess a statue of him. It has been suggested that the bronze shows Hadrian at about the age of 30, whereas his visit to Britain took place when he was 46. There is no reason to regard this as an insuperable objection for acceptance of the statue in about A.D. 122, for the artistic conventions for the period favoured the age of 30 for portraiture.

(*British Museum.*)

were thousands of fragments of Samian ware, "burnt," says Mr Waddington, "to every shade from its pristine sealing-wax red to a glossy black which gave it the appearance of being carved in jet." From the scores of potters' marks and the style of decoration[1] it was possible to place the disaster in the reign of Hadrian, *i.e.* between 117 and 138, while other evidence has narrowed the margins to the middle five years of the reign.

A very notable fact was the paucity of roofing tile fragments that have been found in all this débris. It appears with little room for doubt to point to thatch or wooden shingles. The latter may have been used, but there is no evidence for this, and there seems to be no alternative to picturing the Londinium of the first half of the second century as having only its important buildings and the houses of the more wealthy citizens tiled; the rest would have been thatched. Further than this, the evidence of the great conflagration points to many buildings with walls of wattle and daub on timber framing.

The tendency to imagine that the great cities of the Roman Empire were entirely constructed of stone, brick or marble with more or less uninflammable roofs covered with massive tiles is unjustified by facts. Rome itself suffered frequently from extensive and disastrous fires. To find support for this statement it is only necessary to turn to the pages of Aulus Gellius[2] in order to realise the situation in the Eternal City at this period. Of one incident he writes: "We friends of his [the rhetorician Antonius Julianus] therefore thronged about him on all sides and were escorting him home, when, as we were on our way up the Cispian Hill we saw that a block of houses, built high with many stories, had caught fire, and that now all the neighbouring buildings were burning in a mighty conflagration. Then some one of Julianus' companions said: 'The income from city property is great, but the dangers are far greater. But if some remedy could be devised to prevent houses in Rome from so constantly catching fire, by Jove I would sell my country property and buy in the city.' And Julianus replied to him in his usual happy and graceful style: 'If you had read the nineteenth book of the *Annals* of Quintus Claudius, that excellent and

---

[1] This pottery is in the Guildhall Museum.
[2] *The Attic Nights of Aulus Gellius* (trans. J. C. Rolfe, Loeb Series), Book XV. 1. Gellius was probably born about A.D. 123.

faithful writer, you would surely have learned from Archelaus, a praefect of King Mithridates, by what method and by what skill you might prevent fires so that no wooden building of yours would burn, even though caught and penetrated by the flames.'

"I enquired what this marvel of Quadrigarius was. He rejoined: 'In that book then I found it recorded, that when Lucius Sulla attacked the Piraeus in the land of Attica, and Archelaus, praefect of King Mithridates, was defending it against him, Sulla was unable to burn a wooden tower constructed for purposes of defence, although it had been surrounded with fire on every side, because Archelaus had smeared it with alum.' "

In 209 Severus I., with his two disreputable sons, arrived in Britain and must have passed through Londinium on his way to Eboracum. At that fixed camp of the Sixth legion—the chief military headquarters of the north—he laid his plans for those wearisome Caledonian campaigns that filled the closing years of his life.[1] It is clearly stated that while Severus took Antoninus "Caracallus" with him to the front beyond Hadrian's Wall, Geta was left behind as viceroy of the province, and it may be that he divided his time between Eboracum and Londinium. It has been suggested by various writers, including the younger Arnold[2] and others who apparently followed him,[3] that Eboracum was the capital of Britain. In support of this theory there appears to be no evidence at all; on the contrary, every indication, archaeological and historical, emphasises the overwhelming supremacy of Londinium. The fact that two Roman Emperors died at Eboracum is merely incidental. Both Severus and Constantius I. were engaged in military operations of which the camp of Legio VI was the natural base. It is quite true that Spartianus writes of a *domus palatina* at Eboracum, but seeing that Severus had had his headquarters there for two years it may be taken that some special group of buildings had been put up to accommodate the large staff that accompanied him. It does not appear that more is implied; the residence of the Emperor, even if it were only a tent, was the *domus palatina* for the time being.

[1] See the author's *Roman York*, chap. iii.
[2] W. T. Arnold, *Roman Provincial Administration*, p. 151.
[3] See p. 37 in booklet on Roman Britain, in the World's Manuals.

After the death of Severus on the 4th of February 211, Londinium unquestionably saw his two sons, now joint emperors, as they journeyed back to Rome, where Geta was shortly to perish at the hands of assassins ordered by "Caracallus." With the two brother emperors was Papinianus, the famous jurist, then *Prefectus Praetorio*, who was to fall a victim with Geta to the savagery of "Caracallus" after having vainly attempted to keep the peace between them.

Thus, although historians are silent concerning this period of Londinium's existence, archaeology makes it possible to build up a picture of the city within the limitations that have been indicated.

The visitor, arriving from Rutupiae by the historic highway through the country of the Cantii (now called Watling Street), would enter a somewhat ill-defined quarter to-day represented by Southwark. He would find that the traffic converged upon a long wooden bridge wide enough for an inward and an outward flow, and that from it he would obtain an arresting view of the central part of the city, its low-pitched red or creamy-red roofs contrasting with the varied shades and steep pitch of the thatch showing over red stuccoed or stone walls with here and there uncovered red brick as a glowing contrast. Pillared porticoes would now and again break the monotony of the roof-lines, but otherwise a somewhat featureless outline no doubt presented itself. If a temple of Jupiter occupied an elevated site, as would be almost inevitable, its roof-line and imposing colonnade would be a conspicuous feature. Below the buildings, the stranger would note busy quays with a number of large as well as small square-rigged ships made fast against them. Coming closer to the north end of the bridge, the cosmopolitan origin of the seamen and loungers would be easily noticeable. The traffic would break up into various narrow streets going out from the head of the bridge and the visitor would soon be involved in a stream of vehicles, litters, and foot passengers proceeding to or from the forum. Unless he were wary he might be jostled a good deal and even be lightened of his purse before finding himself in the teeming centre of the city's civic life.

How and when Christianity first made its appearance in Londinium is a matter of pure speculation, but there is no reason to regard it as impossible that there were professing

Christians among the arrivals from the Continent not very long after the conquest of Britain in A.D. 43. Equally, none may have reached the island until many years later, and those in Londinium may have been so few throughout the first century after Christ that they would have been compelled to

ROMAN SAILING SHIP, SECOND CENTURY A.D.

(Crown Copyright. From an exhibit in the Science Museum, South Kensington.)

It was vessels like the one illustrated above which maintained contact between Rome and Londinium. They were square rigged; and usually had one main-mast and a subsidiary mast projecting over the bows, a kind of half foremast half bowsprit, known as an *artemon*, on which was set a spritsail. A few of the largest vessels had two masts in addition to the *artemon*. Two triangular topsails were often set above the yard. These vessels were seldom of more than 250 tons burthen. Their length was probably about 95 feet and their average sailing distance about 55 sea miles on a summer day. Though not markedly inferior to the ships of Columbus, the Roman ships could not sail so close to the wind. Such vessels would, more often than not, be manned by Greeks, who were the chief sailors of the Roman Empire. The use of the swan design as finish to the stern seems to have been practically universal in merchantmen.

practise their faith in private. The progress of Christianity north-westward was undoubtedly slow. It was only in the partly Greek towns of the Rhône Valley that any large numbers of adherents were found as late as the second century. There is, however, the evidence of Tertullian and Origen, who wrote in the early part of the third century, that there was an appreciable Christian element in remote Britain. The legend of the "British" King Lucius and Pope Eleutherius (*circa* 180) is, however, without foundation as regards this country. Lucius was Prince of Edessa, and the supposed Britannia may be a misreading of *birtha*,[1] the citadel of his town.

The martyrologies supply a certain amount of information as to the progress of Christianity in the third century, but the earliest of these (called after the name of St Jerome) was probably not compiled until the sixth century. It contains two names concerning Britain, those of Augulus—an other-

SCULPTURED STONE.
From Duke Street, Aldgate.
(*Guildhall Museum, 20 in. by 11½ in.*)

wise unknown bishop of Londinium—and Albanus, who is said to have suffered martyrdom in about 303. For what this late compilation is worth, it affords evidence of a bishop of Londinium possibly as early as 250.

Gildas conjectures that St Alban was martyred in the persecution of Christians that occurred under Diocletian in A.D. 284. There is, however, no evidence that this persecution ever spread to Britain, and it seems therefore more likely that it took place in either the persecution of Decius (250-1) or of Valerian (257-60). Both Gildas and Bede refer to the *Passio Sancti Albani*, a presumably early writing long since lost.[2]

[1] *Liber Pontificalis.*
[2] *Dict. of Eng. Church Hist.* (E. F. Warren), p. 70.

Chapter V

DURING the middle period of the third century the Roman Empire was suffering from an accumulation of evils that was destined to weaken it beyond the limits of recovery. The decline had begun, and the titanic empire whose great reserves of strength had been so terribly depleted was unable to recover its former prosperity. Perpetual invasions and frequently recurring civil war, with the added misery of protracted periods of plague and famine, were the lot of nearly all the provinces from the English Channel to the Euphrates. Alone among them Britain seems to have escaped all but the slightest injury from these malefic influences.

Despite the fact that the literary evidence is very scanty, there is considerable archaeological testimony to prove that the country was at peace. The overseas trade of Londinium and other ports must have been affected on account of the state of economic wreck that supervened in Gaul, consequent upon the invasions of the Alemanni from Germany in the latter half of the century. On the other hand, there is considerable reason to believe that the volume of exports actually increased, on account of the augmented demand for foodstuffs and other necessaries the Gallic provinces could no longer produce for themselves. Writing in 296, Eumenius[1] the Gallic panegyrist of Constantius "Chlorus," refers in glowing terms to the remarkable wealth and prosperity of Britain, a country notable for its vast wealth in corn and cattle, its numerous and productive mines yielding a huge revenue, and also for the busy harbours with which it was girdled. Later authorities[2] down to Zosimus speak of the great exports of corn from Britain to impoverished Gaul. As an inevitable result of this large external demand, the price of corn would have risen steadily. Yet another evidence of the abounding prosperity of the country is provided by Eumenius, who says that the ruined Augustodunum (Autun) was rebuilt by means of skilled craftsmen sent from Britain "in whom those provinces

[1] Eumenius, *Panegyric*, V.

[2] Emperor Julianus, IV., *A Letter of the Athenians*; and Ammianus Marcellinus, Book XVIII. chap. ii. sec. 3; Zosimus, III. 5.

abound."[1] It is, therefore, possible that the work of British masons still exists at Autun, a town that has preserved a number of its Roman buildings. Londinium, as the great emporium of the island, must have profited enormously through the needs of its neighbours.

In the last quarter of the third century, however, the faint mutterings of the storm gathering in North-west Germany were beginning to be heard, a tempest that in the end was to bring catastrophic destruction upon the flourishing Roman dominion. On account of causes still quite obscure the tribes

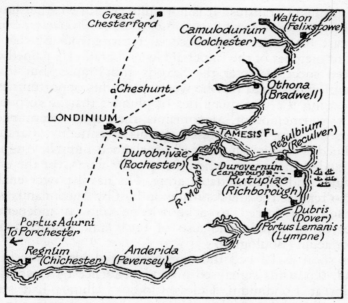

SKETCH MAP OF THE OUTER DEFENCES OF LONDINIUM.

at the mouths of the Ems, Weser, and Elbe, generically called Saxons, but accompanied at this time by Franks and (probably) Frisians, began to indulge in piracy on the sea, and thus Britain, immune during the earlier stages of their activities in Gaul and elsewhere, began to suffer loss and inconvenience. An effort seems to have been made to check their activities by the debauched and short-reigned Emperor Carinus who, for

[1] Eumenius, *Paneg. Const. Caes.*, 18, "Quibus illae provincae redundabant."

some reason, assumed the additional title of "Britannicus Maximus." As there is no trace of Pictish trouble at this time, it seems probable that the cognomen was adopted after a victory gained by the British fleet either in the Channel or the North Sea. But it was not until Carinus had been replaced by the great Diocletian that a definite policy was adopted to ward off the piratical attacks.

In 285 Diocletian's adopted colleague, Maximianus, organised a fleet in the Channel, probably at Gesoriacum (Boulogne) and placed in command an experienced naval officer, a Gallo-Roman of the tribe of the Menapii, named Maus(onius) Carausius. It is not quite certain whether he was officially styled *Comes Litoris Saxonici per Britannias*, but in any case his duties were those later carried out by that important member of the Imperial General Staff. He gained very marked successes over the Saxons and Franks, but it was presently whispered that he was abusing his opportunities by embezzling the vast quantities of plunder that he recovered. The western emperor, Maximianus, thereupon determined to supersede him, but, foreseeing this eventuality, Carausius mutinied with his whole fleet, proclaimed himself Augustus and landed in Britain, where he quickly won over the entire province and its formidable army. His naval power enabled him to repulse the attacks made on him by Maximianus who, in 289, was forced to acknowledge him as independent Emperor of Britain and also of the Gallic district around Gesoriacum (Boulogne).

As soon as he had thoroughly secured his power in the island, Carausius signalised his independence by establishing a mint at Londinium. Unless Clodius Albinus had struck coins in Londonium when he became junior Emperor in 193, the capital for the first time since its Romanisation now began the issue of coined money.[1]

In spite of the temporary break of political relations with Gaul, the trade of Londinium may have continued with comparatively little interference; in fact, seeing that Carausius soon made peace with the Franks, a small zone of business enter-

---

[1] The evidence as to mints of Carausius at Camulodunum and Rutupiae rest only on the letters "C" and "R," and the latter might equally well represent Rotomagus (Rouen). See Percy Webb's articles on the "Coins of Carausius," in *Numismatic Chronicle*, 1907-8.

prise may have been opened, and undoubtedly after 289, when Maximianus had reduced Gaul to a certain amount of order, there may have been a temporary wave or boom of prosperity. In any case Carausius maintained his great fleet and a large army, including thousands of German mercenaries, without, so far as appears, any undue strain upon the resources of Britain. The real test of its prosperity is afforded by the fact that, while the money of all the rest of the Roman Empire was in a hopeless condition of depreciation and disorder, Carausius was issuing an abundant coinage at Londinium in pure gold, silver, and copper washed with silver.[1] All his gold coins are, however, so rare that it appears that the number struck was comparatively small. Sir Charles Oman thinks that the variety of honorific designs and eulogistic inscriptions on the Carausian coinage testifies to a real feeling of gratitude for his enlightened care of the country.

Having established his power he, like the rival emperors whom he now designated his colleagues, naturally assumed a pompous title. His full imperial name was Marcus Aurelius Valerius Carausius with, in some cases, his indefinite Gallic name Maus . . . besides. Amongst the laudatory inscriptions on his coins are found: VBERTAS AVG = "wealth (or wealth-productiveness) of the Emperor"; FELICITAS TEMPORVM = "Happiness of the Times"; RESTITVTOR SAECVLI = "Restorer of the Age"; and yet another motto, perhaps selected by himself, is RENOVATIO ROMANORVM = "Revival of the Romans," that appears with a representation of the wolf suckling Romulus and Remus.

The four years of peace that followed the recognition of Carausius as local Emperor ended in 292, when war was declared upon their intrusive colleague by Diocletian and Maximian, who were anxious to regain control of the most flourishing province of the Empire.

The command was entrusted to Flavius Constantius "Chlorus," Caesar or sub-emperor of the West. All that he could do at the moment was to capture Gesoriacum, for in face of the formidable fleet the British Emperor had created, no attempt could be made to cross the Channel. It seems, however, that with the failure to retain his last conti-

[1] H. Mattingly, in J.R.S., xi., pt. 2, p. 260, makes the statement that the Carausian coinage was the first certainly issued in Britain.

nental foothold, Carausius lost prestige among his officers, for in the next year he was assassinated by a certain Allectus, whom Eumenius calls *satelles* (=underling) and was therefore probably one of the usurper's generals or admirals.

Allectus seems to have had little of the ability of his predecessor, and in any case his throne would appear to have been insecure from the first, probably on account of a certain loyalty to Carausius's memory among the regular legionaries. Eumenius states that in the last struggle Allectus could only rely on his Germanic mercenaries; in any case he remained inactive for some three years, during which time Constantius built an overwhelming fleet in the harbours of Gaul.

The crisis came in 296. The fleet of Allectus was lying in the Solent awaiting the expected attack. One division of the opposing naval forces, commanded by Asclepiodotus, the *Praefectus Praetorio,* sailed directly to the attack, possibly from Rotomagus (Rouen), while Constantius, with the other division, put to sea from Gesoriacum, apparently intending to operate on the Kentish coast. The Caesar's division, missing its course in a thick fog, wandered round the North Foreland and sailed up the Thames to Londinium.

Asclepiodotus, on reaching the coast of Britain, burnt or disabled all his ships and marched upon Londinium with every man available for the fighting line. The "tyrant" also abandoned his fleet and hastened to bar the march of the Praetorian Prefect upon his capital. He had with him the *veteres illius coniurationis auctores* (=the ancient promoters of that conspiracy), in other words the veteran marines who had established the power of Carausius together with the hated barbarian Germans. It is not known where the armies met, nor does the fact that a great hoard of Gallic coins mixed with a small percentage of those of Carausius and Allectus found at Blackmoor, near Woolmer Forest in Hampshire, give much, if any, aid in locating the battlefield. Hoarding had become so prevalent late in the third century that it would be unwise to regard this Blackmoor hoard as a hurriedly buried pay-chest. Wherever the battle was fought, Asclepiodotus inflicted a heavy defeat upon the usurper's forces. Allectus was killed in the rout, and a great slaughter was made of the marines and Franks; but hardly a single Roman citizen is said to have fallen,

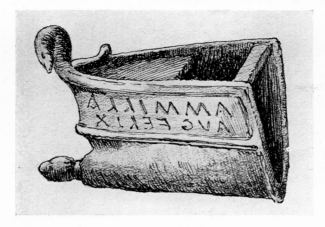

PROW OF A ROMAN WARSHIP IN BRONZE (MINIATURE)
DREDGED FROM THE BED OF THE THAMES.

Inscribed in retrograde *"Ammilla Aug Felix,"* and commemorates a ship of
that name (*British Museum*).

GOLD MEDALLION COMMEMORATING THE RELIEF OF LONDINIUM BY CONSTANTIUS IN 296.

A female figure kneeling at a city gateway symbolises London indicated with the letters LON, and Constantius,
the deliverer, on a charger and armed with a spear, is shown above a galley with a massive prow and single bank
of oars. The mint mark is that of Trèves. The medallion was dug up at Beaurains near Arras and is in the
museum of that town.

(Enlarged from 1⅝ inches in diameter.)

REMAINS OF A ROMAN SHIP DISCOVERED IN 1910 UNDER 7 FT. OF THAMES MUD ON THE SITE OF THE COUNTY HALL, LONDON.

It is the central part of the vessel and is of oak. It was carvel-built—that is to say, its planks were flush and not over-lapping as in clinker-built ships. The length of what has survived is 38 ft. and the breadth 18 ft. The estimated dimensions of the complete vessel are 60 ft. long by 16 wide (*London Mus. Catalogue No. 3*, p. 152). The four bronze coins found in and under the ship were: 1. Tetricus the Elder, 268-273. 2. Carausius in Britain, 286-293. Both were beneath ribs. 3. Carausius, 286-293; and 4. Allectus in Britain, 293-296. The last two were discovered in the vessel. In addition, "several large rounded stones" weighing about 3 lbs. each were found, one of them "partially embedded in a strake," and thus indicating that it had fallen from a height. The coins and the owing to the fact that the usurper had not dared to bring his regular troops to the front.

The disorganised mob of fugitives fled to Londinium, where they succeeded in entering the city, and were proceeding to indulge in indiscriminate sack and massacre when, in the very nick of time, Constantius arrived and his fleet dropped anchor in the Thames. Troops were promptly put ashore and Londinium was soon rescued from the mercenaries, who were slaughtered in the streets of the city.[1]

Making every allowance for exaggeration on the part of the panegyrist, there can be no doubt whatever that the citizens of the capital felt unfeigned gratitude at the almost providential succour brought by Constantius at a critical moment, for although the army of Asclepiodotus was no doubt pressing on by forced marches, the mob of semi-savage mercenaries could have wrought immense havoc in a very few hours.

Further confirmation of this episode in the history of Londinium is afforded by the gold medallion struck at Trèves to commemorate the triumph of Constantius as "Caesar Invictus." This fine example of the numismatic art of the time shows on the reverse a representation of the Emperor, on horseback and carrying a spear, while the city is indicated by a figure kneeling before him in front of a turreted gateway under which appears the abbreviation LON. Below is a galley with a single bank of oars representing the arrival of the fleet in the Thames. The inscription, reading, "*Redditor lucis aeternae*," implies the idea of the re-entry of Britain into the eternal daylight of the World Empire.

An interesting object, that may perhaps be associated with this event, is the barge or galley found embedded in the Thames mud when the foundations of the County Hall were being excavated in 1910. With it coins of Tetricus, Carausius and Allectus, together with other objects, including horseshoes and sherds of pottery, were discovered, and it seems possible that it was a unit of the fleet of Allectus sunk by those of the rescuing flotilla. There is also a miniature representation in bronze of the prow of a Roman vessel bearing the inscription AMMILLA AVG FELIX. It was in the Roach Smith collection and is included by him among other objects dredged from the bed of the Thames near London Bridge.

[1] Eumenius, *Paneg. Const. Caes.*, chap. xvii.

The lettering is late and on the whole it is fairly safe to ascribe this very interesting object to the end of the third or to the fourth century. The fact that the lettering is picked out in niello lends support to a late date. It is possible that the object commemorates a famous ship, and the palm branch shown on the starboard side indicates a victory. This may have been the success gained by Constantius. It is certainly the most impressive naval episode connected with the capital in the Roman period that history has recorded. Alternatively it is possible that the bronze prow may have been cast to commemorate a victory won far from London by a ship that specially distinguished itself in one of the naval exploits of Carausius or Constans I.

In any attempt to picture the background of this event it is not yet possible to decide whether the river front had been fortified or not at this time nor whether bastions had been added along the landward defences. The destruction of Hadrian's Wall by the Maeatae in about 197 may have led to the strengthening of London's town-wall early in the third century, but it is perhaps more likely that the construction of bastions and the building of the riverside wall did not come about until the Saxon threat from overseas became a source of anxiety towards the end of that century.

The entry of Allectus's mercenaries into the city, apparently without difficulty, may indicate that the gates were flung open by a garrison consisting in part, at least, of others of his hired supporters. The behaviour of the Franks having been of such a savage nature, the civil population would no doubt have contrived to let in the relieving force of Constantius with small difficulty, and if the wall facing the Thames had not yet been built, the naval detachments would have had a comparatively easy task in finding ways into the city from wharves and waterside entries.

The chief monument to the Carausian interlude is the prolific coinage, of which the bulk was struck at the Londinium mint. Not only are there the purely provincial types, to which reference has been made, but in addition there is what may be called a fraternal imperial coin in which the head of Carausius appears side by side with those of his late rivals. Over and above this, Carausius struck large issues of coins bearing the names and emblems of legions, both those in Britain and on the Continent, the reason in the latter case being that he was endeavouring to win them over to his side by donations and flattery.

The authority of the Roman Empire being re-established in Britain by the victory of Constantius, Londinium was once more without restrictions or embarrassment in its relations with the Continent, and trade handicaps would doubtless have been removed, although the very heavy taxation imposed by Diocletian may have tended to produce a depressing influence on commerce. High taxation, as is well known, inevitably produces an increase in the cost of commodities, and Diocletian, an emperor of the successful "working-class" type, had the proletarian's ignorant belief that economic evils can be cured by legislation. Thus, in 301, he issued his Edict of Prices, in the confident expectation that thereby the distress resulting from bad harvests and enormous expenditure on perennial warfare would be relieved, and the cost of living reduced from its abnormal figures. From the causes mentioned the price of necessaries had soared 800 per cent. Accordingly Diocletian drew up a long list of maximum prices for food, clothing and rates of salaries and wages. Anyone exceeding the figures laid down was liable to capital punishment or, in the case of slight infraction, to deportation. It was ordered that the list of fixed prices should be exhibited in all markets and public places throughout the Empire, and Londinium, being a very important centre of trade, would no doubt have learnt the details as soon as the Edict was enforced. In the East, where Diocletian ruled directly from Nicomedia in Asia Minor, there was a determined attempt to enforce the provisions of this new legislation, for Lactantius has much to say of the Emperor's sanguinary measures to that end. Whether this state of things applied to Londinium may be questioned, for there is reason to believe that Constantius, a humane and tactful man, used much latitude in interpreting the letter of laws with which he did not altogether agree. It is also possible that the distress that the Edict was intended to combat was not nearly so severe in relatively prosperous Britain; but that Diocletian intended the enactment to apply to the West as well as the East seems clear from the reference to British cloaks that were, with the Gallic mantle, the most highly-priced outer garments in the list. Some of the grain prices may have been intended to apply to Britain, then so active in exporting

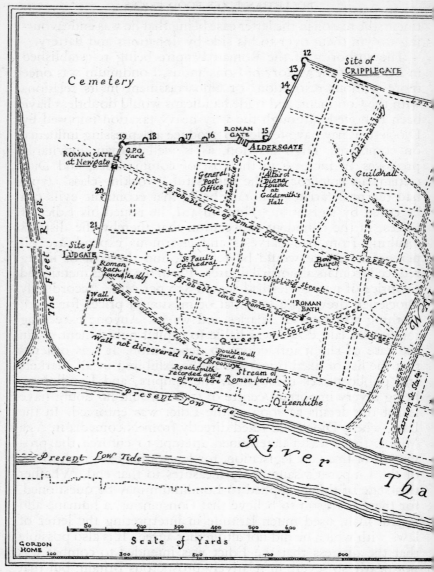

Cemetery

Site of
CRIPPLEGATE

12
13
14
15

ROMAN
GATE

ALDERSGATE

19 18 17 16

ROMAN GATE
at Newgate

G.P.O.
Yard

General
Post
Office

20

St. Martin's Gt.

Altar of
Diana
found
at
Goldsmith's
Hall

Probable line of Roman Street

Guildhall

Aldersgate St.

Wood St.

21

Site of
LUDGATE

The Fleet River

Roman
bath
found in 1667

Wall
found

Suggested alternative line

St. Paul's
Cathedral

Probable line of Roman Street

Watling street

Bow
Church

Cheapside

Roman
BATH

Watling street

Cannon Street

Cannon Street

Queen Victoria Street

Wall not discovered here

Double wall
found in
Brooks'm

Stream of
Roman period

Roach Smith
recorded angle
of wall here

Queenhithe

WATL...

FLEET ST.

Cannon St. & Ca...

Present Low Tide

River

Present Low Tide

Tha

50   200   300   400   500   600

Scale of Yards

GORDON
HOME

100   300   500   700   900

A PLAN O...

The landward wall that enclosed the city is shown with double lines from Ludgate to the Tower and where i...
is still known to exist the space between the lines is filled in solid black. Dividing the area of 326 acres into tw...
somewhat unequal parts is the Walbrook, that formerly flowed between the two hills enclosed by the great tow...
wall. This stream and its feeders now exist only in the form of underground drainage. The eastern position of the
city contained the Great Basilica (or Town Hall), the great forum and probably most of the temples and publi...
buildings. Taking the few places where streets have been found, the Basilica and the positions of the gateways as ...
basis, a possible layout in rectangular blocks has been suggested. It follows the plan published by R.C.H.M. i...

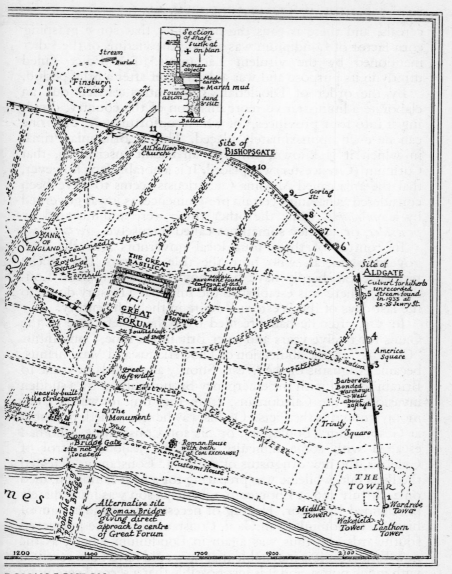

ROMAN LONDON.

its volume on Roman London. The position of the Roman Bridge has not yet been discovered. Such indications as have been brought to light are mentioned on p. 189. It was probably a little to the east of the site of Old London Bridge. The positions of the 21 semicircular bastions of the town-wall so far discovered or recorded are numbered from east to west. Those shown in solid black were built solid. They form an eastward group and may have been added to strengthen the wall at a time of great danger from the east. The wall facing the Thames may have been built or rebuilt at the same time. The group of hollow bastions to the west contain no re-used material and may have been added at a later date.

cereals, and there is thus the possibility that some grasping corn-factor of Londinium was among the victims of the Edict mentioned by the virulent Lactantius.[1] The Edict failed utterly in its purpose and was a dead letter after a brief period.

By the order of Diocletian, Constantius carried out an elaborate administrative reorganisation of the country, dividing it into four provinces,[2] of which, unfortunately, only one can be even approximately placed. This is Britannia Prima, in which it is known, through an extant inscription, that Corinium (Cirencester) was placed. It is a notable fact, however, that the area called Maxima Caesariensis seems to have been considered as having a certain pre-eminence, as it was governed by a *consularis*, while the other three were administered by *praesides*, or, as they sometimes called themselves, *rectores*.

In control of these four local governors was the civil governor-general, who bore the title *Vicarius*. His official residence can hardly have been anywhere else than in Londinium, where was established the Imperial Treasury down to the last days of the Western Empire in the fifth century.

In 305, after he had presided over the Praefecture of the Gauls for twelve years and over Britain for nine, Constantius "Chlorus," by the abdication of Diocletianus and Maximianus, became Augustus of the West. Shortly afterwards he came to Britain to deal with the emergency brought about by a sudden invasion of the Caledonians, from this time onwards commonly known as the Picts. On his way he was joined, probably at Gesoriacum[3] (Boulogne), by his son Constantine, who had escaped with some difficulty from the jealous control of Galerius, the new Augustus of the East. Constantius defeated the Picts but, while he was preparing for a final campaign, died on 25th July 306 at Eboracum, where his son was immediately proclaimed Emperor. Having of necessity to make certain of his father's dominions in Gaul, Constantine at once journeyed southwards and thus was again in Londinium where, as the new Emperor, it is inevitable that he would have been received with much pomp, and it is just possible that a second ceremony of acclamation took place in the capital.

[1] Lactantius, *De Mortibus Persecutorum*, chap. vii.
[2] They were: Maxima Caesariensis, Flavia Caesariensis, Britannia Prima and Britannia Secunda.
[3] Later called Bononia.

Gaul being secured, Constantine returned to Britain to finish the Pictish war, a task that he successfully accomplished. In the years that followed up to 312 he may often have been in his island dominion, and it is hardly to be questioned that during this period he would have from time to time resided in Londinium. There is no doubt that Britain claimed much of his attention, and it is quite possible that the river wall and at least the eastern group of bastions were added now; milestones of his reign are found widely spread throughout the country, showing care for the road system at this time.

The mint of Londinium was active; large numbers of coins were issued from it during the reign of Constantine. Villa-building also appears to have been active, almost inevitably the direct result of a great increase of private wealth due to a trade "boom."

It was probably in 326 that the mint of Londinium was closed. It had been first put into operation by the usurper Carausius (286-293) and issued gold, silver and copper washed with silver, and, according to Mr G. F. Hill,[1] this was the first of the British mints to begin production. Allectus (293-296) continued to issue gold and

SILVER INGOT found at the Tower of London bearing the inscription Ex OF-FE HONORINI [= Ex Officina Felicis Honorini].
From the workshop of Honorinus.

silvered copper from London, but no silver was minted. The reorganisation that took place in 296 brought to an end the issue of gold and silver except during the five years of the reign of Magnus Maximus.

The great stream of copper coins issued in London during the reign of Constantine appears to have ended with the deaths of Crispus and Fausta in 326 or, as there are no coins of Constantius II., possibly two years earlier. It need not be imagined that this closing of the mint, which had been established by military necessity, was any indication of a

[1] R.C.H.M., *Rom. Lond.*, p. 187.

decline in the wealth of Londinium. The height of prosperity and importance that the city attained soon after this time is very clearly indicated by the new and illustrious title of Augusta[1] conferred upon it on some occasion between 337 and 368. It could hardly have been given by Constantine, for all the coins struck by him at the London mint adhere to the old name. Coins struck by Magnus Maximus (383-388) bear "Aug" as the mint-mark, and Ammianus Marcellinus, writing in the last quarter of the fourth century, mentions the new name as though it had been recently conferred. Besides these approximately datable references, Augusta is also used in the *Notitia Dignitatum*, the martyrology ascribed to St Jerome,

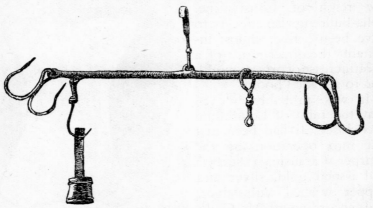

BRONZE SCALES FOUND IN LONDON WALL.
(*Guildhall Museum.*)

and by the Ravenna geographer, to none of which can a date be given.

The development of Christianity in the country may have been stimulated by the favour bestowed upon it by Constantine, and it is at any rate certain that, in 314, the British Church was a body of sufficient importance to send three bishops to the Council of Arelate (Arles). One of these prelates was Restitutus, Bishop of Londinium; another was Adelphius, "Bishop of the *Civitas colonia Londinensium* (probably an error for Lindensium = Lincoln)"; and the third was Eborius, Bishop of York. Although the evidences of Christianity in the city are very slight indeed, it is reasonable to suppose that,

[1] *Ammianus Marcellinus*, Book XXVII. chap. viii. 7; also coins.

after 312, the date of Constantine's "conversion," the community provided itself with churches of some type.

Fifty years of unbroken peace and uninterrupted commercial intercourse with the Continent, in which Britain played to a great extent the part of exporter, had no doubt carried the country and its capital to the highest level of affluence it was to reach again for a great many centuries to come. How the balance of exchange worked, if it is to be understood that British needs were small in value compared with those of the volume of the country's exports, is a problem difficult to solve. The imports of wine, oil, fruit, marble, copper and other metals, together with pottery, glass, silken goods and articles of luxury and ornament, may not have built up a balance without some other considerable item. Was this furnished by the import of slaves? Rough labour in Britain might have been cheapened by this means, and possibly the wealthy landowners were glad to purchase sturdy Teutonic workers in order to increase the cultivated area of their estates. It should not be forgotten that there were still at this time very large areas of forest in Britain, also fens and marshes that by means of draining and damming could be made profitable. In any case the great market in Gaul for British corn could not have failed to result in a steady encroachment of the arable zones on the primeval forest and waste lands.

The expansion of Londinium went hand in hand with all this rise in wealth, and its population must have grown in proportion. It has been calculated[1] that by the middle of the third century the city may have contained about 45,000 persons, and the extent to which it had grown a hundred years later requires consideration.

There are some fairly reliable figures as to the population of London in the Middle Ages, when all the conditions militated against so high a level of population, prosperity and health as during the Roman period. In the year 1199 Peter de Blois, Archdeacon of London, stated to Pope Innocent III. that London contained 40,000 souls. Creighton[2] considered this estimate to be fairly correct, and came to the conclusion that during the next three centuries the population

[1] See p. 80.
[2] "The Population of Old London," *Blackwood's Magazine*, April 1891.

ranged from 40,000 to 50,000. In the year 1631, when a famine was apprehended, an actual enumeration showed that the number of persons "within the walls," that is to say to all intents and purposes the Roman walled area, was 71,029, and Southwark added 18,660, bringing the total to 89,689. This does not include any other suburbs or outlying quarters and, in addition, it is possible that owing to the special reasons for this census, the exclusion of temporary residents and paupers would give a total lower than the normal number.

If conditions in seventeenth century London may be regarded as at all parallel with those in the fourth, Londinium with its suburbs may not improbably have held, about the year 350, as many as 90,000 inhabitants if the "floating" elements—traders, visitors, and seamen, and also the suburbs—are included. This would be a very high figure indeed if Professor Collingwood's estimate of half a million for the whole population of Roman Britain[1] is at all near the facts. He considered that the prehistoric technique of agriculture on upland soils was incompatible with the support of any greater number and that the towns founded by the invaders were too great a burden for this limited rural economy: hence their decline. This was countered by Mr H. J. Randall,[2] who argued in favour of a considerably higher figure in view of the greatly increased rural prosperity in the Constantinian Age (*i.e.* the second quarter of the fourth century), and he was followed by Dr Wheeler, who, in surveying the two points of view, drew attention to the presence of extensive prehistoric tillage on both upland chalk and oolite as well as lowland gravels, these soils being comparatively easy to clear in comparison with heavy soils producing timber of great size, and that it is due to the villa-system that there occurred in Romano-British times a partial movement into forest land. If it is accepted in addition that the prehistoric standard of agriculture was not a low one, the outcome of the discussion points to a population of a million and a half, which would make the figure of London's population suggested above much more justifiable.

Londinium Augusta by the middle of the fourth century had undoubtedly attained a prominent position among the

---

[1] *Antiquity*, vol. iii. (1929), pp. 261-76.
[2] *Antiquity*, vol. iv. (1930), pp. 80-90.

cities of the Roman Empire, being excelled by perhaps not more than a score of places in East and West.

The cloud in the East across the grey waters of the North Sea was gathering, but at this time it can hardly have been perceptible; the first threat to the profound peace in Britain since 306 occurred in the far north, perhaps beyond the Wall of Hadrian, where there is some reason to think that Constantine had established a form of protectorate.[1] The attack seems to have been made by the Picts in alliance with the Scots (*i.e.* North Irish). It was so sudden and violent that the danger called across the Channel in the depths of winter the last "legitimate" Emperor who is known to have visited Britain—Constans I., the third son of Constantine the Great. His success was rapid and complete, and was celebrated in high-flown language by the Christian Gallic writer Julius Firmicus Maternus.[2] Both in his journey from Bononia (Boulogne) to the seat of war and on his return Constans cannot have avoided passing through Londinium—to have lengthened the voyage in winter beyond Rutupiae would never have been contemplated by a Roman, especially a general whose object was to reach the danger zone with the utmost rapidity. That on reaching the north he engaged in some form of naval operations seems clear from the words of Firmicus, who writes of the waves of a sea hitherto almost unknown trembling beneath the oars of the imperial galleys. It was therefore probably in 343 (the year is a little uncertain) that the people of Londinium came for the last time into the streets to witness the entry of a Roman Augustus.

Possibly it was from the son rather than the father, as already suggested, that the capital of Britain received its title of Augusta, and in that case it was Constans I. who made the unsuccessful effort to supplant the name of Londinium. It is also just possible that this danger aroused the Emperor to take the precaution of strengthening the fortifications of the city, but again there is no evidence for this, and certainly the remoteness of the danger hardly gives support to the idea.

So far as is known, the victory just mentioned secured external peace for another seventeen years; there was, however, a certain amount of internal disturbance some ten years after

[1] Sir C. Oman, *England before the Norman Conquest*, p. 153.
[2] *De Errore Profanarum Religionum*, I. 125.

the meteoric campaign of Constans. In 350 that energetic ruler was slain by his British general Magnentius. It should be mentioned that at this time there were four grades in the high command of the Roman army. They were: (1) *Magister Militum* =Field-Marshal—either of Infantry (*Magister Peditum*) or Cavalry (*Magister Equitum*); (2) *Comes* =General; (3) *Dux* =Lieut.-General; and (4) *Praefectus Legionis*, roughly equivalent to Major-General commanding a division.[1] Magnentius at the time of his revolt was in charge of a detachment comprising two legions of unknown strength. He created his brother Decentius his Caesar or co-Emperor, and his rule seems to have been accepted by Britain without demur. These two Romano-Britons had a very stormy reign of three years in the west, being almost continually engaged in warfare with Constantius II., Emperor of the East—the last surviving son of Constantine the Great. After a decisive defeat in 353, Magnentius committed suicide and his brother was killed in Gaul.

Having re-established his authority in the West, Constantius, with the object of punishing the connections and supporters of the usurper, who were naturally very numerous, sent across to Britain Paulus, the *Notarius*, a Spanish Secretary of State whose evil reputation for "loading the bodies of freeborn men with chains and crushing some with fetters" had earned for him the unpleasant nickname of "*Catena*" (*i.e.* chain). The centre of his activities was evidently Londinium, for Ammianus Marcellinus[2] records that his methods quickly brought him into conflict with Martinus, the Vicarius or Governor-General—a man of totally different character in every respect. Such a clash of character and authority could only result before long in open hostility.[3] Martinus, concerned with defending the British citizens involved in the inquiry, many of whom he considered to be innocent of the accusations brought against them, exerted himself more and more strenuously, until Paulus, finding himself thwarted and hampered, allowed his anger to show beneath the imperturb-

[1] The modern division reaching 14,000 and upwards, it might be more accurate from the present-day standpoint to use the term brigade.

[2] *Amm. Marcellinus*, Book XIV. chap. v.

[3] The prisoners were not merely heavily chained, but on reaching the Emperor's camp they found racks prepared and the executioner busy preparing "his hooks and other engines of torture." *Amm. Marcellinus, ibid.*

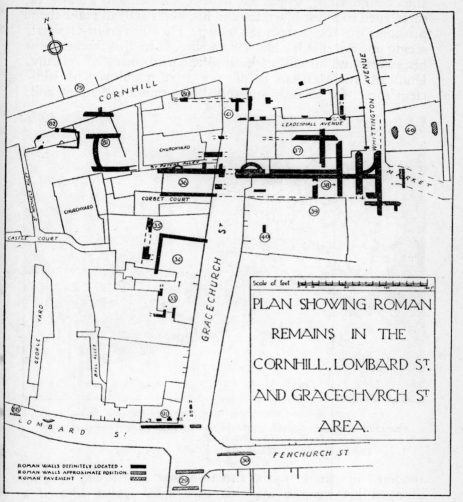

This locality is one of the most important in Roman London. It includes the site of the Great Basilica or Town Hall of the city and, south of it, that of the chief forum. The foundations came to light at widely separated intervals, and when previous editions of this book were published (1926) the whole plan had yet to be pieced together. The foundations show where it would be expected to find the N.W. portion of the forum and indicate that the great open space had at least one considerable structure in it markedly out of alignment with the basilica.

By Permission of the Royal Commission on Historical Monuments.

able countenance which he usually maintained. Finally he threatened to arrest Martinus and his whole staff and take them prisoners to the Emperor's court. The Governor-General, seeing at once that his life was endangerd by this threat, drew his sword and struck at the insolent instrument of tyranny. Unluckily for Martinus he did not drive his blow with sufficient force, for he only succeeded in wounding Paulus, and,

THE BASTION OF THE WALL NORTH OF NEWGATE (No. 19 ON PLAN).
The wall had sagged outwards above the modern supporting concrete as shown on the left.
This bastion is preserved under the Post Office yard in Giltspur Street.

rendered desperate by the situation that confronted him, he plunged his weapon into his own side, giving himself a mortal wound.

The Secretary recovered and, relieved of opposition by this tragic event, completed his unsavoury task, upon which he returned to the Emperor, taking with him in chains a number of prisoners condemned to torture and death. That these included persons of wealth and position may be inferred from Marcellinus's reference to the confiscation of their property. Since the imperial treasury was unquestionably at Lon-

dinium and the official residence of the Vicarius most likely
at the capital, it seems reasonable to suppose that the events
just described took place there: it is indeed difficult to imagine
where else they can have occurred. The scene may have
actually been enacted in the Basilica or in the Governor's
Palace.

Apart from this inquisition, that may have only affected a
small number of the wealthy and more influential classes,
Londinium continued to thrive, and this chapter closes with
the city prosperous, busy and probably still expanding. It
brings the story of Roman London to about the year 360,
when the storm brewing on the coasts of northern Germany,
and in the wildernesses of Hibernia and Caledonia, began at
last to make itself felt with ever-increasing severity.

THE last chapter ended with a hint of dangers brewing in more than one quarter, and the commerce of Londinium may at this time have begun to feel the first effects of the invasions of the Alemanni and Franks in Northern Gaul. By 360, the energy of Julian, the Caesar of the West, had much improved the situation in Gaul, but, while passing the winter in Lutetia (Paris), he received information that the Picts and Scots had violated the truce forced upon them by the victory of Constans, and were ravaging the country near Hadrian's Wall. The first reports were disturbing enough for Julian to think of proceeding himself to Britain, but being unable to leave Gaul on account of the threatening situation there, he sent over in his place his *Magister Armorum*, one Lupicinus. Of this highly-placed officer Marcellinus mentions that he was a man of talent in war and especially skilled in administration, but so haughty in his demeanour that he suggested the tragic actor, while at the same time he was notoriously avaricious and cruel.

Lupicinus landed at Rutupiae in the depths of winter and marched straight to Londinium,[1] where he established his headquarters and remained there while studying the situation. He brought with him two Moesian *numeri* (detachments) and some units of Batavi and Aeruli. Before, however, he had commenced active operations he was recalled, his presence being required on the Persian frontier. He took with him the Batavi and Aeruli, but doubtless the Moesian soldiers were sufficient to reinforce the danger point of the north, for the outbreak seems to have collapsed, and an interval of four years elapsed before any further hostilities in Britain were recorded.

The visit of the senior Field-Marshal of the western Empire to Londinium in 360 brought to the capital for the first time for many years the pomp and circumstance of war. With the haughty Lupicinus there would have been a brilliant staff representing nearly every race in the Empire, while the troops

---

[1] *Ammianus Marcellinus*, Bk. XX. chap. i.

TESSELLATED PAVEMENTS FOUND IN LONDON.

Above : Part of a pavement of a passage 6 ft. wide found in Threadneedle Street in 1841. The design, with its curious labyrinths, has a most unusual—almost "crazy"—effect.

Below : Brought to light in 1805 at the Bank of England 20 ft. W. of the W. gate of the Bank leading into Lothbury. 11 ft. square (*British Museum*).

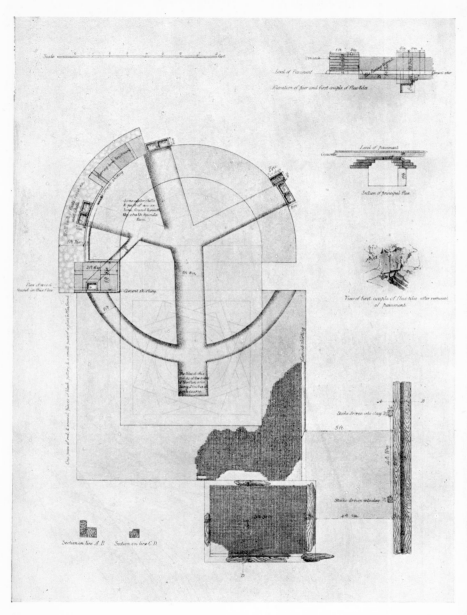

PLAN OF A ROOM IN BUCKLERSBURY FOUND IN 1869 AT A DEPTH OF 19 FT. BENEATH THE
ROAD SURFACE AND CLOSE TO THE BANK OF THE WALBROOK.

The tessellated pavement that covered the floor is illustrated on p. 171 and the warming system or hypocaust is
shown here. At the ends of the arms of the flues under the floor there were placed in pairs flue tiles that carried
the heated air through the walls and thus produced an even warmth all over the chamber. The position of the
furnace was not discovered.

themselves, largely composed of Teutonic mercenaries, must have been objects of much curiosity and interest to the citizens, and doubtless the various houses of entertainment, especially the wine shops and taverns, were exceedingly busy during the cold winter evenings, when the hard-drinking Teutons were making merry during the period of waiting for orders to march.

What impression these uncouth defenders of the Empire made upon the people of the city may be gathered from the interesting description given by Tacitus,[1] in connection with his account of the entry into Rome of the soldiers of Vitellius three centuries earlier. He writes of them as being unused to crowded streets, and mentions the rough way in which they conducted themselves among the populace, pushing the foot passengers with some violence when they found them in the way, and sometimes slipping down on the pavements through the pressure of the throng, accidents that they resented with abusive language and even sword blows. While it is not necessary to imagine that any extreme behaviour took place in Londinium when the Batavi and Aeruli entered its streets, this illustration of the behaviour of a rough soldiery in the crowded thoroughfares of a city, although not contemporary, is to some extent illuminating.

Londinium having resumed its normal existence with the departure of the troops, four years passed—then it was that the storm burst in all its fury. Julian had fallen in Mesopotamia, and the Roman Emperors were now Valentinian I., whose father had commanded in Britain, and his brother Valens. They assumed the purple in a whirlwind of trouble. Marcellinus, in a sentence breathing real vigour and emotion, writes of the trumpet giving the signal for war throughout the Roman world.[2] All the frontiers of the Empire from Britain to the Euphrates and along the desert boundaries of the African provinces were simultaneously assailed. Britain was attacked by all her enemies at once, Picts, Scots, Attacotti and Saxons making incessant raids. Effective help from the Continent could hardly be expected at first, for Valentinian had to face invasions along the whole of the northern limits of the Empire. For three years, therefore, the forces

[1] Tacitus, *Historia*, Book II. lxxxviii.
[2] *Amm. Marc.*, Book XXVI. chap. iv. para. 5.

8

in Britain were obliged to meet the general onslaught unaided, and to make matters worse, there was divided command.

The almost inevitable collapse came in 367, when two simultaneous disasters occurred, leaving the defences temporarily wrecked. The *Dux Britanniarum* named Fullofaudes, who commanded in the north, was defeated and apparently captured, and at the same time Nectaridus, the *Comes Litoris Saxonici*, was killed. This latter disaster brought the danger to the very gates of Londinium, and in no long space of time the whole country in its neighbourhood was being subjected to the horrors of invasion at the hands of barbarians, while the great city itself was soon in a state of blockade—"submerged in extreme difficulties,"[1] as the soldier-historian records the situation.

Whether parties of the invaders actually reached the suburbs of the capital or not, the alarm must have stimulated the authorities to set in motion every measure of precaution possible to secure the safety of the city. If the bastions had not already been built the strengthening of the town-wall by this means would have been a most reasonable precaution, and if those of the eastern group were by this time standing, the hasty erection of others to the north-west and west to complete the scheme may have taken place at this time together with a similar reinforcement of the river front.[2]

The Emperor Valentinian I. was naturally alarmed on hearing of the disaster that had befallen prosperous Britain, hitherto immune from anything more serious than frontier affairs. He was in Gaul, and actually on his way to Treveri (Trier) from Ambiani (Amiens), when the tidings of disaster were brought to him.[3] His first step to meet the emergency was the sending of Severus, the *Comes Domesticorum* (Commander of the Household Troops) to report on the situation, but he was quickly recalled. It is, however, possible that it was this officer who initiated the plans for strengthening the defences of Londinium and other places. His reports seem to have been alarming, and when he returned, the Emperor

---

[1] *Amm. Marc.*, XXVII. viii. 8, "mersam difficultatibus summis."
[2] See chap. ix.
[3] *Amm. Marc.*, XXVII. viii. He is the authority for the events up to the appointment of Civilis.

directed Valens Jovinus, the *Magister Equitum* (Field-Marshal
of Cavalry), to make another report on the position of affairs.
Having seen the extremes to which Britain was reduced, he
hurriedly despatched to the Emperor an officer named Prover-
tuides, with a message stating that conditions were so desperate
that unless powerful reinforcements were sent all would be
lost. Without further delay Valentinian appointed to the command in Britain Count Theodosius (the Elder), of Spanish
birth and undoubtedly at that time one of the ablest men in the
Empire, being possessed of rare ability both for war and
administration. To this trusted subordinate the Emperor
assigned a strong force of field legions and auxiliary cohorts.
Landing at Rutupiae, he found the road to the capital blocked
by roving bands of invaders, and was therefore compelled to
await the arrival of the first sections of reinforcements, consisting of the Palatine Guard regiments Jovii and Victores,
and some units of the Batavi and Aeruli, that had already been
in Londinium, as mentioned above.

As soon as the disembarkation had been carried out,
Theodosius moved to the relief of Londinium. To effect this,
his troops had the arduous task of clearing the surrounding
country of the many invading parties that were plundering far
and wide. The strength of the soldiers was taxed to the utter-
most, but the operation was successfully carried through, and
Theodosius entered the capital amidst the acclamation of the
rejoicing citizens, bringing with him thousands of provincials
whom he had rescued from the slave-gangs of the invaders,
together with enormous quantities of recovered plunder. It
is an interesting fact that he took especial care to see this
plunder restored to its proper owners. Only a small percentage was deducted as a reward for the troops who had
already, as the first-fruits of the campaign, effected so much.

There can be no doubt that Theodosius spent several
months in the capital reorganising the shattered and demoralised army of Britain round the nucleus of his victorious
troops. As many of the provincial soldiers had disbanded,
and were therefore technically guilty of desertion, he issued
proclamations guaranteeing immunity from punishment to all
who rejoined the eagles without delay. The result was the
pouring into Londinium of stragglers, who were soon re-
embodied in regular units, and in this manner the forces at

Theodosius's disposal for taking the offensive grew steadily throughout the winter of 368.

To aid his great general, Valentinian sent over to him one Dulcitius, an excellent officer, to replace Fullofaudes, the Dux Britanniarum. A new Vicarius or civil governor was also appointed in the person of Civilis, a man with a high temper, but inflexibly just—perhaps an indirect comment on his predecessor. Thus Londinium, throughout this crucial winter, was the very focus of the military and administrative activity of the three men who were preparing to restore Britain once more to peace and security.

The open spaces surrounding the city must inevitably have been the camping grounds of the growing army; huts and tents would have been everywhere in evidence; the strengthening of the wall may have been in progress, with transport vehicles adding congestion to the streets; a busy coming and going of orderlies from the camps and the administrative offices was a daily sight, and the feeling of great events impending would have been experienced in every quarter of the city. Wagon trains from Rutupiae laden with clothing, munitions and supplies of all descriptions must have rumbled over the bridge at all hours of the day and night.

No doubt the social side reflected the temporary militarisation of the place, and the reception chambers and dining rooms were enlivened by the presence of brilliant and often barbaric uniforms among the more sober garb of the citizens. Londinium was an opulent city. Its wealthier families could make considerable display when occasion required, and such an occasion was the present one, when hospitality to the saviours of the city was both a duty and a pleasure. Although the hours of work were long and strenuous, there were moments when relaxation was possible, and no attempt to reconstruct the life of Londinium during this winter would be complete if the element of a certain social brilliance were overlooked.

Preparations for the offensive having been completed, Theodosius launched his attack. Ammianus[1] describes the departure from the capital in a few telling words:

"And now Theodosius, that general of immortal fame, in the very fullness of his vigour marched forth from Augusta

[1] *Amm. Marc.*, XXVIII. iii.

(Londinium as the ancients called it) with an army which had gathered together with wonderful energy."

The campaign, in which the whole province was cleared of its invaders and retaliatory raids made by sea into Ireland and as far north as the Orkneys, was uniformly and completely successful, and Theodosius, having achieved a very great task, returned to the south and re-entered Londinium "after distinguishing himself by as many helpful victories as Furius Camillus or Papirius Cursor," the founders of Rome's dominion in Italy. So says the admiring Marcellinus, and he may be believed when he tells us that the inhabitants of Britain were "dancing for joy." The reception of their deliverers by the citizens of the capital must have been a more brilliant, joyous and heartfelt ceremony than had yet occurred in its annals. It is good to know that Theodosius was received by his somewhat unamiable Emperor with scarcely less cordiality, and was forthwith promoted to succeed Jovinus, the commander of the cavalry forces, whom the Emperor Valentinian considered to be lacking in energy.

The victory of Theodosius gave to Britain a further spell of peace that was not broken until about 383, a period of some fourteen years, during which it is permissible to suppose that much although not all of the damage caused by the invaders was repaired. There is a good deal of evidence for stating that many isolated homesteads and villas destroyed by the invaders were never rebuilt. No doubt the owners and their employees had in some instances been killed.

There is no other mention of Britain or British affairs in the pages of the invaluable Marcellinus except in 371, when he states that the Emperor Valentinian sent to the island a military settlement consisting of Bucenobantes, a tribe of the Alamanni, whom he had subjugated and deported. Where these Teutonic soldier colonists were settled is not known, but if sent anywhere north and west of the Thames on their way to their assigned locations they would have passed through Londinium.

Nothing more is recorded of Britain or its capital for twelve years. During this period great disasters overtook the Roman Empire. The able, though cruel, Valentinian I. died in 375, and was succeeded by his young son Gratian, who presently

earned much unpopularity among his soldiers by his undis-
guised liking for barbarian dress and habits. The discontent
affected the troops in Britain, who in 383 revolted and proclaimed as Emperor their most distinguished general, the
Spaniard Magnus Clemens Maximus.

While preparing for an invasion of Gratian's continental
dominions, he made his headquarters in Londinium, where he
re-established the Mint for the issue of gold and silver.
Troops on their way to Rutupiae, the usual point of embarka-
tion, must have passed through the capital, and thus once
more the streets echoed to the tramp of the legions. If, as is
sometimes suggested, Legio XX, that had been at Deva for
more than three centuries, formed part of this fourth-century
expeditionary force, it may be that Londinium now saw the
famous badge of the wild boar for the last time. There may
have been much military pomp in the city at this period, but all
thinking men must have viewed with alarm the diminution of
the country's defensive forces. Maximus, however, persisted
in his designs, and defeated and slew Gratian, only to hear
that the Picts had at once seized the opportunity and had
invaded Britain behind his back. He acted promptly, and the
attack was speedily defeated, presumably by reinforcements
sent from the Continent.

For five years Maximus reigned over Britain, Gaul, and
Spain, allowing Valentinian II., the half-brother of Gratian,
to retain Italy and Africa by an agreement with Theodosius
the Great, son of Britain's deliverer—Count Theodosius. But
when, in 387, Maximus, breaking the pact upon which his
power rested, invaded Italy, he was defeated in the following
year by Theodosius and beheaded near Aquileia (north-east
of Venice).

The five years of the reign of Maximus may have wrought
little change in Londinium, but if, as is said, his ambition led
him to drain Britain of its man power, it cannot be doubted
that a sense of increasing anxiety and insecurity, in face of the
growing overseas menace, would have indirectly hampered
trade. It is also stated, it is true by enemies of the Emperor,
that he was avaricious and grasping, in other words that his
taxation was very heavy—another cause for the curtailment of
enterprise and a consequent diminishing demand for labour.
At that time, however, rough labour was to a considerable

extent performed by slaves, and thus no very acute social problem presented itself. But at the same time it must have been becoming increasingly clear that the most prosperous days of Londinium Augusta were past, and although there may have still been intervals when the optimists began to think that the more flourishing years were returning, the city's existence henceforth was to be one of growing precariousness and uncertainty.

The population may not have diminished at this time: it may even have increased through the tendency in troubled times for the inhabitants of an exposed countryside to take refuge within the walls of fortified cities.

Whether the fresh waves of invasion began to distress Britain as early as 383, or whether the barbarians hung back until "Maxen Wledig," as Maximus is called in Welsh legend, had fallen is unknown, but it is quite certain that soon after his death Britain was being harassed on every side. The worst enemies during this troubled period were the Irish, who overran all Wales and harried the western and south-western coasts for many years, led by the famous King Niall of the Nine Hostages.

The position deteriorated between about 390 and 397, for the poet Claudianus,[1] who had the best possible sources of information, writes of Britain as living in continual dread of the painted Pict and the dart-throwing Scot, and watching anxiously for Saxon raids with every shift of the wind. It is possible that the coast flotillas, after the triumph of Theodosius, had fallen into a state of inefficiency, possibly owing to inability to spend money in this direction. The distress of the province evoked about 397 a special effort at defence on the part of Flavius Stilicho, the Romanised Vandal who, as *Magister Militum*, ruled the Western Empire in the name of Honorius, the weak-minded boy who had succeeded his great father Theodosius. To the beneficial results of his activity Claudianus[2] bears witness. He says that Stilicho (that is Stilicho's officers) defeated the Picts and Saxons. The poem was written about the year 399, and since it dates these victories in the reign of Honorius, that began in 395, the operations must have taken place between that year and 399.

[1] Claudianus, *De Consulatu Stilichonis*, Book II. 247-55.
[2] Claudianus, *In Eutropium*, I. 391-3.

Earlier dates have already been suggested for the adding of bastions to the town-wall, and as there is nothing that indicates any further strengthening of the city's defences, whatever took place at this time of alarm and danger is not known. The obscurity enveloping the occasions that led to the building of the two

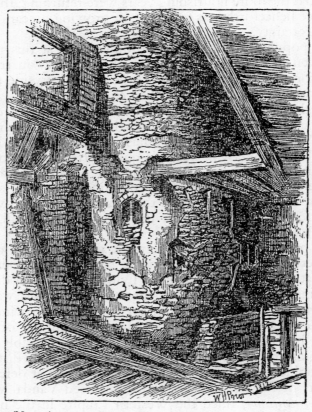

A Bastion (No. 15) of the Roman Wall of London, now demolished, as it appeared exposed at the Rear of No. 7 Falcon Square, Aldersgate.
Two courses of bonding bricks appear in the upper portion.

groups of bastions is so impenetrable at present that there is no reason to rule out the possibility that the later of the two was constructed at this time. The same state of uncertainty applies to the river front, concerning which there is just enough discovered to show that two periods of walling took place at least in one portion of the mile and a quarter facing the Thames.

When Stilicho's officers had completed their work, Claudianus proudly declared that Britain was secure from external attack. Unfortunately for the island province, events were soon to disprove this confident statement. Only three or four years later, when Stilicho's rival, Alaric, threatened to invade Italy, the great *Magister Militum* thought himself obliged to withdraw part of the garrison of Britain, and it seems nearly certain that one of the three legions that had been in Britain since the conquest by Claudius was now sent to the Continent.

The people of Londinium would have seen with still greater dismay in their hearts the passing through the city of a large number of the units of the army that had stood between them and repetitions on successive occasions of the fearful experience of 367 and the following year. It does not appear, however, that any serious disaster happened for a number of years, in fact it seems probable that the provincial troops were successful in driving the Irish completely out of Wales. The great Irish King Niall was killed about 405 in the English Channel, and his successor Dathi entered into friendly relations with the Roman Government. In Gaul, however, a catastrophe was soon to take place. A great mass of Teutonic invaders crossed the middle Rhine on New Year's Eve, 406, and made a devastating irruption, penetrating as far south as Tolosa (Toulouse). The whole of central Gaul was laid waste, and its chief cities, including Treveri (Trèves), Remi (Rheims), Ambiani (Amiens), Atrebates (Arras), Lutetia (Paris), Aureliani (Orleans) and Burdigala (Bordeaux), sacked. This invasion cut apart Britain from Stilicho at his headquarters in Italy. As far as Londinium was concerned the situation must have created a financial panic.

The ultimate result was to cause a burst of indignation in Britain, that, so far as can be seen, determined the country to throw off its allegiance to the half-imbecile Honorius and his Teutonic regent, who had shown their incapacity to protect the Empire. Naturally, as on previous occasions, the officers and officials determined to set up an emperor of their own. Their first choice was a soldier named Marcus, who was almost immediately assassinated. In his place was elected an official named Gratianus, who is described as a *municeps*. This is interesting, for it indicates that he held high office in one of the cities of Britain, and that city may have been

Londinium. If its preponderating size, wealth and influence be considered, the power to impose on the Province an emperor of its own choice is manifest.

Gratianus held power for only four months,[1] possibly a period when civil strife prevailed, for, like his predecessor, he came to a violent end. It is probable that the reason for his death was that he was unwilling to send the army away from the country to the help of Gaul. Acting on its own initiative, the army chose as emperor a man who is stated to have been no more than a private soldier, meaning, perhaps, that he had risen from the ranks. He is said to have claimed descent from Constantine the Great, and assumed the imperial names of Flavius Claudius Constantinus. He crossed to Gaul without delay, and the defensive forces of Britain were again weakened. Thus when, in 409, a fresh onslaught on the British coasts was made by the Saxons, the new Emperor, with the best of his troops, was far away. The situation was critical, but the province rose to the occasion, organised new regiments to fill the gaps, and completely defeated the invaders. Zosimus gives the impression that some of the cities were attacked, and it is just possible that hostile ships came up the Thames as far as Londinium itself, only to meet so stout a resistance as to regret their temerity.

One of the results of this invasion was the decision to revert to allegiance to the legitimate Emperor of the West, and although Honorius and his ministers, with Alaric in their very midst, could send no reinforcement to the defenders of Britain, they legalised the measures they had taken by a formal edict that would have been proclaimed in the capital. In fact throughout this period Londinium must have played a part of vital importance. The very fact that the invasion was a Saxon one brought it into the forefront of the defence, and its citizens must have provided not only man-power but supplies of all kinds and the essential financial resources.

Some half-dozen years later—exactly when is not known—the capital saw a brief glimpse of sunshine in the gathering clouds, when reinforcements came from the now recovered Gaul to strengthen the defence of Britain against Saxon raids that were again becoming formidable, this enemy being able to resume the offensive after the defeat of 409. Although the

[1] *Zosimus*, Book V.

authority for this is Gildas, who did not write before 540, there
are grounds for thinking that until about 440 Britain remained
in touch with the imperial government, that continued to
organise energetic resistance to its encircling enemies.

Between 427 and 430 the great general Aetius gained a
succession of victories on the Continent and, in response to
requests from Britain, appears to have sent reinforcements to
aid its defence. It was possibly about this time that the last
edition of the *Notitia Dignitatum* was compiled.[1] It was an
official and confidential list of the whole civil and military
hierarchy of the Roman Empire. In it appears the diocese of
Britannia with its five provinces, its Vicarius, Consulares and
Praesides with the Treasury at Augusta (Londinium). Thus
the last known official survey of the Western Empire shows
that the capital of the province was Londinium.

A sidelight is turned upon Britain and its cities at this time,
i.e. 429, in the life of St Germanus, who was present at the
synod at Verulamium with his friend Lupus, Bishop of
Augustobona Tricassium (Troyes), on a mission from Pope
Celestinus I. Although the country was still facing raids from
Picts as well as Saxons, an impression is obtained of a certain
wealth and prosperity. Attention is drawn to the magnificent
appearance of the magnates against whom the two bishops
argued. Germanus and his friend also venerated the shrine of
St Alban outside Verulamium, a fact revealing some evidence
of fairly peaceful conditions in that part of Britain if not elsewhere, for Germanus found it necessary to turn from the main
purpose of his visit—the denunciation of the Pelagian heresy[2]

---

[1] A very thorough examination of the question of the date of the
Notitia and the details of the information it contains concerning the
officials and units of the army stationed in Britain is given in *Roman
Britain and the English Settlements*, R. G. Collingwood and J. N. L. Myres,
1936, chap. xviii.

[2] Pelagius was born *c.* 360 and was most probably a Briton by birth
who left the island for the Continent in about 380—"an elusive and
gracious figure beloved and respected wherever he goes, travelling in
Italy and Africa and the East with his friend the Irishman Coelestius"
(R. G. Collingwood). Through his disciples he taught (*a*) that Adam was
mortal and that he would have died had he never sinned; (*b*) that man
might be saved by his own merits without the special Grace of God;
(*c*) that infants do not inherit original sin and are as pure as Adam when
he came from the hands of his Creator; and (*d*) that the general resurrection of the dead is not the result of Christ's resurrection.

—to lead to victory with shouts of "Hallelujah" the British levies hastily brought together to repel Saxons as well as Picts. The magnificent appearance of those with whom the visiting bishops conferred at the Synod of Verulamium assorts ill with the floors patched with clay and the hand-made pottery that recent exploration of the site has shown to be typical of this period of the city.

If the much-decayed municipium on the little river Ver could impress visiting ecclesiastics with a display of wealth and physical well-being the great centre of commerce and government would surely have been able to excel it with ease at this period.

Although the greatest days of Londinium were certainly passing, yet it was still the large and influential capital of an important Roman province, with prosperity sufficient to allow its officials and wealthier inhabitants to enjoy considerable luxury. Since Gaul had been restored to a state of comparative peace there may have been a slight revival of trade, especially in view of the fact that the Gallic cities of the north and west had formed a kind of federal league within the Empire, and thus had been in a position to make a stand against the disruptive influences. Even allowing that their purchasing capacity had been much reduced, there may have been resources upon which to draw sufficient for the Gaelic merchants to maintain a certain volume of trade.

Up to this time no permanent foothold had been obtained in the country by any of its numerous invaders, except in one perhaps doubtful instance on the Yorkshire coast.

Among the very large number of Roman coins found in London and recorded, R. G. Collingwood,[1] after prolonged research, did not come across any later than a deposit of c. A.D. 393, while the hoard at Stanmore (Middlesex) contained only one coin later than Honorius and this, of Constantine III, 408-411, brought the numismatic link with the Imperial mints no later than the first decade of the fifth century.

[1] *J.R.S.* XII. pt. 1, p. 95.

Chapter VII

AFTER the visit of St Germanus in 429 there seems to have followed an interval of twelve years of apparent peace—a brief period of calm before the overwhelming storm of invasion broke upon Roman Britain. Although no definite abandonment of the province was made by the central Roman Government at Ravenna, yet, about the year 440, there appears to have been a large withdrawal of troops for the defence of Italy; and these troops did not return. The only authority is Gildas, but his testimony is indirectly borne out by events elsewhere. In the preceding year the terrible Vandal king, Gaiseric, captured Carthage and thus not only seized the great granary of the Western Empire, but was only three days' sail from Rome itself. The effect was immediate and disastrous. He at once began to ravage the coasts of Italy, and the great Aetius, who hitherto had successfully defended Gaul and perhaps indirectly Britain, was obliged to hurry back to protect the centre of the Imperial power.

Preparations for this withdrawal were, according to Gildas, organised and much attention paid to fortifications in the north and south. The raising of new regiments from the Romano-British population to fill the expected chasm was also put in hand, and Gildas goes on to mention that private subscriptions were raised in order to assist in providing the cost of these measures. In this Londinium, as the largest and most important city in the country, must have played a very prominent part.

If the bastions of the defensive wall had, as can scarcely be doubted, been added at one of the earlier periods referred to already, the people of Londinium must have rejoiced in the wisdom of their forbears. The magnitude of the danger, however, was so great that the wall must have been very carefully surveyed for any signs of decay or weakness. It is certainly more within the accepted limits that the building of the bastions should be placed between the beginning of the third century and the last decades of the fourth.

The news of the weakening of the garrison to save Rome from Gaiseric appears to have quickly crossed the North Sea and become common knowledge in the villages of the Saxons and their kindred tribes. The attraction of Britain was increased by the fact that in the Saxon hinterland, at no great distance for mounted men, were the destroying hordes of Attila—yellow-skinned, slant-eyed and brutish-looking Mongoloid raiders, of whom the average Teuton went in dread. It is not surprising, therefore, that the Teutons eagerly embraced the opportunity of securing a hold on the fertile and now inadequately defended shores of Britain. They lost no time, for only about a year later, a Gallic Chronicle[1] records that "the Britains (*i.e.* the five Provinces), which up to the present time have been exhausted by a series of defeats and disasters, are being reduced under the Saxon yoke." This conveys the impression that the defence was definitely giving way. Although Gildas wrote only about a century after the events, his description of the newly-embodied defenders of the Wall as unwilling to fight and ready to run away is not reliable and must not be taken as fact, however probable it may seem.

It is questionable whether Londinium was actually attacked at this time, but seeing that the southern parts of the island had been so completely overrun that the Gallic chronicler writes that the Romano-Britons were being conquered, the Saxon bands and perhaps ships may have been within sight from the hills round the city. Having easier prey at their mercy it is fairly certain that the invaders would not have wasted their strength against walled cities.

It is possible that not long after the first visit of St Germanus the fast-shrinking remnants of Romano-British civilisation isolated in country districts were being driven more and more into walled towns. Dr Wheeler[2] thinks it is permissible to imagine small Saxon fleets "passing up-river beneath the closed gates of a London which may have regarded them with the same wary indifference wherewith, four centuries later, Saxon London often enough regarded the roving longships of the Vikings."

This view is confirmed by the silence of Gildas as to the fall of towns at this time. The city no doubt did its best to organise the resistance that was soon afterwards successful in

[1] *Chronica Gallica Patrologiae Cursus Completus*, vol. liv. p. 863, 18th year of Theodosius II. "Britanniae usque ad hoc tempus variis cladibus eventibusque laceratae, in ditionem Saxonum rediguntur."

[2] R.C.H.M., *Roman London*, p. 65.

driving back the Saxons and their allies to the ships in which they crossed, but it must at this time have suffered greatly from the effects of famine consequent upon the interference with cultivation. Probably the population of the capital was considerably reduced by losses in war and the inevitable effects of hunger and disease. The suburbs no doubt became sparsely occupied; indeed, particularly daring raiders may have burnt outlying houses, while others that were built of stone are likely to have been dismantled to provide materials for repairing the walls.

The cessation of overseas trade, caused by the new wave of invasion, must have had a paralysing effect upon the already diminished prosperity of the great port. The result of this cutting off of the main industry of Londinium cannot have failed to be disastrous to the whole social structure of the city. In place of the steady activities of warehouses and quays in the old days of security, there was now little to be done by sea that was not attended by extreme risks. Vessels due in did not arrive; the means of executing such orders for goods as were received gradually shrank. Since the disaster of 367 Londinium had experienced no comparable period of distress and danger.

But the end was not yet. Although, in 446, matters had reached such a pitch that the Romano-Britons—very probably the citizens of Londinium itself—sent a pathetically-worded appeal for aid to Aetius, they were actually on the threshold of a surprising victory. Apparently, as later during the Danish invasion, many of the attackers had returned home, presumably to secure their plunder, while the new British troops were learning experience in the hard school of necessity. In any case, it seems that almost immediately after dispatching the appeal, the military situation took a turn for the better, so that in a surprisingly brief space of time the country was cleared of its ravagers, except perhaps on the north-east coast.

There is indirect proof that this was the case, for, in 447, St Germanus, now in extreme old age, paid another visit to the country accompanied by Severus, Bishop of Treveri. His biographer has nothing to say, either of danger in crossing the Channel or of any war-like activity in the island. It seems quite impossible, had the most eminent and revered figure in Roman Gaul been exposed to perils of this description, that the fact would have been left unrecorded by the adulatory hagiographer. St Germanus's errand, as on the former occasion, was the combating of the heresy of Pelagius, and during the mission it is stated that he performed many miracles. The single point of historical interest, however, is that during the visit he came in contact with a certain Elafius, a personage of high rank. The chronicler's words are so extremely obscure that it is impossible to draw from them a definite meaning, but he appears to imply that he was the Governor. If so, he may have been the last *Vicarius* appointed to preside over the island province.

According to the hysterical Gildas, who is the single writer who gives anything remotely resembling a connected narrative of events during this obscure period, the victory of 446-7 was followed by a brief period of remarkable recovery. Amongst other things he mentions that there had never been such a succession of abundant harvests. This prosperity, however, was accompanied by an outburst of luxury and moral laxity that much shocked the monastic writer. There was also considerable civil disturbance, owing to the fact that the Roman administrative system had been totally dislocated, and there were violent quarrels among the nobles who aspired to the positions of generals and local governors, or as Gildas calls them, *tyranni*. Among these were two competitors, with both of whom Londinium was probably well acquainted. They were a certain Ambrosius,[1] who seems to have belonged to a powerful family with strong Roman sympathies, and a Welsh baron from Glevum named Vortigern. The latter presently obtained an unquestioned supremacy, and it was he who on receiving news of an impending invasion of the Picts, took the ill-advised step of enlisting against them Teutonic mercenaries, who were led by two somewhat shadowy chieftains named Hengist and Horsa (= stallion and mare).

The engagement of these adventurers was the true beginning of the English conquest of Britain. Having obtained, by the grant to them of the Isle of Thanet, a definite foothold in the country, the intruders gradually pushed westward until, by the year 596, they had conquered two-thirds of its area. During this long period of nearly one hundred and fifty years (about 450 to 596) Londinium is only mentioned in 457. In

---

[1] *Not* the Ambrosius Aurelianus who afterwards became the ruler of the Romano-Britons, but probably his father.

A LENGTH OF THE ROMAN TOWN WALL OF LONDON AT TRINITY PLACE, TOWER HILL.

It is a part of that shown on p. 162 reproduced from Roach Smith's *Illustrations of Roman London*. This is the outer face of the wall facing towards the east and therefore belonging to that part of the city's defences that would have opposed all invaders who approached by water.

(*By permission of the Society of Antiquaries.*)

MARBLE TOMBSTONE TO THE MEMORY OF MARTIALIS, A GLADIATOR.

It was erected by his wife [Ant]onia. Found at Islington and is now in the Guildhall Museum. 22 by 15 inches.

that year Hengist overcame the Southern Britons at the passage of the Cray in Kent and the defeated troops "forsook Kentland and fled in great fear" to Londinium.[1] That is all the information given: there is, however, not a word to warrant the supposition that the city was stormed by the victors. As there seems to be no justification for imagining that the capital had by this time become a deserted and burnt-out shell, the taking and sacking of the most important place in the whole country would have constituted a triumph of so outstanding and sensational a character that it cannot be imagined that the chronicle of the conquerors would have omitted to record it. In marked contrast the capture of the isolated fort of Anderida[2] on the Sussex coast is celebrated in a manner indicating that it was regarded as a remarkable victory. But as regards Londinium the Anglo-Saxon Chronicle is silent, and it seems impossible to interpret its silence otherwise than by concluding that, whatever may in other respects have been the fate of the once great and wealthy Augusta, the English never captured it by military force.

The last gleam of light in the gathering murk of that age of disruption shows the English ravaging and settling in Kent under the kingly rule of Hengist; it also shows the defeated British troops abandoning the defence of the south-east, and in full retreat upon Londinium. But athwart the path of the advancing invaders stood the grey bastioned walls that had been built long ago in view of such a contingency. It is not unlikely that for some time they formed the south-eastern buttress of the area defended by the Romanised British.

History, however, is silent as to the fate of the capital. It is not known what happened to it during the long period of nearly a century and a half that succeeded the last definite reference just mentioned. When all hope of saving the central portion of Roman Britain from the Anglo-Saxon invaders had vanished, it is possible that it opened its gates by formal capitulation to one of the rulers in its neighbourhood. All statements as to the storm and sack of Roman London by the English are based on conjecture alone, for there exists no historical evidence whatsoever. The people of London have always shown themselves to be of very tough fibre, and

---

[1] *Anglo-Saxon Chronicle*, sub-anno 457.
[2] Now called Pevensey.

capitulation on honourable terms is a far more likely occurrence than a failure to defend its walls. On the other hand, the city might have been starved out and subsequently, with its inhabitants reduced in numbers to a very few hundreds, would have been incapable of further maintaining itself against plunder, fire and decay.

If the passing of a living Roman Londinium into an English London did take place, a likely date for such a transition is about 570, for only a few years later King Aethelberht of Kent was defeated by Ceawlin of Wessex at Wimbledon. The site of the battle suggests that the Kentish King had taken up a position to defend London, and if so the inference is that at some previous time the city had become subject to him or a predecessor.

Londinium by 570 may have been isolated from the nucleus of Romano-British territory still kept together around Corinium through the advance of the invaders into the Chilterns, and its much-diminished population would have felt incapable any longer to keep in repair and garrison more than three miles of wall. The lapse of time had doubtless softened the earlier asperity of the struggle: Englishmen and Britons had learned to know and respect one another: there was not now any question of a policy of annihilating massacre on the part of the intruders; indeed, unless Bede be indulging in quite unscrupulous idealisation, the conquerors of Kent were a decidedly attractive and reasonable people, possessed of certain elements of high civilisation. King Aethelberht's answer to Augustine, when the latter explained his mission, is full of the good sense and kindly feeling characteristic of the modern Englishman of the ruling classes.

Thus, in the middle of the sixth century, there was no absolute bar to the conclusion of an honourable agreement between the citizens of London and the enlightened and powerful prince who ruled the country almost up to the walls of the city. With the revival of civilisation in Kent industry and commerce must have tended to develop in a certain degree, and the interests of the Londoners would have been in the direction of coming to a satisfactory *modus vivendi* with the new settlers of the country. If the later Romano-British rulers were as unamiable and addicted to dynastic warfare as indicated by Gildas, the Londoners might well have thought it time to break away from them: in that case inclination and self-interest would, not for the first or last time in history, have coincided.

Therefore it may be that at some time between the years 570 and 580 London passed into the political position of an English city. Its exact status cannot be defined: it has always, throughout its long history, occupied a curiously distinctive position in England—that of a somewhat self-contained unit in the body politic—as it were, a kingdom within a kingdom. There are many points that cannot easily be cleared up, but certain features in its civic constitution appear to indicate that this independent status was recognised by the English princes; and thus, perhaps without violence, Londinium would have passed from the position of a Romano-British city-state to that of a great river-port of the nascent English kingdom.

In view of the fact that there has been a tendency to believe that Londinium, wrecked and depopulated by the Teutonic invaders, lay for a considerable period a ghostly and deserted waste, every contribution to the discussion is worth consideration, for archaeology has not yet been able to discover the facts.

The level of Roman London is found as a rule from 12 to 20 feet below the present surface, and the fragmentary plans of Roman buildings that have been pieced together show that the modern streets do not at all coincide with Roman buildings. These facts suggest at once a great gap during which all traces of streets were obliterated under a vast accumulation of ruin and subsequent vegetable deposit. Whether such an inference is correct or not may be judged from a comparison with Rome itself. Reproduced here is a portion of the very centre of the Imperial City showing the relation of modern streets to the buildings and thoroughfares of its greatest days. It will be seen that the streets of to-day cut regardlessly across the sites of temples and other large buildings of first-class importance. Further than this, the classic structures so ignored are at depths beneath the surface ranging up to as much as 40 feet. And yet it is known that except for a period of forty days Rome was never deserted. It should, nevertheless, be remembered that Rome suffered from frequent fires, some of them so extensive that they devastated large areas of the city. In addition there were at various times vast levelling works undertaken in order to get rid of steep ridges and cliffs that in the early period had been desirable from the advantages they gave for defence. The amount of destruction caused by such attacks on Rome as that of Robert Guiscard in 1084 must also have been considerable and may have resulted in a certain amount of rearrangement of streets.

In favour of continuity during the transitional period it has been frequently stated that the survival of the name of the city is in itself sufficient evidence and that the British flavour of the names of two of the gateways[1] gives further support to the theory of an unbroken occupation of London. More recent opinion discards the gate names as unreliable and it would have been easy for the city's name to have survived many years of abandonment.

Sir Laurence Gomme[2] made his contribution to the theory of unbroken civic life in London when he quoted the will of John Mabb, citizen of London, dated 1578. This man left one-third of his property to his wife, one-third to his children, and the remainder in various other ways, and he mentions that this division into three equal parts was "according to thauncient custome of this citye of Londoun." The law of London was only abolished in the reign of George I. (II. cap. 18) and Gomme claimed that it had come through from the days when Britain was a Roman province, the Anglo-Saxons finding their customs opposed by a solid body of codified municipal laws.

The Historical Monuments Committee for Roman London in 1928 favoured the idea that there was a gradual settlement of Saxon invaders in the fifth century "without completely obliterating the walled towns." Another aspect of the problem also noted was to the effect that although the Saxons occasionally found the Picts and Scots convenient allies, their objects and traditions were so fundamentally different that, as invaders, they could not avoid a hostile attitude to each other. It was suggested that this incidentally led to the survival of some of the remaining Romano-British cities, for the northern tribesmen out for plunder would, on reaching the midlands, find themselves not only confronted with strongly-walled towns, but between them a countryside fast filling up with

---

[1] See p. 209.
[2] *The Governance of London*, p. 139.

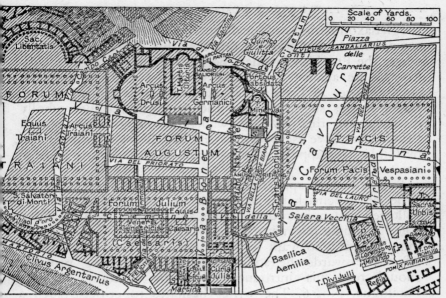

A PORTION OF ANCIENT AND MODERN ROME.
Present streets shown white and blocks of existing buildings shaded.

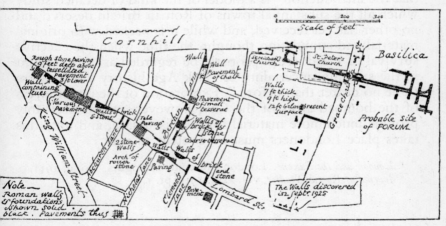

STREET PLAN OF A CENTRAL PORTION OF LONDON, SHOWING THE RELATION OF MODERN
STREETS TO ROMAN BUILDINGS.

In both cases the modern streets bear scarcely any relation to the ancient ones, and in those of Rome they cut diagonally across buildings and forums.

London suffered terribly during the Danish invasions in the ninth century, and Rome, south of the Capitol, was laid waste in 1084. To each city came a great disaster at a comparatively late date, and to these calamities may perhaps be attributed a great deal of the wiping out of streets and important buildings.

tough Saxon settlers as little disposed to disturbance as were the townsfolk. It was pointed out that this happened in Gaul, where the Frankish invaders became defenders of the Gallo-Roman life against Huns and Visigoths, and although the circumstances in Britain may never have developed to this extent it was suggested that the situation was not wholly dissimilar. In this way the walled towns in south-eastern Britain may have escaped the complete destruction described by Gildas that appears to have come upon the more isolated cities of the north.

In 1935 there appeared from the pen of Dr. R. E. M. Wheeler a remarkable statement of the evidence he has collected that points to London's survival through the Dark Age.[1] Nothing relevant to his subject appears to have escaped him, and all who want to be possessed of the latest lines of advance towards the solution of this fascinating problem should read his introduction to the London Museum Catalogue, No. 6. The writer hesitates to criticise such a masterly marshalling of new materials and instead quotes a review by Mr. J. N. L. Myres[2] which he concludes by saying that the introduction "is a model of the kind of detailed study which all the substantial towns of Roman Britain deserve and no other has yet received, and while it is packed with original material and stimulating thought, the time when the effective survival of London can properly be regarded as a fixed point in the swirling uncertainty of Dark Age history would seem to be no nearer than before." Exploration of the upper layers of the bombed areas of the City, however, may conceivably provide much more material for the discussion, and until this takes place Londoners must be content to wait.

[1] *London and the Saxons.* London Museum Catalogues, No. 6, 1935.
[2] *Journal of Roman Studies*, vol. xxvi. 1936, pt. 1.

Chapter VIII

LONDINIUM IN RELATION TO THE ROAD SYSTEM OF BRITAIN

IF a map showing the Roman roads of Britain is studied, it will at once be apparent that Londinium stood at the centre of the whole system. In all directions great arterial thoroughfares led to every town of consequence in the province. While actually only six of the great routes leave the capital, it will be seen that these soon fan out considerably, giving direct access to every part of the country.

No other town has anything remotely approaching this central position except Corinium, and there it will be seen at once that while this important place stands at the meeting-place of five roads, yet two of them are accounted for by the Fosse Way—a lateral thoroughfare joining the somewhat remote districts of the Fens and Dumnonia (roughly Devonshire). At the most Corinium was a western ganglion of ways subsidiary to the national system centred on Londinium.

How far these Roman ways radiating from London followed the primitive Celtic roads or tracks cannot be ascertained. Attempts have been made at various times to pick out certain thoroughfares and to suggest that they are of pre-Roman origin, but one is compelled to admit that there is little or no evidence to work upon beyond probabilities and the presence of prehistoric tumuli. The study of the ridge-ways in the southern counties of England in relation to the earliest land charters points to their great antiquity, and there can be little doubt that the Pilgrims' Way along the hills of Hampshire, Surrey and Kent is of pre-Roman origin. Geographical conditions caused the pre-Roman ways to take approximately the same routes as those followed by the great road-makers. That the ancient tracks went with general directness to their objectives is quite possible. H. M. Stanley and others have commented on the directness of primitive roads in Central Africa. That there was a very ancient route from Kent to a point where the Thames was fordable and onwards to the tribal capital at St Albans is beyond dispute, but where it crossed the river remains in doubt. Possibly a ford at Chelsea might have been used at some seasons of the year and another lower down when conditions were favourable. The map on pp. 138 and 139, if carefully studied, will give certain basic information and will suggest ideas, and the reader whose appetite is whetted should read Mr Reginald

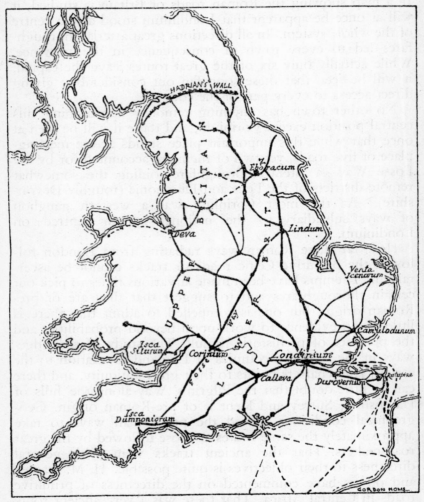

MAP OF BRITAIN SHOWING THE PRINCIPAL ROMAN ROADS.

Apart from the Fosse Way, all the principal roads focus on Londinium. Although the actual boundaries between Upper and Lower Britain are not known, the available evidence points plainly to the division having been based on highland and lowland zones. (*See* Appendix III, p. 272.)

A. Smith's highly illuminating article printed in *Archaeologia*.[1]

Whatever may eventually be discovered as to the relation of prehistoric London to the Celtic tracks or chariot ways, there can be little doubt that soon after the Roman occupation all the roads led into the city, and, since the place had acquired outstanding importance as early as A.D. 60, it is a rational inference that by that time it had become to some extent the main focus of provincial communications. By the third century that system was fully developed as regards all the arteries of major importance, and an impression of it is afforded by the catalogue of routes called the *Itinerarium Antonini*. Although this list is of immense importance, being almost the only surviving example of its kind, it may be described as only an amateur and second-rate production, defective in several respects and not scientifically arranged.[2] Its special merit is that it gives a fairly accurate list of distances from point to point,[3] thus enabling the investigator to locate the sites of many lost stations.

Of the great roads entering Londinium, that from Rutupiae (Richborough) must have always ranked as the most important. It was the link that joined the British capital with the continental world of the Roman Empire. Almost everyone of consequence who came to the city from Gaul traversed the ninety odd miles of what, in post-Roman times, came to be known as the Watling Street. Military units marched along that pleasant Kentish highway, and supplies and equipment, that did not come by water to the Thames, must have been brought in wheeled transport wagons or on the backs of animals by the same route. Subsequently, no doubt, the southern road, now called the Stane Street, and also that from Clausentum (Bitterne, near Southampton) brought Continental produce to Londinium, but the route from Gaul to the British capital was pre-eminently that which traversed the northern side of Kent.

[1] "Roman Roads and the Distribution of Saxon Churches in London," *Archaeologia*, vol. 68, pp. 229-62.

[2] "The Legacy of Rome," article on Communication and Commerce by G. H. Stevenson, Fellow of University College, Oxford, p. 159.

[3] In a number of instances, however, where it can be checked the Antonine Itinerary is inaccurate in its mileage.

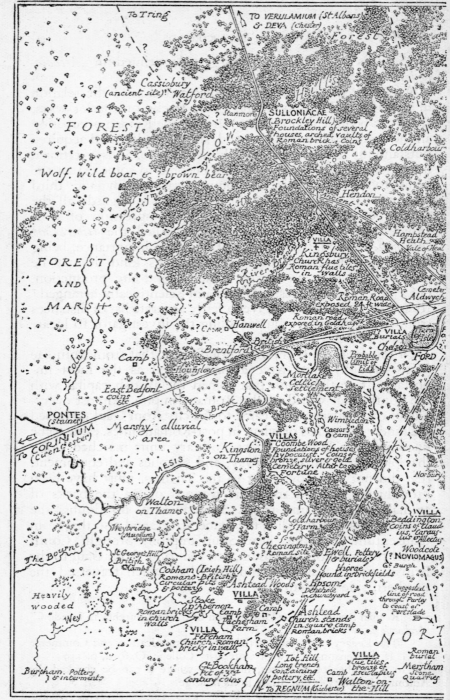

The Roman roads which are fairly well ascertained are shown with double lines, and
those that are uncertain are indicated with a single broken line. It will be noticed
that on the hills to the south of the city have been found a fair number of villa or
country house sites. These were probably the homesteads of wealthy agriculturalists.
The cold clay soils north of the Thames have given very few traces of the existence of

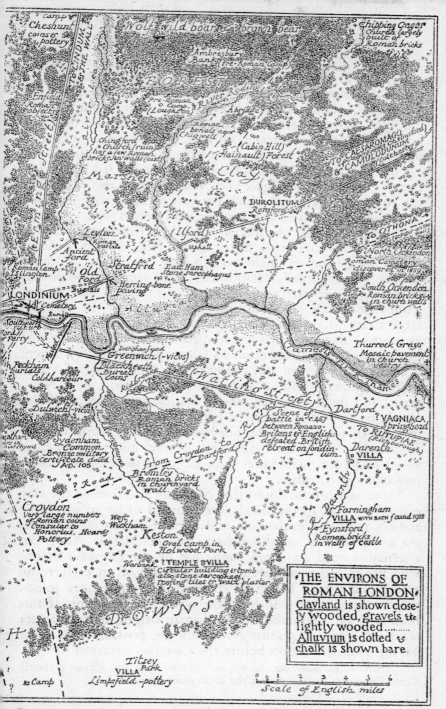

THE ENVIRONS OF ROMAN LONDON. Clayland is shown closely wooded, gravels &c lightly wooded......... Alluvium is dotted & chalk is shown bare.

Scale of English miles

Romano-British houses. Sulloniacae appears to be the only place where foundations have been found. Many minor discoveries, mainly burials, have been omitted in the southern suburbs of London. There are practically no indications of Roman roads in Essex definitely recognisable as such. Those in that county, shown with broken lines, were suggested by Mr R. Miller Christy.

Idlers in the city, who wished for inexpensive amusement, and were in search of bright scraps of information as to coming events, would have gravitated towards the quays and the bridge, where they could watch the stream of human life, fed by at least four Kentish ports and one or two on the coast beyond the great dendrogenous zone to the south—almost an unexplored no-man's-land to the citizens of Londinium.

North of the Thames, probably six gateways led out to important highways. Ludgate and Newgate were the outlets for the routes to the west, which converged as they approached the Brentford loop of the Thames, and united went onwards to the tribal capital of Calleva Atrebatum (Silchester). There three roads directed towards the capital met. They came from Venta Belgarum (Winchester), where the army clothing factory was eventually established;[1] from Isca Dumnoniorum (Exeter), at the extremity of the south-western artery; and from Corinium Dobunorum (Cirencester), the second largest city in Britain. This thoroughfare not only received, at a short distance, that from Aquae Sulis (Bath), but was prolonged beyond Corinium to Glevum (Gloucester), where it crossed the Severn and followed the south coast of Wales to the legionary base at Isca Silurum (Caerleon, near Newport), and finally reached far-off Maridunum (Caermarthen). It was by one of the western gateways, therefore, that those in need of the cure at the hot springs on the Avon left the city, and by the same roads went officers and men on their way to take up their duties with Legio II on the confines of mountainous Cambria.

There seems little doubt that Newgate also formed the way out of the city to the north-west, for, in order to reach the ancient road to Verulamium and beyond, it was necessary to go as far as the neighbourhood of the Marble Arch. An alternative road has been suggested by Mr Reginald Smith, who has traced to some extent the course of an early route across Hampstead Heath to Hendon, that must have joined the Watling Street a little to the north of the Brent. If this road may be accounted of pre-Roman origin, it is a further scrap of evidence pointing towards the possibility of there having been a London before the Claudian invasion.

[1] *Notitia Dignitatum*, occ. xi. 60, as "Venta" only, but almost certainly Venta Belgarum on account of the local wool supply.

Whether the Watling Street was joined near the site of the Marble Arch or north of the point where it crosses the Brent, it was one of the two great routes that traversed Britain diagonally, and after passing the Fosse Way at a point where a "half-way house" might be expected, ended at Deva (Chester), the fixed camp of Legio XX. From this great military base ran the western highway to the Wall of Hadrian, and also the road to Segontium (Caernarvon) and Anglesey.

Either Cripplegate[1] or Aldersgate may have been the exit for the link with the Watling Street just mentioned, otherwise the purpose of these gates does not seem too clear.

From Bishopsgate went the main trunk route to the north leading to the great potteries at Durobrivae (Castor, near Peterborough), on to the Colony of Lindum (Lincoln), and so to Eboracum (York), the third and most important military centre of the province, where at first Legio IX and afterwards Legio VI held with Deva watch and ward over the danger zone of the north. Beyond Eboracum this great artery, in medieval days named Ermine Street, was prolonged through the country of the Brigantes to the eastern end of the Wall at Corstopitum and Pons Aelii. Onwards to the north yet farther ran this highway, for passing Hadrian's imposing barrier, it continued over the bleak hills to Trimontium (near Melrose), and until 211 it was prolonged far beyond the Tweed to the Turf Wall that ran between Clyde and Forth.

Through the arches of Roman Bishopsgate therefore came and went all who had business in the eastern midlands and the far north. One may imagine the marked difference in the attitude of mind between those who left Londinium by the ways to the north and north-west, and those who went out of the city at dawn by way of the bridge, or westward with the sun full behind their backs sending long shadows ahead on the well-kept roadway. Farewells in the first instances may have been tinged with no little anxiety, while in the latter one may picture envious comment, congratulation, and all sorts of pleasantries.

The last important exit from the capital was that by way of Aldgate, the portal for the low countries of Britain, and for one town at least of no little consequence—Camulodunum,

[1] The existence of a Roman gate at this point is not yet established.

upon which Claudius had bestowed the dignity of capital—a position it was so soon to lose to its prosperous neighbour on the Thames.

If the map of the environs of Londinium is examined, it will be seen that the villa sites discovered up to the present time are very much more numerous on the south side of the Thames than they are to the north. From Kingston along the Mole, and thence by the North Downs to Titsey and Keston, and so to the valley of the Darenth in Kent, there is a chain of habitations. The fact that nearly all Essex churches that go back as far as the twelfth century contain Roman brick and perhaps other re-used materials in their walls suggests the presence of ruined houses in the vicinity of each where the church-builders were in search of materials. At Kingsbury, in Middlesex, the church also contains Roman materials, and at Brockley Hill, Stanmore, foundations of houses have been found. Surrey and Kent seem to have been the favoured parts, and perhaps good corn-lands there led to the acquisition of riches. Possibly wealthy citizens had their country seats in the pleasant positions indicated on the map. With a well-kept road and a pair of good horses, a chariot would soon take banker or merchant a dozen miles out of the city.

Chapter IX

THE DEFENSIVE WALL OF LONDINIUM

UNTIL the second half of the eighteenth century the ancient nucleus of the city of London was engirdled by the Roman town-wall erected in the first or second century of the Christian era. As late as 1477, Sir Ralph Josceline, Lord Mayor of that year, restored the whole of the northern face from Aldgate to Aldersgate, and it was only in 1766 that the Commissioners of Sewers sought permission from Parliament to sweep away this only surviving monument of the Roman epoch of London. The work of destruction was fortunately by no means carried to completion, many long sections having been left for piecemeal destruction in later years, and, happily, builders have often preferred to utilise portions of the ancient structure rather than face the heavy work of demolition. Thus, buried out of sight and almost forgotten by its citizens, the historic bulwarks of Londinium still exist in fragmentary fashion throughout nearly the whole of their length. Had a voice been raised in defence of the city's venerable defences and the destructive energy of the Georgian age been thereby arrested, London would have possessed an impressive visible link with Imperial Rome. No appeal against the order for demolition appears to have been made, Londoners rejoicing in the airiness and spaciousness brought about by the disappearance of the gateways, the posterns and a considerable proportion of the wall. Chamberlain,[1] writing at the time of this destruction, mentions that the wall "between Cripplegate and Moorgate . . . and in several other places was razed from the foundation." Fortunately this was an overstatement for, so far as records exist, the Roman foundations and, as a rule, 10 feet or more of this part of the structure were left undisturbed. In at least two places the wall with its medieval additions still remains standing to heights of between 20 and 35 feet.

These scattered relics of the great defensive work are, however, not easy to find, and when seen in the dim light of a warehouse or the basement of a block of offices do not greatly

[1] Henry Chamberlain: *History and Survey of London and Westminster*, 1770, p. 410.

stir the emotions of those uninformed on Roman military architecture or the earliest phase of the city's history.

The one great monument of Roman London would, therefore, have probably remained in this melancholy state of inaccessibility had not German bombs, flung indiscriminately on the city, in 1941, suddenly altered the situation. The widespread destruction in the neighbourhood of Cripplegate left that angle of the wall so much revealed that it has now become a subject of keen interest not only to Londoners but to the British people as a whole.

In spite of the formidable difficulties that have confronted archaeologists ever since questions as to the age and appearance of the earliest defences of London have engaged their attention, a considerable amount of information has been accumulated. It is now quite clear that the wall enclosed the area from the Fleet River to the Tower of London, and thus both the hills were included. The three landward sides of the somewhat irregular oblong were built first, probably between the years of recovery after Boudicca's burning of the town and soon after the destruction of the Ninth Legion about 119. This first walling effort consisted of featureless lengths of curtain wall without turrets or bastions extending from gateway to gateway with possibly one or two posterns.[1] Angles were probably without towers and would have been rounded. The danger at the time of this first defence scheme was obviously not water-borne, for the river front was left undefended.

In time the political situation changed and it was considered necessary not only to strengthen the land wall with bastions but to rely no longer on the river alone for the protection of the southern side of the parallelogram. The instability of the foreshore made it necessary for the additional mile and a quarter of walling to be built between two rows of piles, but even with this reinforcement of the foundations it early developed weakness and by the end of the twelfth century had all fallen. Up to the present time no indication of bastions has been discovered on the river front, but Fitzstephen describes it as walled and towered, and there is further evidence

[1] There was discovered in 1935 part of the north wall of an internal turret under No. 19 Tower Hill. It is illustrated in *London Wall through Eighteen Centuries*, 1937, p. 25.

A LOCK, KEYS AND LAMPS FOUND IN ROMAN LONDON.

1. Bronze lock with hasp for a box.　2. Bronze keys.　3. Earthenware lamp with a stopper in the filling hole.　4. A mould for a lamp.　5. Earthenware lamp in its tray for holding the oil drip.　6. Bronze hand lamp.　7 and 8. Bronze lamps for suspension—one with six burners.　9. Highly finished bronze lamp with two burners and a handle ornamented with a ram's head.

(6 and 9, *London Museum ; others, Guildhall Museum.*)

CONJECTURAL BIRD'S-EYE VIEW OF T

In the right centre is shown the Great Basilica or Town Hall with the Great Forum to the south o
forum running towards Bishopsgate.   It is not yet known where the Roman bridge stood and it is poss
feeders is shown to the left.   It probably ran nearly dry at low tide and its upper arms would have b

CENTRAL PORTION OF ROMAN LONDON.

bridge is shown leading to the street that has been discovered over 30 ft. wide on the east side of the
its position was more to the west and close to the site of Old London Bridge. The Walbrook with its
sed by a number of wooden bridges —*From a drawing by the Author*.

HYPOCAUST DISCOVERED UNDER THE CORN EXCHANGE IN LOWER THAMES STREET.

Shows the closely-placed supports for the concrete floor and tessellated pavement between and under which the hot air was passed from an external furnace.

(Reproduced by permission of the Royal Commission on Historical Monuments.)

in this direction in the outer defences of the Tower of London. There the Wardrobe Tower is built upon the base of a Roman bastion and stands about 200 feet from the Lanthorn Tower. The same distance separates the Wakefield, Bell and Middle towers that punctuate the river front of the Tower defensive wall, and the intervals between the Roman bastions from the water-side to Aldgate are identical. From this it is difficult to

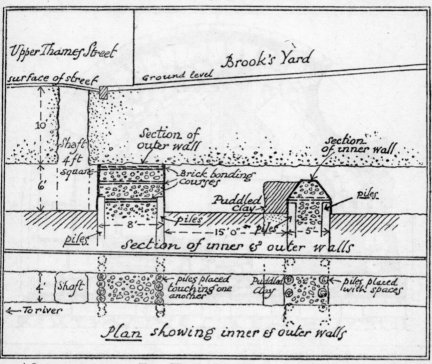

A Section through the Town-Wall of Londinium on the South or River Front.
Found during the making of a sewer under Brook's Yard in Upper Thames Street.

avoid the conclusion that the mediaeval builders took advantage of the Roman structures if they were still standing.

There is no doubt whatever that the bastions on the land sides were additions, for, in every instance where examination has been possible, the wall with its carefully constructed plinth runs on continuously and without the slightest recognition of them. The builders of the bastion found in Camomile Street did make an attempt to form a bond with the curtain

10

wall, but in spite of this fact the bastion was very obviously an addition.

From existing remains or records of a reliable nature the sites of twenty-one bastions on the landward sides are known, and for archaeological purposes are numbered from east to west, the first being under the Wardrobe Tower in the Tower of London and the last (No. 21) being north of the site of

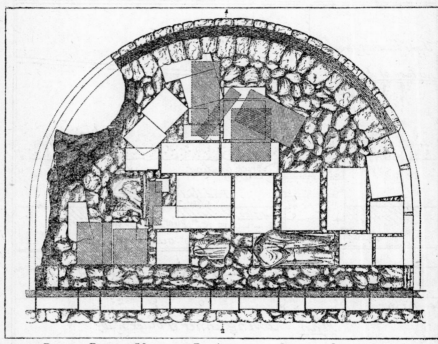

PLAN OF BASTION (No. 10 ON PLAN) FOUND IN CAMOMILE STREET IN 1876.

It contained a great deal of reused materials from among which a number of sculptured stones of considerable interest were found and are now in Guildhall Museum.

Ludgate. Assuming that the average spacing of the bastions maintained the 200 feet that is found among the positions that are known, the land fronts would have been strengthened by forty-four bastions and the river side by twenty-eight, making a total of seventy-two. In addition, the three and a quarter miles of wall had from six to eight gateways flanked with massive guard rooms or towers.

From the bastions that have been examined it has been

found that structurally they fall into two groups, the dividing point being at Moorgate. With the exception of the Wardrobe Tower bastion all the eastern group were constructed with solid bases and contained re-used Roman sculptured stones; those to the west, again with one exception—namely, that numbered 17 on the site of Christ's Hospital—were built hollow from the base and no re-used Roman materials were found in them. In each group there is a bastion that contains evidence for its having been built in the Romano-British period; apart from this, however, the evidence so far available is insufficient to provide a clue as to which group was built first. The lack of re-used stone in the western group suggests a slightly later date for that side, where there would seem to have been less danger at the period when it was most probable that this strengthening of the defences took place.

The evidence collected and discussed by Dr Wheeler in 1928[1] points towards a third-century date for the bastions. His opinion is that from the comparative evidence available it is "possible only to affirm that neither series of bastions in London is likely to be prior to the third century" and, he adds, "which series is the earlier it is impossible to say." Dr Wheeler accepts the eastern half of the city as more important for strengthened defences, being nearer to attack from the sea, and writes: "The presence of danger from this source is emphasised by the apparently contemporary building or re-building of the river wall." It is just possible that the explanation of the problem may be a simple one. If the eastern half of the town-wall and the river front were to receive attention first, materials available from disused buildings and cemeteries would be absorbed in the earlier stages of the operations, and by the time the eastern half of the land fronts and the new (or renewed) river front was completed this source may have quite easily been exhausted.

The builders would thereafter be obliged to continue the work using only new materials, and if the north-western and western fronts had seemed of less importance than the rest, economy of time and materials would suggest entirely hollow bastions. This is merely a conjecture, but it appears to cover the difficulties.

At a distance of between 10½ and 15 feet from the base of

[1] R.C.H.M.. *Roman London*, pp. 80-82.

the wall was a V-shaped Roman ditch. In the four places where it has been exposed and measured, two of them to the east and two to the west of the Walbrook, the width varies between 10 and 16 feet and the depth was found to be between $4\frac{1}{2}$ and $6\frac{1}{2}$ feet. The berm or flat surface between the base of the wall and the ditch averaged about 12 feet broad. The Anglo-Saxon castle-builders would have regarded this ditch as a very trifling addition to the strength of the defences.

Although there may have been eight gateways in the wall,

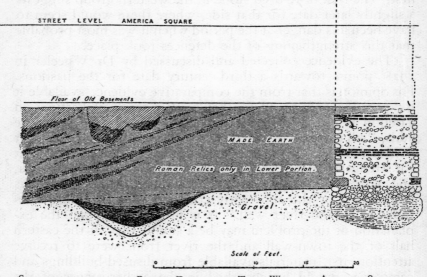

STREET LEVEL   AMERICA SQUARE

Floor of Old Basements

MADE EARTH

Roman Relics only in Lower Portion.

Gravel

Scale of Feet.

0   5   10   15   20

SECTION THROUGH THE ROMAN DITCH AND TOWN-WALL IN AMERICA SQUARE.
(From *Archaeologia* LXIII.)

at the present time structural remains of only two have been discovered. One is Newgate, the plan of which has been brought to light piecemeal since 1875, and the other is at Aldersgate, whose Roman foundations were met when boring a tunnel during the present war. The available evidence points to the great probability of there having also been Roman predecessors to Aldgate, Bishopsgate, Cripplegate, and Ludgate, and there must have been another facing the Roman bridge that spanned the Thames a little below the site of Old London Bridge. This would give a total of seven gateways with the slight possibility of an eighth at Moorgate.

Nowhere does the wall exist to its full height, the greatest stature that has been recorded being 14½ feet above the plinth. This may be only half the full height to the top of the parapet. The materials employed were Kentish ragstone divided at fairly uniform intervals by bonding courses composed of large Roman bricks laid in thick cement.

The foundations were formed by digging into the gravel of the site a trench from 3 to 4 feet deep and about 10 feet wide, or very slightly broader than the wall itself. The trench was then filled with rammed flint and puddled clay or with broken ragstone in place of the flints. This might appear to be somewhat inadequate to support a structure of such dimensions and weight, and yet, wherever it has been exposed, the wall has been found standing quite upright and without cracks or sagging. So far as it has been examined, nowhere does the landward wall or its foundation reveal the presence of re-used materials, and the materials employed are the same throughout, from which it is clear that, excluding the river front, what appears to have been the first defensive wall of London was erected at one time and under one control.

Upon the foundation came a plinth 9 feet thick and from 2 to 3 feet high, composed of a core of ragstone set in a very hard white cement with the same stone indifferently squared, forming two or three courses on the external face. Outside special trouble was taken with the finishing of this plinth, a fourth course being composed of a dark ruddy-brown, ferruginous type of sandstone with a chamfered edge. Within, the plinth was finished with three courses of brick that form a facing only, and the top layer is sometimes inset to conform with the reduced thickness (about 8 feet) of the wall immediately resting upon it. This second level is about 3 feet high, with a facing of squared Kentish ragstone finished on top by a double or triple layer of brick running through the structure and showing as a feature on each face. Internally the top course is inset about 6 inches, thereby reducing the wall to 7 feet 6 inches. The same form of construction is then repeated except in regard to the brick bonding that is usually composed of not more than two courses, the upper one inset as in the lower section. The rubble core remains the same throughout except that the stones are in places laid in the herring-bone manner. At this level the wall is about 9 feet high and its thickness above is reduced to 7 feet. The next layer of construction repeats what is below, being again completed with double bonding courses of brick. Above the wall continues at the same thickness as far as records of it exist. Where it is standing to-day at greater heights than a little less than 15 feet the upper portions are later reconstructions or repairs that rob the wall of anything that can be recognised as Roman, from

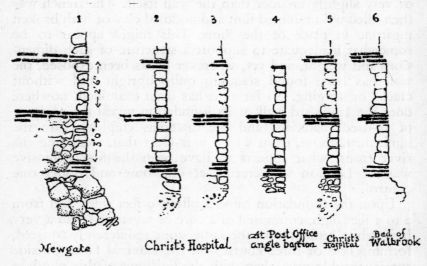

SECTIONS OF THE INTERIOR FACE OF THE TOWN-WALL SHOWING THE VARIATIONS IN
THE ARRANGEMENTS OF THE OFF-SETS AND BONDING BRICKS.

which fact it may be assumed that the thinner upper portions were destroyed or damaged sufficiently to require extensive rebuildings in the millennium between the fifth and the fifteenth centuries.

Taken as a whole, the defensive wall of London may be considered to be a roughly finished example of Roman building. That it was strong and adequate for its purpose is proved by all that has survived to the present time. Much irregularity can be seen in the laying of the facing stones, which appear to have been largely shaped with the hammer. Where the workman found them too small for the spaces they were to occupy it was the practice to fill up the gap with additional cement rather than look for, or cut, a more suitable stone. It should also be noted that there was much lack of uniformity in the thickness of the wall, for at its base it varied

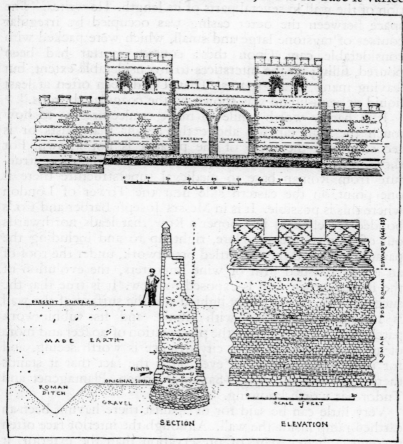

THE TOWN-WALL OF LONDINIUM.

Showing the method of construction to the average height of 15 feet. Above is a suggestion of the appearance of the Roman Newgate based on the dimensions and levels of its foundations.

between 7 and 9 feet, with an average of 8 feet. In detail there was also a certain amount of divergence, particularly in the offsets on the interior face and of the bonding courses, although, for all practical purposes, these small variations were of little account.

As the method of making the concrete core of the wall is of considerable interest it is important to quote Dr Philip Norman,[1] whose study of the structure covered a number of years during which he witnessed the uncovering and demolition of the wall in several parts of its length. He writes: "The space between the outer casing was occupied by irregular courses of ragstone large and small, which were packed with considerable care. Upon these courses mortar had been poured, filling up the interstices to a considerable extent, but leaving many vacant spaces. That it had been often at least liquid or semi-liquid was shown by the coagulated drops."

It is hardly worth while to make conjectures as to how much the wall tapered above the height that exists or is recorded and the form of the parapet is not known. For those, however, who wish to see a section of the great structure from Roman base to medieval superstructure there is one point on the eastern side near the Tower of London where this is possible. It is in Messrs Joseph Barber and Co.'s bonded warehouses in Cooper's Row that leads northwards out of Trinity Square. Here, right up to and including the parapet walk and the embattled breastwork, under the roof of an old-established firm of wine importers, the evolution of the Roman town wall is exposed to view. It is true that the successive floors are dimly lighted and the surface of the wall is indistinct, begrimed with smoke and its rubble-work patched and irregular, yet the presentation of 20 feet and more of an ancient and massive city defence is worth seeing, and for those who cannot set eyes on it the fact that it stands there still—Roman, Anglo-Saxon, Norman, Plantagenet and Tudor—is worth knowing.

Very little can be said for or against there having been an earthen ramp inside the wall. Although the interior face often presents a better state of preservation than the exterior, it would not be safe to regard this by itself as any evidence of value, for the accumulation of rubbish and soil inside a wall is inevitable, and the convenience of construction of lean-to structures that a wall offers helps towards the same result. Slight indications of a bank were found on the Christ's Hospital site, and ramps have been discovered against the walls at Silchester, Reculver and a number of fortified towns.

[1] *Archaeologia*, Vol. 59, pt. 1, p. 127.

THE TOWN WALL OF ROMAN LONDON SOUTH OF NEWGATE.

This portion of the wall viewed from within—the absence of the plinth course is noticeable—was disclosed on the site of Newgate Prison in 1903. The top end of the plank on the left marks the base line of the wall and the bottom of the foundation is indicated by the lower end of the plank and the large piece of stone lying loose on the ledge in the middle of the photograph.

GORDON HOME. 1944

THE ROMAN WALL OF LONDINIUM NEAR CRIPPLEGAT

Above : The neighbourhood of St. Giles's Church, Cripplegate, after the debris caused by bombing in the sec
two other bastions. *Below :* A suggestion for the preservation of this portion of the defences of Londinium in wh
inside and outside the wall, office buildings of a suitable style erected, and a museum of Roman antiquitie
monument of the first period of its existence, in the same manner in which the Tower of London memorialises
angle bastion (1944).

GESTED UNVEILING OF THE PAST.

World War had been cleared. In the centre is an angle bastion of the Roman town-wall and to the right are ain wall, bastions and the Roman ditch are fully exposed. It is here proposed that streets should be formed in the form of a temple built on the spot (right). This would give London an impressive and enduring age. *Inset—Left :* A length of the wall exposed east of St. Giles's Church. *Right :* The interior of the

THE INTERIOR OF THE HORSESHOE-SHAPED BASTION NORTH OF AND CLOSE TO
THE SITE OF THE GATEWAY AT NEWGATE.

This bastion (No. 19 on plan) is on the site of Christ's Hospital and is now a few feet below the yard of
the General Post Office in Giltspur Street. This bastion was hollow, as were all save one on the western
half of the landward sides of the town wall.

(*By permission of the Society of Antiquaries.*)

Of the two gateways in the wall of which there is definite evidence only Newgate has so far revealed enough of its foundations to provide materials for making a fairly complete plan; the other, Aldersgate, having been discovered accidentally during the War (1939-45), there has been no opportunity for making more than a few measurements and plotting its position on the line of the wall.

It was in 1875 that E. P. L. Brock recorded the first unveiling of the remains of Roman Newgate. Sufficient was discovered of the northern tower or guardroom to plan it approximately. The external dimensions were 32 by 30 feet and the interior space was reduced to 22 by 15 feet owing to the northern wall being 10 feet and the others about 6 feet thick. More than a quarter of a century passed before the discovery was made of any part of the southern tower. Then, in 1903, Dr Philip Norman recorded the finding of indications of more than half the east wall with its plinth as far as the southeast angle.[1] This was just sufficient to make it possible to complete the plan of the gateway, revealing a distance between the guardrooms of 35 feet that allowed space for a normal double entrance with a dividing wall to give central support to the arches, each about 15 feet in width.

This very interesting discovery was described in detail in a paper read by Dr Norman at a meeting of the Society of Antiquaries in 1903. He gave its position as "57 feet east of the western face of the substructure of the later City gate . . ., completely involved in the foundation of its eastern wall, here about 7 feet wide, and a little over 13 feet south of the northern front of Dance's prison facing Newgate Street." At this point, as the work of demolition proceeded, there was exposed "the end of a massive plinth composed of yellowish oolite closely resembling Barnack ragstone, which had formed part of the south-west corner of a Roman building."

Dr Norman described the angle stone first found as having a broad chamfer, its height was about 13 inches and, what is a unique constructional feature so far found in London's Roman defences, each of the stones was fastened to its neighbour with iron clamps fixed in place with lead.

The whole of the plinth was laid in pink mortar "as hard as the stone itself," a feature otherwise entirely absent from the

[1] *Archaeologia*, Vol. 59, pt. 1, pp. 130-132.

town-wall, where the mortar is white or creamy-white throughout.

Beneath the plinth there was a layer of ragstone laid in mortar 1 foot 10 inches thick and under it ragstone fragments in puddled clay 4 feet 10 inches thick. It was at a depth of 13 feet below the Newgate Street level and rested on the virgin gravel, and Dr Norman noted that "these footings as a whole were quite of the same character as those found under

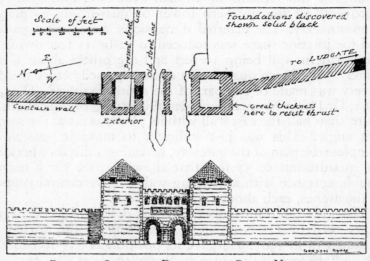

PLAN AND SUGGESTED ELEVATION OF ROMAN NEWGATE.

In addition to the lengths of foundations that are shown solid black in the plan, there are those discovered in 1909 on the west side of the north tower.

the Roman wall to the south . . ., excepting that there was a much greater depth of puddled clay."

This recording of the discovery of the southern portion of Roman Newgate was made in the worst possible conditions for the watching archaeologist, for Dr Norman mentions how, after the corner-stone was exposed, those secured to it along the eastern face of the gate tower "were broken up as the work proceeded," and that "the last, 3 feet 5 inches long, and extending partly under Newgate Street, was not completely uncovered until November, 1904"—that is to say, about a year later.

The gateway was placed out of line with the wall running

southwards, revealing what appears to be the obvious intention of being placed at right angles to the medial thoroughfare leading to the Walbrook and the centre of the city; thus it projected inwards twice as much at its northern end as the 8 feet of encroachment at the south.

The only further discovery on the Newgate site was made in 1909, when Dr Norman and Mr F. W. Reader recorded another portion of the west side of the north tower. This also revealed a length of the plinth, and it was at the same depth as the remains of the southern tower—namely, $6\frac{1}{2}$ feet lower than the level of the pavement discovered. It was also revealed that the plinth of the town-wall was $4\frac{1}{2}$ feet below that of the gateway, from which it may be inferred that the level inside the city had risen so much that a rebuilding of the gate had been necessitated during the Roman period, for it is not doubted that the gate is Roman, although the medieval successor very much confused the earlier foundations.

As at Newgate, the recently discovered foundations of the Roman predecessor of Aldersgate are askew with the line of the wall. It would seem that between Cripplegate and Aldersgate the wall was built to conform with a pre-existing highway that entered the city by this gate.[1]

In connection with this discovery it is interesting to recall that in 1888 Mr G. E. Fox examined the city ditch to the west of and close to Aldersgate Street. Here "in the bottom of the ditch appeared a slightly raised mound of unknown length, as it ran under the street and could therefore only be traced for a short distance. It was 22 feet high and 7 feet 2 inches broad at the top and 11 feet 10 inches at the base and was traceable for a length of about 10 feet . . . It was not placed in the middle of the ditch, but was nearer the outer than the inner margin." It has been suggested that this mound supported a wooden trestle-work supporting a bridge. Although the very broad ditch found at this point—its total width was $74\frac{1}{2}$ feet—has been accepted by some authorities as Roman, Dr Wheeler considers that its unusual dimensions "throw grave doubt upon this attribution."[2] It seems possible that the Ealdredsgate mentioned in the laws of Ethelred c. 1000

---

[1] The writer is indebted to Mr Quintin Waddington for this information concerning the discovery of the Roman Aldersgate.

[2] R.C.H.M., *Roman London*, p. 94.

was either an Anglo-Saxon structure erected on the Roman foundations or was a restoration of the earlier gateway. This question will doubtless be cleared up when further exploration of the site becomes possible.

Of the Roman Aldgate, the only discovery was made in 1907 when a sewage-tunnel was being bored under the roadway on the south side of Aldgate High Street. At a depth of 16½ feet solid masonry was found, consisting of work of two periods built close together. One portion was of comparatively recent date, but the other bore all the indications of

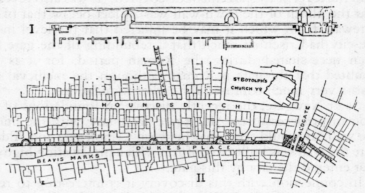

TWO PLANS OF THE TOWN-WALL WEST OF ALDGATE.

1. From the Holy Trinity Priory Survey made in 1592, showing Aldgate as it then existed with semicircular towers. The two bastions are those now numbered 6 and 7.

2. From Ogilby and Morgan's map dated 1677. Bastions 6, 7 and 9 are given. No. 8 at the eastern end of Bevis Marks is omitted. The plan of Aldgate has here undergone a great change.

Roman work, being built very solidly of ragstone and hard white mortar in which were fragments of Roman tile. Further out and under the roadway was found the face of another wall. It was composed of dressed stones from 9 inches to 2½ feet in length "running diagonally in a south-easterly direction." Unfortunately this wall was opened up for a length of only 2 or 3 feet, and it is therefore impossible at present to go further than regarding it as probable that part of a late Roman gate had been encountered.

At Bishopsgate discoveries in 1905 and 1921, at depths as shallow as from 3 to 5 feet, walling was found having Roman characteristics that may have formed a part of the internal projection of the Roman gate, but beyond this it is unsafe to go.

It is an interesting fact that the remains of gateways that have been discovered up to date are those that Stow regarded as "the first four gates of the city."[1] He had sources of information no longer available and from one of them "a booke called *Beware of the Cat*," he obtained materials for his notes concerning Aldersgate. Newgate, Aldersgate and Aldgate have all three revealed enough of their Roman origins to make it safe to regard them as the west, north and east gates. That facing south would have been the bridge gate of whose foundations nothing has yet come to light. They must be looked for on the waterside of Lower Thames Street.

Although as long ago as 1766 Entick, in describing the remains of Roman London[2] writes of fifteen bastions on the landward sides of the wall and Hughson,[3] in 1805, mentions only nine, it is remarkable to find that that very careful archaeologist, Roach Smith, appears to have known very little about them when in 1859 he wrote his *Illustrations of Roman London*, while twenty-one years later J. E. Price[4] went so far as to question whether the bastions or the wall belonged to the Roman period. "I venture to think," he wrote, "the evidence goes far to prove that the former [the Camomile Street bastion he was describing] was an addition, erected, if not as late as the Middle Ages, at a time long subsequent to the occupation by the Romans, and that the wall itself must no longer be assigned to a period so remote."

Until recent times only one of the bastions found its way into books that described the antiquities of London. This was the angle bastion to be seen in Cripplegate Churchyard, that once withdrawn and shadowy spot overlooked by the backs of high masses of office buildings. There, in comparative silence, in the heart of the closely packed City, it was possible for those of an enquiring mind who loved to explore its byways to look upon the medieval superstructure built upon a deeply buried Roman predecessor. It was a much

---

[1] *A Survey of London*. Ed. Kingsford. Vol. I. p. 34.

[2] *A New and Accurate Survey of London, Westminster and Southwark.* Rev. John Entick, M.A. Vol. I. p. 15.

[3] David Hughson: *London and its Neighbourhood*, 1859, Vol. I., pp. 36-37.

[4] John Edward Price, F.S.A.: *On a Bastion of London Wall*, 1880, p. 5.

patched and mouldering tower of semicircular form with a growth of soot-laden weeds and moss upon its brick, stone and tilework. To many it could not have been very impressive, but to the imaginative mind it did convey a feeling that here was something of great, if uncertain, age that certainly belonged to a time when people preferred to live within the shelter of a great protective wall if it were obtainable.

To-day, instead of being overshadowed, the Cripplegate bastion stands out as a feature of some consequence in a great space from which all but a very few buildings have vanished. Nearby is the burnt-out shell of the historic church of St Giles, in which John Milton was buried and Oliver Cromwell was married. A little farther off stand a fire station and one or two large warehouse blocks burnt but serviceable. It is now difficult to reconstruct in the mind the courts, passages and narrow streets of yesterday, but exceedingly easy to see the defences of Roman and medieval London at this point. If the City is wise it will preserve this new atmosphere of Cripplegate by digging out to their foundations the Roman town-wall and the three bastions now exposed, and in addition excavating the defensive ditch along the re-entrant angle.

So far the Cripplegate bastion has done little to help in deciding its date or that of the western series of hollow bastions; this it will perhaps be able to do when extensive excavations take place at and around it.

Between 1908 and 1909 the first opportunity of recent times occurred for the complete exploration to its foundations of one of the bastions. The occasion was the clearing and excavation of the old Christ's Hospital site and the erection upon it of new buildings for the General Post Office. It was here that the angle bastion adjoining Newgate on its north side was discovered and completely exposed. This was found to be of horseshoe form and hollow, with walls 7 feet thick at the base. The foundations go down to a depth of 7 feet below the base of the plinth of the Roman wall itself. It was one of the western series already mentioned that contain no re-used materials, being entirely of ragstone set in white mortar.

It is regrettable that it is not more widely known that this bastion in Giltspur Street has been carefully preserved and is accessible to the public if application to the Secretary of the G.P.O. is made by letter in advance.

The two bastions numbered 13 and 14 in the plan on pp. 100 and 101 are now exposed internally to the level of the basement floors that extended into them, and any scheme for permanently revealing the larger one at the re-entrant angle in the churchyard of St Giles', Cripplegate (No. 12 on the large plan), would include them. Both are hollow and no re-used materials have up to the present time been found in them.

Of the bastions that have been demolished two or three have been well recorded, and that found in Camomile Street (No. 10) in 1876 had a quarto book written on it by Mr J. E. Price.[1] It was solid and the materials employed for the filling included quantities of re-used sculptured stones that have added considerably to the collection in the Guildhall Museum.[2] Price thought that the discovery of a handle of green glazed ware "beneath the lowest bed of stone and near the centre of the structure" was sufficient evidence for regarding the bastion as post-Roman, although he himself mentions a number of places in the Roman Empire in which the unearthing of similar green glazed ware is recorded and examples are exhibited in museums. Dr Wheeler, in the Historical Monuments Commission's volume on Roman London, wrote "the sherd may well have been Roman," and there seems little doubt that the green glaze in question was being produced at the period when the bastions were added to the wall of London.[3] The foundation of this structure stood "upon the natural soil of London clay, which had been levelled by compressing together masses of chalk into the clay for a thickness of 2 or 3 inches." Apart from the re-used stone the material was Kentish ragstone both for the external facing and the core.

The bastion (No. 9) found in Castle Street (now Goring Street) in 1884 was recorded by Henry Hodge, who made plans and sectional drawings of it. The foundation consisted of flint and puddled clay surmounted by a bed of chalk. The dimensions were 26 feet wide with a projection of 15½ feet; it stood nearly 11 feet above the foundation, which was 5 feet below the plinth of the town-wall at this point. At a height of 8½ feet from the foundation was a double band of bricks

[1] John Edward Price, F.S.A.: *On a Bastion of London Wall*, 1880.
[2] See illustrations on p. 198 and facing p. 193.
[3] The writer has seen a number of examples of this glaze discovered on Roman sites in North Africa.

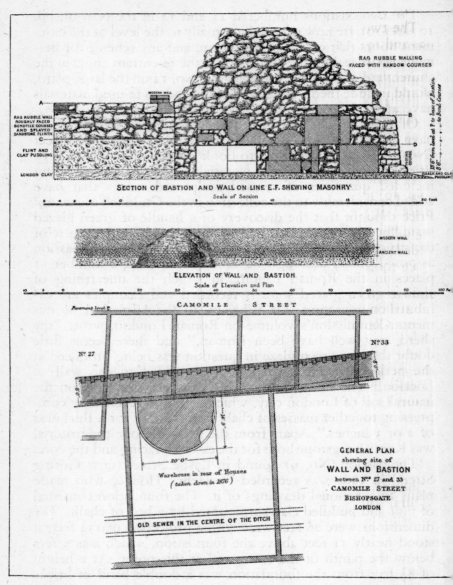

Labels within the figure:

RAG RUBBLE WALLING
FACED WITH RANDOM COURSES

RAG RUBBLE WALL
ROUGHLY FACED
BONDTILE COURSES
AND SPLAYED
SANDSTONE PLINTH

FLINT AND
CLAY PUDDLING

LONDON CLAY

MODERN WALL

SECTION OF BASTION AND WALL ON LINE E.F. SHEWING MASONRY
Scale of Section

MODERN WALL
ANCIENT WALL

ELEVATION OF WALL AND BASTION
Scale of Elevation and Plan

CAMOMILE STREET

Pavement level P

Nᵒ 27   Nᵒ 33

Warehouse in rear of Houses
(taken down in 1876)

20' 0"

OLD SEWER IN THE CENTRE OF THE DITCH

GENERAL PLAN
shewing site of
WALL AND BASTION
between Nᵒˢ 27 and 33
CAMOMILE STREET
BISHOPSGATE
LONDON

SECTION, ELEVATION AND PLAN OF THE TOWN-WALL AND BASTION BETWEEN
27 AND 33 CAMOMILE STREET, BISHOPSGATE.

This bastion (No. 10) is one of the eastern group with one exception of solid construction; it is notable for the quantity of re-used stone employed.

(From *On a Bastion of London Wall*, by J. E. Price, 1880.)

that was not carried through the solid core. Among the sculptured stones recorded were a portion of an inscription, a fragment of a frieze carved with swags and running hares and a cornice, all now in the Guildhall Museum.

At All Hallows, London Wall, the vestry was built into the adjoining bastion (No. 11), a fact that was revealed when, in 1905, Dr Norman and Mr F. W. Reader had, during building operations, an opportunity of examining the entire structure, of which 8 feet of Roman work had survived. This had a diameter of only 19 feet, or 7 feet less than No. 9 (described above), with a projection nearly the same at 15 feet. It stood 3 feet below the top of the plinth of the town-wall. The exterior was of random rubble laid in white mortar which stood on a plinth of large re-used ashlar, and this was supported by a rectangular platform composed of much thinner ashlar, also re-used. After the bastion had been built the evidence showed that the ditch had "clearly remained open for some time . . . accumulating mud and rubbish against the obstruction of the bastion footings."

Notwithstanding the fact that Roach Smith[1] described the feature destroyed in 1852 as merely a "buttress" of the Roman town-wall at Tower Hill (No. 2), he was only able to give a somewhat vague report on it, and the drawing by Fairholt published with this only indicates a small piece of rubble standing against a well-preserved piece of the town-wall. Forming a part of the rubble mass are shown large worked stones with moulded sides. It was here that the Classicianus inscription[2] was found in two instalments separated by eighty-three years. No measurements of the structure have been published, and there is no information as to the external treatment nor of the foundations. There can, however, be little doubt that this conformed fairly closely with the rest of the eastern series of solid bastions.

The bastions numbered 4, 20 and 21 are known to have existed from early maps of London. No. 4 appears only in the survey by Ogilby and Morgan in 1677, and the other two are given in John Leake's map engraved by Hollar in 1666.

Before leaving the town-wall of Roman London it would be well to refer, if only briefly, to the gradual gathering of

[1] *Illustrations of Roman London*, p. 15.   [2] See p. 254.

THE REMAINS OF BASTION (2) IN TRINITY PLACE, EAST OF TOWER HILL.

It was found built against a well-preserved section of the town-wall and it was here that sculptured stones from the tomb of Julius Alpinus Classicianus, the Procurator of Britain at the time of Boudicca's insurrection in A.D. 60, were found in 1852 and 1935.

(From *Illustrations of Roman London*, C. Roach Smith, 1859.)

evidence that has made possible the formation of the most recent inferences and views on its age. In the previous editions of this book the writer was inclined to accept Professor Haverfield's suggestions, but during the twenty years that have elapsed the many discoveries made and the exhaustive work of the committee of the Royal Commission on Historical Monuments that was responsible for the volume on Roman London have thrown fresh light on the problems and more convincing views have now been put forward.

It is helpful to quote here the evidence as presented by Haverfield. "The material facts," he writes, "appear to be the following: First, the wall itself, as I have stated, stood entirely on the clean gravel subsoil; no sign has been noted that it anywhere crosses earlier buildings or even graves. This would suit an early date, though perhaps our records are too imperfect to give us certainty, at least in the matter of such small remains as burials. Secondly, the line of the wall was seemingly laid out so as to include almost all the buildings of the town which were in existence when it was constructed. The area thus enclosed is very large, and this suggests considerable growth and a late date. Thirdly, the absence of buildings, other than graves, close outside the wall suggests that it was built late in the life of the town; there was no subsequent period during which more suburbs could develop. Fourthly, the structure of the wall, with its courses of small stones and its bonding-tiles, is generally ascribed to the later empire. This, however, is not quite so certain as is generally alleged. Bonding-tiles were certainly used very freely in the later empire. We have datable instances in the forts of the Saxon Shore, and in the city of Trier and on other Gaulish sites. But, at any rate south of the Alps, they were known and used in the first century A.D. They may favour, but they certainly do not prove, a late date for the London wall. Lastly, we have the general probability that wall-building would be carried out in Britain, as in Gaul and elsewhere in the empire, under the pressure of some evil, such as the attack of the barbarians. It is plain that these considerations permit of no definite conclusion. We must wait and see. But some of the facts seem to have rather more weight than others. In particular, the large area included by the wall, and the scarcity of buildings outside it, and the need of some historical cause for wall-building, combine to make me think that perhaps the end rather than the beginning of the 3rd century is the more probable date. The bastions might easily have been added in the course of the 4th century, when the dangers from Saxon pirates became even more acute."[1]

Dr Wheeler assembles the evidence in three groups:

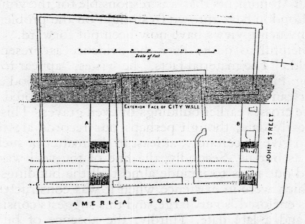

Plan of ditch in America Square　From *Archæologia* LXIII.

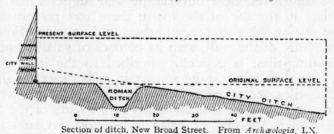

Section of ditch, New Broad Street. From *Archæologia*, LX.

The berm at this point was about 15 feet broad and the ditch 3 feet less.

(1) The actual evidence provided by the remains; (2) that provided by the form and compass of the wall, with special reference to burials within and without its circuit; and (3) evidence of analogous sites in Britain and Gaul.

Under the first group he presents the fact that the landward wall nowhere reveals the presence of re-used materials. The use of bonding courses of bricks or tiles occurs freely at

[1] *Journal of Roman Studies*, i., 158.

Pompeii and Herculaneum before A.D. 79 and also at Colchester, where the walls are regarded as late first century A.D.

There is no evidence of any previously laid down deposit or of buildings under the wall; it stands everywhere on the undisturbed and original surface of the ground.

A deposit of from 6 to 7 feet yielding only indications of the Roman period of the town was found against the wall and above the ditch in America Square. At Newgate also there was the considerable rise in level already mentioned. The

BLIND ARCHES IN THE ROMAN TOWN-WALL OF LONDON.
Discovered in 1857 near Aldermanbury Postern.
(From a woodcut published in *Illustrations of Roman London*, C. Roach Smith.)

bastions were added at a later date without being bonded into the wall and they cut into the Roman ditch.

Where the Walbrook passes through the base of the wall there has been found evidence that points to the lowest level of the silt having accumulated *c*. A.D. 100-130.

At whatever date it was built the wall was laid out to enclose the two hills, the westernmost of which was only partially occupied to the north-east. All the cemeteries lie just outside the wall.

The excavations carried out by Dr and Mrs Wheeler at

Verulamium since 1930 showed that the town-wall there belongs to the period 120 to 150, and it was observed that the work has a number of features that resemble those of London.

Geographically the two places were similarly placed if danger threatened overland, particularly from the north. Outstanding events in Boudicca's revolt were in living memory at the period when Verulamium felt it desirable to put up a strong defensive wall, and the people of London could not therefore have forgotten that in A.D. 60 both towns shared the same fate. In about 119 the Ninth Legion stationed at York was entirely destroyed; the situation caused by this great gap in the defences of the province was so alarming that the Emperor Hadrian considered it necessary to send without delay a new legion to replace it, and in 120 himself came to Britain to take command of operations to restore the situation.

No indications of the site of any other town-wall have been found in London, and it may thus be accepted that at the time of this disaster the place was undefended. If the erection of a wall had been discussed at an earlier date the problem would have been where to place it, for it is clear that in this period the growth of Londinium was so rapid that to put restrictions on it would create almost immediate inconvenience and congestion. If the threat from the north was sufficiently heavy with alarm and all objections had to be over-ridden, that of constriction could be overcome by placing the boundaries generously outside the built-up area. That this actually did take place seems indicated by the thinning down of occupation that occurs in the areas nearest to the northern line of the wall.

In Hadrian's reign Rome was at the zenith of her world power, and the building of vast and imposing monuments of her greatness in the form of public works gave added security to her far-flung frontiers, and it would be almost inevitable that the period that witnessed the consolidation of Hadrian's Wall by a very formidable building effort should also see the walling of the two great and very vulnerable cities of the south. There is also some significance in the fact that the only monument to a Roman Emperor so far discovered in London commemorates Hadrian.

Nearly everything that archaeology contributes to the discussion points fairly closely to the date of the great military disaster mentioned above as having occurred in Hadrianic times. A comparison of the areas of Gallic cities built in the early and late Imperial periods reveals a marked tendency to enclose large spaces in the Early Period and very much less in the Late Period. London, with its 326 acres, falls easily into the average size of the earlier series and is a giant in comparison with the 30 acres that may be regarded as the normal area in the later period.

Chapter X

THE PUBLIC LIFE OF LONDINIUM

IN none of the scanty references to Londinium is any mention made of its rank as a city. That it had attained sufficient importance by the middle of the fourth century to be honoured with the proud name of Augusta has already been mentioned, and yet this furnishes no information as to the category in which it was placed. If it were eventually to be proved that Londinium never possessed any distinctive municipal rank, no deduction could be made to suggest that it had an inferior position among the towns of Britain. Corinium, probably the second city in importance of the province, was in the same undefined position, while Camulodunum, which, as the first British town given the rank of colonia, had claims to seniority, was certainly in size, population and influence scarcely in the second rank. There were many instances in the Roman Empire of cities of great importance that did not possess any municipal rank, and notable among them was Capua.

There were serious difficulties in the way of making the port into a municipium, for it required the presence of a large number of landowners to compose a local senate or *Ordo*. The merchants and bankers, who constituted by far the most important class, would have lacked the leisure to fulfil the largely ornamental and expensive duties of the *decuriones* or municipal councillors, quite apart from the fact that, important as they were, there was an inherent tendency in the Roman political system to regard the commercial class as of inferior status. Besides all this, when Londinium was rising into importance as one of the great cities of the West, the most flourishing period of the coloniae and municipia was already past. The control of a city's finances by the *ordo* was already showing signs of failure as early as the days of Trajan, and thirty years later the *decuriones* of Tergeste (Trieste) were complaining of impoverishment due to the drain of gratuitous service upon their private resources.[1]

Britain as an imperial province was governed by a legate and a procurator, "the first," as the Britons put it, "to tyrannise over our lives and the procurator to tyrannise over our

[1] Mommsen in *C.I.L.*, vol. v. 53.

property."[1] This was in the early years of the Roman occupation. The holders of these two high offices quarrelled so much that it was considered remarkable that when Agricola was Governor of Aquitania he had had no contention with his procurator. When Catus Decianus, who had made himself conspicuous by his precipitate flight from Londinium at the outbreak of the Boudiccan revolt, was succeeded by Julius Classicianus there soon developed a state of hostility between him and Suetonius, the legate, that culminated in dispatches from the procurator to Rome pressing for the governor's recall.

The post of procurator often developed into that of emperor's spy upon the legate and there was a marked tendency for the lower post so to increase its authority that it confronted the legate on almost equal terms. It was natural that under a bad emperor, who used his procurators for underhand purposes, the situation should become strained, if not intolerable, especially in view of the fact that the two officials belonged to different orders of society.

The *juridici* who assisted the legates were appointed directly by the emperor. Those who formed the legal council that assisted the governor were in time known as assessors. The *comites* or attachés, as they would now be called, were appointed by the governor, who was responsible for their good behaviour. These were the posts open to young Romans of good birth who wished to acquire the knowledge of administrative methods and practice.

Londinium, as capital of the province, would have been the base of the governing structure, with the consequence that a considerable proportion of the population consisted of the legate's assistants, their juniors and those attending to their requirements. There were clerks, messengers and postmen, and, in addition, the military units attached to the governor and the procurator.

There can be very little doubt that the city was unique among the others in Britain on account of its outstanding importance as a port as well as for its possession of a very cosmopolitan population. While it is clear from recent discoveries at Verulamium and Viroconium that British towns

[1] Tacitus, *Agricola*, XV.
[2] W. T. Arnold, *Rom. Prov. Administration*, p. 67.

had greatly decayed by the middle of the third century, the causes that brought about their decline could not have affected Londinium to any great extent. However heavy may have been the imperial exactions on the city, the volume of trade represented by the general prosperity of the country, apart from the towns, continued so long as British exports were in demand, and beyond this there was the steady flow of civil and military pay from Rome that helped to keep the shops in a flourishing condition.

The *collegia* of the city were no doubt popular, as in all Roman towns, for these guilds, clubs or corporations gathered together in groups, traders, civil servants, priests and others. Here could be found much of the friendly social life of Londinium, where, no doubt, much business was carried on without formality, where religious matters were discussed, and where those in official positions could forgather. A guild required state permission before it could function. Presumably the Government wished to know who was who in these clubs in case of trouble, for the members would have discussed a great deal more than the question of providing the burial expenses of those enrolled on the membership list.[1]

Although, so far as is known, there were no aqueducts on a large scale in Britain, and none have been traced near London, water may well have been led into the city by means of surface conduits, for allowing that an abundance of wells provided to a great extent the requirements of the small consumer, yet for large establishments and baths some other source of supply may have been provided.[2] It is a remarkable fact, however, that some of the springs in London tapped by deep wells yield a very copious supply of water.[3]

High among the officials of the city would have been those whose duties were the conservancy of the Thames. In view of the fact, pointed out by geologists, that the level changed considerably throughout the latter half of the Roman occupation, there must have been much embanking to organise and

[1] *Rom. Brit. and the Eng. Settlements*, Collingwood and Myres, p. 201.

[2] From the Bank of England site have come lengths of squared oak, $7\frac{3}{4}$ by $4\frac{1}{2}$ inches, with circular piercing $1\frac{3}{4}$ inches in diameter. These wooden water-pipes seem to indicate one of the various forms of supply. Examples are to be seen at the London Museum.

[3] The well under Whitehall Court adjoining the War Office supplies the whole requirements of that great building.

foreshore rights to settle. Dredging and general supervision of quays and docks were also a part of the conservators' duties.

The *portoria*, or customs duties levied upon imports and exports, required a bureau of officials, who may have been

ROMAN TESSELLATED PAVEMENT FOUND IN
BUCKLERSBURY IN 1869.
It measured 13 feet by about 20, and was unearthed
at a depth of 20 feet.
(*Guildhall Museum.*)

independent of the procurator. At first these duties were very low—from 2 to 5 per cent.—but incoming oriental luxuries were very heavily taxed, and by the time of Diocletian even the ordinary *portoria* were raised to the crippling height of 12½ per cent., the effect of which could only be countered by an exceptional wave of prosperity.

The conditions under which the traffic in slaves was carried on in Londinium is not known nor is there any information as to where this human merchandise was penned, inspected and disposed of.

Hospitals existed throughout the Roman Empire, but if, as is more than probable, there was one in Londinium for the benefit of the officials, civil and military, nothing is known of it. In connection with such an institution, and for the benefit of the city in general, especially the poor, there were *archiatri*, or public physicians. These formed a very important feature of Roman municipal institutions. They numbered from five to ten in accordance with the size of the city, and received a regular salary from the public revenue. Their position was regularised by the Emperor Antoninus Pius. Justinian's Codex required the doctors to pay special attention to the poor and not concern themselves too exclusively with their wealthy patients.

During the last century and a half of its existence as a Roman city, if not at an earlier period, there were resident in Londinium several of the most important figures in the high administration and perhaps of the defence of the province. The *Praepositus Thesaurorum*, or High Treasurer, undoubtedly had his residence in the city, and although there is no absolute record, the presence of the *Vicarius*, or civil Governor-General, is clear. Further than this, there is some probability of there having been another official, the *Consularis* or *Praeses* of the particular sub-province in which the capital was situated—possibly, but at present without any certainty at all, Maxima Caesariensis.

Lastly, towards the close of the fourth century, there probably lived in the city the *Comes Britanniarum*, the Commander-in-Chief of the Romano-British forces, a fact that would have provided an element of military pomp not hitherto prominent in a capital whose origin and interests had been largely commercial and financial.

Chapter XI

THIS attempt to recreate a picture of Londinium as far as the archaeological materials will allow must be taken as during the greatest period of wealth and size after the recovery from the disaster in 367.

It is not known whether any careful planning followed the destruction of the town by Boudicca, but this is more than probable, and the extensive exposure of the Roman levels of Londinium that will in due course take place north and east of St Paul's may reveal the existence of well-planned streets. So far very few have been recognised with any certainty.

Notwithstanding this extreme paucity of materials, a suggested lay-out of streets in uniform blocks has been skilfully built up on the basis of the basilica, the bridge, two points on the Walbrook where there are indications that streets were carried across it, and finally Newgate in relation to a small section of a street discovered under St Mary-le-Bow Church. This beginning of a plan of Roman London was published in 1928 in the Report of the Historical Monuments Commission on Roman London. It may be useful should other discoveries fit the framework it offers, and if they do not alternative plottings may become apparent.

Approaching the city by the great western highway from Wales through Glevum, Corinium and Calleva, the traveller is likely to have found himself in pleasant suburbs along the high ground sloping to the Thames between Westminster and the Fleet. On nearing the site of the Savoy the buildings would become more frequent, for there is at Aldwych[1] the possibility of a link with the Roman period. The name appears to have originated in the English appellation given to the deserted houses of this suburb, Aldwych meaning old village or settlement. The deserted Roman town of Isurium near York was named Aldborough, and other instances could be cited.

Passing along what is now Fleet Street, the new arrival

[1] Old Wych until Stuart period.

173

would find the road descending gently to a bridge across a
tributary of the Thames, in later times known as the Fleet
that flowed past the famous prison of that name. With little
doubt this copious stream took the place of the artificial
ditch dug elsewhere. The eastern slope, dotted over perhaps
with the evidences of sundry minor occupations, was crowned
with the massive western walls of the capital. Immediately
above and facing the bridge, the gateway named perhaps after
the Celtic god Lud stood astride the roadway, its arches
allowing for the inward and outward streams of traffic.
Ascending the rise and reaching the gates, there would be
transactions with the customs or "octroi" officials, after which
the wonders of the great city would be free to the gaze of the
new-comer. If in need of a bath he would inquire for the
nearest establishment, and might have been directed to a
building within sight, for there are grounds for believing that
there were baths close to Ludgate.

A reference to such a building is found as far back as the
year 1667, when Londoners were busy in the work of reconstruction after the Great Fire. A certain Mr Span, "a ancient
citizen in Holyday Yard, Creed Lane" [south of Ludgate Hill],
found what is described as a Roman aqueduct passing round
"a Bath that was built in a round Forme with Nitches at an
equal Distance for Seats."[1] Unfortunately no dimensions are
given, but the description appears to indicate a bathing
establishment on account of the circular form of the bath. A
good parallel to this description is afforded by the circular
bath at Aquae Flavianae near Khenchela in Algeria.

The position just within Ludgate is eminently suitable for
such a public establishment where the dusty and travel-soiled
arrivals in the city could obtain the luxury of a bath immediately after entering the gateway.

The sites of three small and apparently private baths have
been located. One was discovered in Cannon Street in 1906,
a little over 16 feet below the street level. It was not quite
rectangular, being slightly smaller at the end where the steps
descended to the water. The dimensions were 10 feet 6 inches
by about 6 feet. The yellow brick sides and the floor were
covered with a layer of fine water-tight concrete or *opus*

---

[1] Strype's edition of Stow's *Survey of London*, vol. ii. Appendix v. 24.
The seats perhaps indicate a latrine.

signinum. A second bath, 5 feet 8 inches square, was discovered in 1895 at No. 63 Threadneedle Street. Its walls were composed of rough Kentish rag and the floor was like the other covered with *opus signinum*.

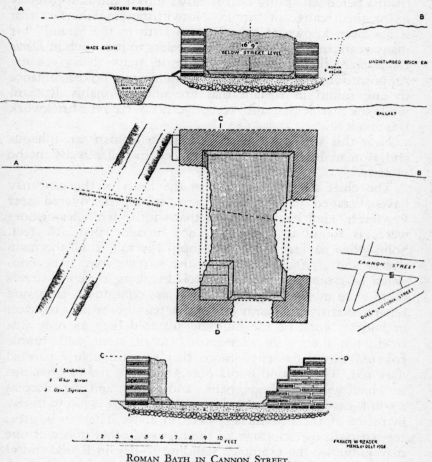

ROMAN BATH IN CANNON STREET.
Discovered in 1906 on the site of the fire brigade station that backs on to Queen Victoria Street.
(From *Archaologia*, LX 214.)

Stone used in Londinium in some instances was an oolite that came from as far off as a district lying between Wincanton and Bath.[1]

[1] *London in Roman Times* (Lond. Mus. Cat.), p. 37.

In Strand Lane, between St Mary le Strand Church and the Thames, there can be seen a third bath with its sides of red brick closely jointed. Its dimensions are 15 feet 6 inches by about 6 feet 9 inches and the western end is rounded. Water from a perennial spring nearby flows into it and is apparently its original source of supply. Notwithstanding the fact that it has been known as "the Roman Bath in the Strand" for many years, and although Dickens refers to it as such in *David Copperfield*,[1] there is nothing besides its shape that gives any support to the claim. The bricks certainly bear no resemblance to any found in Britain that are unquestionably Roman, while the marble that until recent years covered the brickwork was modern.

Near this site was found, in 1741, a Roman sarcophagus and Roman bricks have been noticed in cellar walls in the vicinity.

The chief streets leading into the heart of the city may have averaged 30 feet in width. A section discovered near Pewterers' Hall has more than that width,[2] while lesser ones were, as found in Eastcheap, not broader than 16 feet. Solid stone paving would have been the rule in all the main streets and in the lesser ways the surface may have consisted of rammed flint and gravel. Flanking the chief streets there were most probably more or less continuous frontages separated fairly frequently by narrow passages from 3 to 4 feet in width. Much of the building material then as now was brick, but there was widespread use of stone and rubble covered externally with stucco that was frequently painted dark red. The ground floors possessed wide arched openings in which were the shops, banks and offices, and the effect as a whole may have resembled in essentials what is found to-day in many of the provincial towns in Italy. There was great regularity in the windows of the first and other floors, if one may judge by the examples standing to-day in Rome and at Ostia. The height to which buildings were carried in Lon-

---

[1] *David Copperfield*, chapter xxxv.: "There was an old Roman bath in those days at the bottom of one of the streets out of the Strand—it may be there still—in which I have had many a cold plunge. Dressing myself as quietly as I could, and leaving Peggotty to look after my aunt, I tumbled head foremost into it, and then went for a walk to Hampstead."

[2] See p. 241 *infra*.

SILVER AND POTTERY VESSELS AND A FLUE TILE.

1. A pair of black ware vases from the Marne Valley found in Moorgate Street (*London Museum*).   2. A drinking cup or beaker found near St. George's Church, Southwark (*British Museum*).   3. Two silver vessels (*British Museum*). 4. A flue tile with elaborate design impressed to provide a hold for plaster.   5. Samian globular-shaped olla form 72, found in Cornhill (*British Museum*).

IMPORTED AND BRITISH POTTERY FOUND IN LONDON.

1. Carinated (*i.e.* shouldered) vase of 1st century A.D. found in Liverpool Street (*London Museum*). 2 and 4. Beakers with slip ornament, New Forest type (*London and British Museums*). 3 and 7. Castor (Durobrivæ) ware ornamented with running hares and stags in relief or barbotine. 5. Black-glazed ware imported (*Guildhall Museum*). 8. Vase mica-dusted, from Bell Alley (*Guildhall Museum*). 9. Vessel with handle, from Finsbury Circus (*London Museum*). 12. Fluted beaker from Ivy Lane (*London Museum*). 14. Vase of Upchurch (Medway) ware from London Wall (*London Museum*). 15. Handled cup ornamented with grotesque face, from London Wall (*London Museum*).

dinium can only be estimated by the great thickness of lower walls. On this basis there would have been houses here and there that rose high above those surrounding them. It is not uncommon to find walls 3 feet in thickness—witness the house beneath the Coal Exchange in Lower Thames Street—and such structures would, according to modern standards, have been capable of carrying four or five floors at least. From the foundations brought to light in the heart of the city,[1] it is

ROMAN HOUSES IN THE FIRST AND SECOND CENTURY TOWN OF OSTIA, THE PORT OF ROME.

At No. 42 Lombard Street foundations were discovered in 1925 that suggested the possibility of their having been associated with houses of this type. There were two complete piers and part of a third entirely of brick with openings 10 feet 6 inches between them. The shops or offices that the ground plan seems to indicate fronted a passage 10 feet wide, on the south side of which ran a great wall 4 feet thick. These buildings appear to have occupied a position on the south side of the Great Forum.

evident that buildings were laid out with almost fantastic irregularity in spite of the fact that some of them possessed walls with foundations about 8 feet in thickness. Therefore, if regularity of frontages be accepted for the streets of certain quarters, the conclusion cannot be avoided that the central area, or ancient nucleus of the city, doubtless for very good reasons, presented in some areas an appearance greatly lacking in uniformity. The angles at which houses were constructed in relation to those adjoining, so far as records of

[1] *Archaeologia*, vol. lx. 222, for foundations in Cornhill.

foundations exposed have been kept, show an amazing dis-
regard for one another, and the only inference that can be
made is that space was very precious, as at the present day,
and where it was desired to make the most of a site indi-
viduality reigned supreme.

In 1925 foundations of what might possibly be traces of shop
fronts were laid bare on the north side of Lombard Street at
its   Gracechurch
Street end. From
the   plan   given
here (p. 181) the
basis for this con-
jecture can be seen.
Two openings $10\frac{1}{2}$
feet in width faced
a passage or nar-
row street about

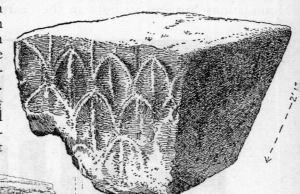

CAPITAL ORNAMENTED WITH A
LEAF DESIGN AND OTHER
SCULPTURED STONES FOUND
IN LONDON.

(*Guildhall Museum*).

$8\frac{1}{2}$ feet wide. The openings were shown by brick piers resting
on concrete foundations and the central one had a short length
of wall running back from it. The passage was bounded on
the south side by a wall 4 feet thick that was exposed for a
distance of about 55 feet. The position of the walls and piers
may indicate that the eastern end of Lombard Street follows
the course of a Roman thoroughfare, for although the earlier
frontage stands some 5 or 6 feet back from the present line it
is nearly parallel with it. It is worth mentioning in this con-

nection that Mr J. E. Price records that in one part of Lombard Street so many fibulae (brooches) were found that it suggested the presence of a jeweller's shop.[1]

At the time of the discovery of these foundations the question was discussed as to their having formed a part of the buildings on the southern margin of the great forum or public square on the northern side of which stood the imposing Basilica. The position is quite in keeping with such a theory, and excavations on adjoining sites in years to come will perhaps throw light upon it.

The Basilica or hall of commerce and government of Londinium must have been the largest building in the city. It was slightly over 500 feet long by about 152 feet in width. The plan reproduced here shows the whole structure as it has now revealed itself from the widely separated pieces of walling that have been found. There was an apse with a radius of some 20 feet at each end of the nave that ran the whole length of the vast structure flanked by broad aisles. The arcade on either side consisted of thirteen massive piers with oblong bases measuring about 10 feet by 5. Behind the northern aisle—a vast corridor about 25 feet wide—ran a range of eighteen offices or shops each some 20 feet square. The site of this notable building is cut through nearly in the centre by Gracechurch Street, the north-west corner lies beneath Cornhill, while most of the eastern half is under Leadenhall Market and part of Whittington Avenue.

In the area south of the Basilica it would be normal to find the chief forum of the city and it is probable that it was situated there. On the other hand, the site has revealed here and there foundations of massively-built structures that may belong to the same period as the Basilica, and, if so, the forum must be looked for to the north of the building unless, for special reasons not easy to suggest, one or two buildings of importance were erected in the open space. Here, as in so many instances in London, the usual circumstances of discovery that make it impossible to date walling deprive the archaeologist of the value of what has come to light and, instead of elucidating the products of previous excavations, merely complicate existing problems.

The foundations from which the complete plan of the

[1] *Jour. of Brit. Arch. Assoc.*, xxx. 186; *Arch. Review*, i. 355.

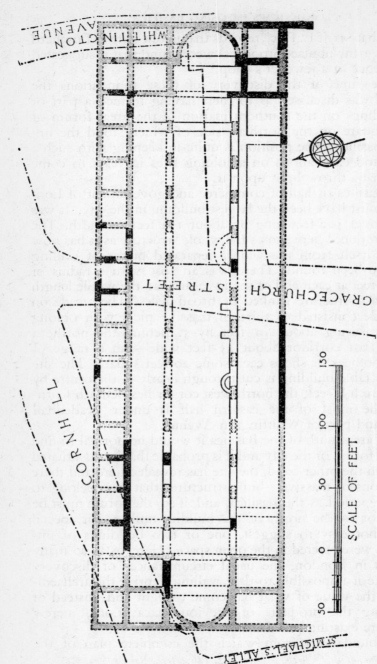

RECONSTRUCTED PLAN OF THE GREAT BASILICA OF ROMAN LONDON. From these and from foundations Mr Gerald C. Dunning has been able to produce the first complete plan of this vast structure. It was a reconstruction of an earlier basilica about half the length of the later one. The first building has been dated approximately to A.D. 60-80 and its great successor to the Flavian period (70-95).

The walls that have been discovered are shown solid black.

(Reproduced by permission of the Society of Antiquaries.)

Roman Basilica has at length been extricated were very much involved by rebuilding that had occurred at various periods, and, had it not been for the fortunate circumstances that caused an extensive rebuilding that included the whole of the eastern half of the site, it is possible that recognition of the importance of piecemeal discoveries in this area might have been delayed for a very long time.

A good many discoveries made in recent years indicate that a first basilica was erected not long after Boudicca's

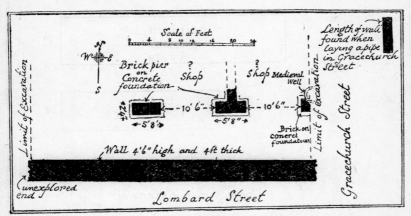

PLAN OF FOUNDATIONS OF ROMAN BUILDINGS DISCOVERED IN LOMBARD STREET IN 1925 AND 1926.

The solidly-built brick bases at regular intervals approximately in line with the present street suggest shop fronts of typical Roman character. These were found in September 1925.

The massive wall of rubble alternating with courses of brick shown about 10 ft. to the south extended along the whole length of the site excavated and thus formed a corridor.

rebellion and that the great structure which succeeded it was completed before the end of the first century A.D.

The basilica at Corinium (Cirencester) was about 340 feet long by 78 broad, and that of Calleva (Silchester) 233 by 58, and thus their lengths were four times their widths. The basilica of Londinium measured no less than 505 feet in length, or only about 8 feet shorter than the existing St Paul's Cathedral.

The oblong piers of the interior were about 10 feet broad by 5 feet thick, and would have been about 28 feet high including base and capital. To the top of the semicircular

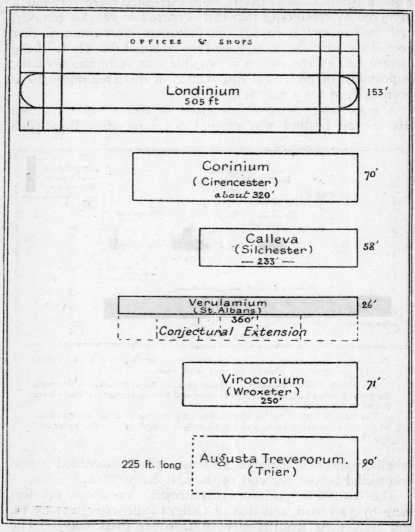

OFFICES & SHOPS

Londinium
505 ft
153′

Corinium
(Cirencester)
about 320′
70′

Calleva
(Silchester)
— 233′ —
58′

Verulamium
(St. Albans)
360′
Conjectural Extension
26′

Viroconium
(Wroxeter)
250′
71′

225 ft. long
Augusta Treverorum.
(Trier)
90′

COMPARATIVE PLANS OF BRITISH AND ONE GAULISH BASILICA.

The measurements are given in English feet. The length of Corinium's basilica has also been given as 285 and 340 feet and that of Calleva as 240 feet.

The Basilica was a hall of public assembly, generally with a court room and offices attached.

arches that they supported the height would have been about 40 feet. Seeing that the foundations of the nave arcades are over 12 feet in thickness there can be no reasonable doubt that the walls supported by the piers possessed a clerestory of the usual basilica form to be seen in the early Christian churches of which those at Ravenna are typical. This would bring the full height of the arcaded walls to scarcely less than 70 feet.

Of the internal decoration of this great structure some slight evidence may be obtained from the fragments of painted plaster showing green foliage on a red ground preserved in the British Museum, and it is more than probable, from the fragments discovered, that at least the lower parts of the walls were lined with marble. Mosaic pavements were found in the area of the excavations, and thus indications of the nature of the necessary component materials of the great pile have been disinterred in the heart of modern London, where the memory of such a structure had been lost for so many centuries.

There are only very incomplete indications of any other individual buildings in this most important quarter of the Roman city, but there can be no doubt that the administrative area contained massively-built structures of large dimensions containing a certain amount of stone masonry and a fairly large proportion of embellishment.

A little to the north-east of the site just described there was found in Leadenhall Street (in front of East India House), at a depth of 10 feet, a very elaborate mosaic floor in perfect condition, showing, in the centre, Bacchus riding on his tiger. The room that this pavement adorned was much larger than the area of the mosaic and was at least 22 feet square, a wide border of plain red tesserae surrounding the design. The discovery of pieces of green porphyry on the same site has been mentioned already.[1] This would certainly suggest a structure of exceptional richness of treatment. Another fine tessellated pavement, including a representation of a bacchante, was unearthed under the old Excise Office between Bishopsgate Street and Old Broad Street. It was part of an elaborate design 28 feet square, and adjoining was another pavement composed of large square tiles. It is interesting to note that rough and unsuccessful attempts to repair the tessellated pavement had been made.

[1] See p. 85.

TESSELLATED PAVEMENT DISCOVERED UNDER THE OLD EXCISE OFFICE.

This fine pavement found in Old Broad Street with other tessellated floors was sufficiently well preserved for the whole design to be reconstructed. The depth was stated (*Gent. Mag.* [1807], I, 415-7) to be about 7 feet from the present surface. The central panel shows a Bacchante on a panther.

In Threadneedle Street and adjoining have been found various well-designed mosaic pavements and parts of others, revealing that this quarter was thickly occupied by well-built houses, and the impression one gathers is that in the area, just to the east of the Walbrook, were grouped a number of exceptionally well-appointed structures having mosaic pavements of considerable merit. Fragments of plaster show that they were decorated with somewhat elaborate designs of green, blue, black and yellow, while others had flowers and foliage in red, yellow, white and green upon a black background.

It has already been suggested that a building containing such a fine pavement as that of the Bacchus may have belonged to the Government House, but it may be that others as skilfully designed have been destroyed in the callous fashion of the nineteenth century.

Two buildings of the greatest importance in fourth-century Londinium were the Treasury and the Mint. It is quite likely that they were in close proximity, but no indications of either have been discovered. The discovery on the site of the Board of Ordnance Office in the Tower of the silver ingot illustrated on page 103 can hardly be accepted as evidence for suggesting that the buildings were in the south-east corner of the city.

Apart from the bath mentioned as being just inside Ludgate, there are interesting remains of a building beneath the Coal Exchange in Lower Thames Street that has frequently been called a private or public bath.

The site was partially discovered when the Coal Exchange was commenced in 1848; eleven years later more of the ground plan was brought to light, so that it became possible to plot the whole with more or less completeness. A considerable portion was covered by the new buildings that were being erected, but the rest is still to be seen in a vault beneath the Exchange.

It is not certain what purpose the structure was designed to fulfil. Although, as just mentioned, it has been described as a bath, there is really no evidence in favour of the hypothesis beyond the fact that the two central rooms possess hypocausts under their floors; indeed, the arrangement of the apartments hardly suggests a bathing establishment, and it is more probable that the building was a private house, perhaps partly used for purposes of business, being in proximity to the quays, and therefore in the heart of the business quarter. That offices should be warmed by hypocausts beneath the floor is not in the least surprising, for any flourishing house would provide its clerical staff with comfortable conditions for the winter. The warmed rooms are not sunk below the level of those adjoining, and there are no indications of any water

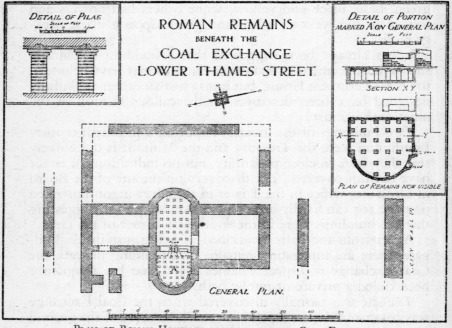

PLAN OF ROMAN HOUSE FOUND BENEATH THE COAL EXCHANGE
IN LOWER THAMES STREET.
Details of the heating arrangements are inset in the corners.
(*By permission of the Royal Commission on Historical Monuments.*)

supply. These foundations form the single link that has been discovered between the average business offices of Londinium and those of our own time, and on this account it is a matter of no small satisfaction that they have been preserved. The style of the brickwork with exceedingly thick joints suggests a late period in the Roman occupation, and there are indications from the raising of the floor level that the existing building superseded an earlier one.

Small workshops that were doubtless very numerous may be almost unrecognisable from their foundation plans, but there are one or two spots where factories have revealed themselves. One of these was discovered in 1677 at the north-west corner of St Paul's Cathedral during the excavation of the foundations for Wren's new structure. It was a quadruple potter's kiln and appears to date back to an early period in the history of Londinium. A certain Mr John Conyers, an apothecary of Fleet Street, who made notes between 1674 and 1677, records that "coffins lay over this loamy kiln, the lowest coffins made of chalk, and this supposed to be about Domitian's time. This kiln was full of ye worst sort of pots, lamps, urns, and not many were saved whole." If Conyers, who might well have discussed the matter with Wren, were approximately correct in his dating, it would seem that the site became a cemetery at some early date in the Roman occupation. In any case, there is here a report of the manufacture of rough pottery in the western parts of Londinium at an apparently early date, indicating that the industry was a well-established local one, and in all probability was carried on until the area was required for other purposes by the growing city.

Another pottery site was discovered underneath the church of St Mary Woolnoth in King William Street. There were found on that site, in 1724, Roman foundations into which the débris of brick kilns and furnaces had been worked—an indication perhaps of the breaking up of a very early pottery. In 1936 there was found a large deposit of potters' wasters and other kiln débris on a site beside the Walbrook under Copthall Court, Moorgate. This pottery was working at the end of the first century.[1]

The site of a glass factory was brought to light in Clement's Lane (King William Street end) in 1840-41. Not only was glass slag and pot glass discovered on the piece of ground, but also a tool that was judged to have been used for the purpose of glass decoration. In addition, the same site yielded a number of large amphorae, but for what purpose they were there is not apparent. There do not seem to have been any indications of their having been fabricated on the spot.

As in every large Roman city, space was devoted to places

[1] For details see pp. 249-250 *infra*.

of amusement, and yet so far the spade of the house-building excavator has provided within the walls no hint as to the whereabouts of theatre, amphitheatre or circus. It is impossible even to find any clue as to which quarter of the city may have possessed any such feature. There is, however, one suggestion that may be a sound one. Londinium, in its process of expansion, must have found its internal spaces of the utmost importance. To abandon any large area for the purposes of amusement where offices, warehouses, private residences and shops required all the available space, would have been anathema to the commercial mind that was, and always has been, paramount in London. Therefore it may be that there was then, as now, a tendency to relegate places of amusement to the outskirts of the city. In that case one of the most convenient positions would have been in the suburb across the water now known as Southwark, and it would, therefore, have been towards the bridge that the inhabitants turned their faces when in holiday mood. No archaeological evidence in support of this conjecture, however, has yet been found. It may be that the custom of using the transriverine suburb for purposes of public amusement, from dramatic entertainments to cock-fights and bear-baiting, continued in London from the Roman epoch. That there are no traces of any amphitheatre need surprise no one, in view of the fact that, wealthy as Londinium became, it is scarcely conceivable that the idea of bringing to the city the vast quantities of stone required for such a structure was ever contemplated by the most spendthrift set of municipal officials. If, therefore, a large amphitheatre stood in Southwark, it may be accepted that its materials consisted of brick, concrete and timber with perhaps a certain amount of iron and bronze. Possibly the foundations were of concrete and brick, and the tiers of seats of wood on an earthen bank. The ground plan of the Roman theatre of Verulamium was fully exposed to view in 1936 and London may even now give up the secret of some of its places of amusement.

The bridge, consisting of wooden arches, perhaps resting on stone piers, whose date has been discussed elsewhere, was doubtless one of the most notable and attractive features of Londinium, thronged as it must have been at all times by people representing every class and a large percentage of the many races embraced by the frontiers of the Empire. The framework of the wooden arches connecting the massive stone piers was with great probability heavily painted, and there may, in such a permanent structure, have been elements of ornament in bronze. At the northern end, after the defensive wall was built, there would have stood an imposing gateway with double arches. It is not unlikely that this was the most important and impressive in its architecture of all the entries to Roman London, and yet it has totally disappeared together with any barbican that may have stood at the southern end of the bridge.

In seeking for the precise position of the bridge not quite sufficient attention appears to have been given to the lines of oaken piles, shod with iron, that were found in the Thames "slightly to the east of the site of Peter de Colechurch's erection." Mr H. Syer Cuming, who makes this statement,[1] describes the line of piles as extending from shore to shore. "There have been traced," he writes, "the remains of stout oaken piles with iron shoes, and huge conglomerates composed of ferruginous matter; and numerous Roman coins, chiefly first and second brass of the higher empire." He then proceeds: "If it be said that this huge abundance of Roman money in the bed of the Thames is due to the frequent upsetting of ferry boats, we have still to account for the iron shoes of piling which speak so unmistakably of the former existence, at this part of the river, of some long and strong erection. And it is most important to bear in mind that these shoes are not wrought of the porous, ropy iron characteristic of the Teutonic forge; and that therefore the structure, whatever it may have been, had no Saxon origin; but the hard, tough, solid metal in the production of which the Roman *ferraria* stood pre-eminent."[2]

Viewed from this approach, the scene must always have been full of life and activity with a variety of ships and small

---

[1] *Journal of the British Archaeological Association*, Vol. 43 (1887), pp. 166-7.

[2] As at least one of these iron-shod piles has been preserved the value of Mr Cuming's statement as to the quality of the iron could be tested. That the successive bridges were built on different sites seems likely for the practical reason that it is always desirable to keep the existing one open for traffic. To erect a temporary structure was an undertaking too slow and expensive for bridge-builders before the invention of steel girders. A new site upstream appears to have been usual for sufficiently good reasons.

boats forming an attractive picture of waterside life. There were large vessels from Gaul and Spain and others from the Mediterranean; smaller coasting craft with and without oars; fishing boats in great numbers, for the river literally swarmed with edible fish, and skiffs and wherries innumerable. At times the Pool undoubtedly saw the long and graceful lines of a war galley lately come up the Thames on some special mission, perhaps to convey to the capital an important official or officer, or the Governor himself.

Interspersed here and there among the public buildings, business and private houses stood the temples of the city, whose sites have not yet been determined. That the more important, if not all, stood up conspicuously upon a massive podium is almost certain, and that their porticoes were composed of stone columns supporting the usual type of pediment is not to be doubted. A certain number of bases and capitals of columns have been discovered and also parts of stone pilasters and cornices, but whether any of these belonged to temples is not known. It might be an occasional feature of street life to witness the passage of a garlanded bull destined to be sacrificed on the altar of Jupiter the Preserver or Neptune the Ruler of the Sea, the gift, perhaps, of an officer who had escaped the perils of a northern campaign or of a sea captain who had brought a valuable cargo safely past the Pillars of Hercules and the uneasy waters of the Bay of Biscay.

During the greater part of the life of Roman London, one would have had to look far to discover a Christian church recognisable as such, if the poverty of the body that has already been mentioned were reflected in its buildings. Perhaps in a byway among shops and small private houses there may have been an obscure doorway, behind which the rites of the unpopular faith were performed with secrecy and in some fear before a small, but fervid gathering. In later times, in the fourth century at any rate, some obvious site would have been obtained for a church of the then established religion, but it may be that no such sites were then obtainable except at a prohibitive cost, and therefore, as at Timgad and elsewhere, the new churches were built outside the city proper.

The custom of burying the dead at the sides of the main roads outside cities was usual in Britain as in other Roman provinces, and it is therefore not surprising to find that the

Scale markings (right side): 40 ft, 35, 30, 25, 20, 15, 10, 5, 4, 3, 2, 1

SCALE OF FEET

GORDON HOME

Dimensions: 3'9" · 2'6"

SUGGESTED RECONSTRUCTION OF ROMAN COLUMNS FROM BASES AND
CAPITALS IN THE GUILDHALL MUSEUM.

The base of red granite shown on the left (separately illustrated on p. 210) supported
a column 3 feet 9 or more inches in diameter. Dr. H. H. Thomas of the Geological
Survey has identified the stone as being of Egyptian granite while another geologist
gives Shap in Westmorland as its origin. The base weighs over five tons, but the
difficulties of transport from either place were not insurmountable. A portion of the
column with a raised lozenge pattern was found in a bastion in Bevis Marks.

cemeteries of Londinium appear to have been concentrated in three groups on the western, northern and eastern thorough-fares as they emerged from the city. On the northern loop of the western outlet the burials are most thickly grouped, and also to the north-east of St Paul's. The second most important cemetery appears to have been on the northern road leading to Lindum, Eboracum and the Wall of Hadrian between Moorgate and Bishopsgate as well as in the Spitalfields area. Outside Aldgate burials have been found in considerable numbers in the Goodman's Fields neighbourhood. In South-wark there was another cemetery, and a fifth in Bermondsey.[1]

An interesting fact, that a study of the positions of the interments brings out, is the gradual pushing out of the en-circling necropolis by the expansion of the city of the living. The fact that only one burial has been discovered in the area immediately east of the Walbrook gives a clue as to the earliest inhabited nucleus, this portion of the city being more or less surrounded by a semicircle of burials all within the area that was eventually walled. Taking the closeness of the interments to the north of St Paul's as a guide, there is a fairly definite indication that the western hill was built upon latest, for other-wise such an extensive cemetery cannot be explained. While there was, doubtless, a tendency for the expansion of the city to cease on the slope down to the Fleet, yet it is probable that houses soon began to appear on the sunny slopes now occupied by the Temple, where also a piece of ground may at an early date have become a public park. The fact that no burials have been found south of Fleet Street between Ludgate and Howard Street (east of Somerset House) points to the proba-bility that this attractive quarter was reserved for other pur-poses, despite the fact that it was upon one of the important roads emerging from the city.

Further corroboration of the growth of the town from a nucleus situated in the angle east of the Walbrook was pro-vided by the fact that the Claudian and earlier coins found in the city are almost entirely restricted to this area. The evi-dence of early pottery, compiled by Mr Frank Lambert and Prof. Atkinson, gave still more support to the same theory.[2] By plotting out the positions of the finds of Samian pottery

---

[1] *The Geology of the London District.* H. B. Woodward, 1922, p. 88.
[2] *Archaeologia*, vol. lxvi. 269-74.

TWO ROMAN SARCOPHAGI FOUND IN LONDON.

On both there is a portrait bust in relief.   *Above* : Marble sarcophagus found at Clapton in 1867.   Beneath the medallion that encloses the head and shoulders of a young woman is a much-worn inscription of which "to his dearest . . . for her deserts" is all that can be read.   The first line may have given a man's name and the word *fil[iae]* = daughter.   The fluted design and the shallow lettering suggest the late empire period (*Guildhall Museum*).   *Below* :   This sarcophagus was found in Haydon Square in 1854.   The head in the medallion is that of a youth and the bones found in the leaden coffin within were those of a boy of about 10 to 12 years of age.   A basket of fruit is carved on each end of the sarcophagus and a gadroon design fills the front on each side of the medallion (*British Museum*).

ROMAN OBJECTS IN STONE, LEAD, GLASS AND EARTHENWARE.

1, 2 and 3 from incineration burials found in Warwick Square in 1881. 1. A very fine vase, 27 in. high, made out of one piece of grey igneous stone. The lid is of the same stone. Contained burnt bones and a coin of Claudius minted in A.D. 41. 2. A leaden cylinder with panels showing a charioteer driving four horses. 3. The glass two-handled ossuary; a beautiful piece of work containing burnt bones found within the lead cylinder. 4. Part of a box flue pipe bearing a raised pattern solely to form a grip for plaster or cement. 5. A stone vase partially hollow. 6. A roughly sculptured head.

(All except 4, British Museum.)

of sufficiently datable types up till that time recorded they endeavoured to show that a form which went out of use between A.D. 80 and 90 was also restricted, with few exceptions, to the same area. Since these reports were made, however, the productions of the South Gaulish potter Bilicatus, whose Samian bowls known as "form 29" were being turned out in the reigns of Tiberius, Caligula and Claudius, have been found at several places along the line of Cheapside as well as in the St Martin-le-Grand area. These discoveries have much disturbed the earlier theories, for there is now material for supporting the idea that the Roman town began to grow more or less simultaneously on both sides of the Walbrook. As a flood of fresh light will clarify the problem of the early growth of Londinium as soon as the destroyed area east of St Paul's is explored to the Roman level, the further discussion of the problem can await with confident expectations the day when reconstruction begins.

The forms of interment are both burnt and unburnt. Up to about A.D. 250 cremation, the ancient practice of the Greeks and Romans, was the most prevalent method of the disposal of the dead. It must not, however, be accepted as by any means universal, for it is well known how some of the great Roman families, including the renowned Cornelii Scipiones, were always, according to their own domestic religious rites, buried instead of burnt. Of the cremated remains, a great many examples have been found, some of them with the urns placed in stone sarcophagi.[1] In Warwick Square, north of Paternoster Row, were found a number of different types of burial, including a very fine urn of grey-green porphyry (or possibly serpentine),[2] together with others in which the incinerated remains were placed in glass or leaden receptacles. The stone sarcophagi, a fair number of which have been found in London, are of all types ranging from the elaborately sculptured examples discovered in Haydon Square (Minories) and at Clapton, to the less pretentious example exhumed at Westminster Abbey and the roughly shaped variety without inscriptions from other sites. Some of these stone sarcophagi enclosed a leaden coffin usually ornamented with a beaded

[1] An example of this type was found under Liverpool Street Station.

[2] In the British Museum. See illustration facing.

and scallop shell design. Good examples of these are preserved in the British Museum.

In some instances square glass ossuaries were found enclosed in cubical oak chests with earthenware lids. This class is unusual. Numbers of interments closely resembled the popular methods of to-day, especially those belonging to a date later than 250. These wooden coffins are sometimes of simple type and others are more elaborate, being banded with iron.[1] Another wooden coffin containing a skeleton found in Smithfield Market is remarkable for the lateness of its date, for in it was a labarum coin of Gratianus I. (375-383). The common form of tile grave, formed of roofing tiles placed tentwise over the remains, has been frequently found in London.

The funeral monuments, apart from sarcophagi, number at least twenty-six. In some cases the inscriptions have disappeared, and in at least two instances the tombstones were lost subsequent to discovery. The inscriptions are given in full in the Appendix. If they are carefully examined, it will be found that out of some twenty-seven inscriptions that may be classified as sepulchral, three are in Greek characters, and otherwise show a certain amount of evidence that the persons commemorated came from the Hellenistic portion of the Roman Empire, while one or two other memorials bear Greek names. In other words, one in eight or nine of the inscriptions of Londinium refers to Greeks, and this fact reveals in some degree how far these pioneers of banking and trading were represented in the capital of Roman Britain.

The tombstone of a gladiator found in Tottenham Court Road is one of those bearing Greek inscriptions and is excluded from the above suggestion in regard to the trading community. It furnishes a reminder that the ranks of that dangerous profession were partly recruited from Greek-speaking peoples in the Balkans and Asia Minor. The memory of this gladiator was perpetuated by his wife, Antonia, who put up the monument to his memory.

That there are no memorials connected with Legio IX "Hispana," which disappeared so tragically in about A.D. 120 after being in Britain for three-quarters of a century, may seem surprising, but the loss in Boudicca's revolt of the greatest part of its strength, the cavalry only being excluded,

[1] An example of this type was found in the line of Houndsditch.

and its obliteration about sixty years later, may provide the
explanation.

Of the remaining inscriptions the majority are those of
soldiers, or persons connected with the army. The three
legions longest in Britain are all represented. Of Legio XX,
"Valeria Victrix," whose base was at Deva (Chester), there is

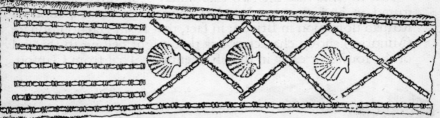

LEADEN COFFIN LID FOUND INSIDE A STONE SARCOPHAGUS.
Discovered in 1854 in Haydon Square between the Minories and Mansell Street. The
sarcophagus is illustrated facing p. 190.

one to a soldier named Julius Valens, who died at the age
of forty, while another bore the name of Saturninus. Of
Legio VI, "Victrix," stationed at Eboracum, there is the
tombstone of a soldier named Flavius Agricola, who lived
to the age of forty-two, and was mourned as a husband
without compare by his widow Albia Faustina. This name

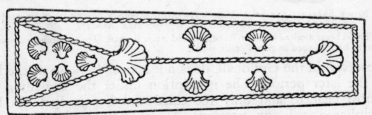

LEADEN COFFIN LID FOUND IN BATTERSEA FIELDS IN 1794
AT A DEPTH OF TWO FEET.

suggests that the period of the monument was after 138, when
Faustina I. was Empress. Legio II, "Augusta," is represented
by a "speculator" or despatch rider, whose name was Celsus,
and with him are associated three other members of the legion
who erected the tombstone to his memory. A second monument to a member of this legion is that of Vivius Marcianus,
erected by his widow, Januaria Martina. A third on a Mithraic

monument is to a veteran named Ulpius Silvanus, who had fulfilled an unspecified vow.

As a whole, it may be taken that rather more than half of the Latin inscriptions are of the pre-Antonine period, or roughly before A.D. 150, while the rest seem to be spread out through the succeeding two centuries.

It is notable that the two elaborately sculptured sarcophagi found in and close to London suggest the later period of Roman dominion in Britain; in fact, that from Haydon Square (Minories) shows characteristics that might belong to the end of the fourth or early in the fifth century. That from Clapton,

STONE SARCOPHAGUS OF VALERIUS AMANDINUS FOUND NORTH-WEST OF THE NORTH TRANSEPT OF WESTMINSTER ABBEY.

The lid bears a raised cross on its surface and is not Roman. The sarcophagus appears to have been re-used in post-Roman times.

preserved in the Guildhall, does not appear to be so markedly of the later period. The inscription under the medallion is almost effaced, and only the third and lowest line can be deciphered with any certainty. A recent attempt to interpret the first two lines suggests that it is a father's memorial to a greatly loved daughter.[1] The arrangement of the altar-shaped panel beneath the medallion portrait in the centre of the fluted front of the sarcophagus is very pleasing, and the pose of the female bust is gracious and skilfully executed. For general quality of workmanship it ranks with the Mithraic sculpture and the monument found in the Camomile Street bastion, both of which are illustrated in these pages.

[1] *Journal of Roman Studies*, vol. xii. 281.

The sarcophagus of Valerius Amandinus found at West-minster Abbey, and preserved in the entrance to the Chapter House, bears a much more simple design than those described above, but it may perhaps belong to as late a period as either of them.

Of uninscribed monuments the most important is that which was found broken up in a bastion of the defensive wall in Camomile Street. It shows an officer or soldier wearing a sword on his right hip and carrying tablets in his left hand. His right arm would appear to have been raised, but for what purpose it is impossible to say. He is wearing the *paenula* or buttoned cloak and a fairly short tunic of the military type. Mr J. E. Price, who wrote at great length on the subject in 1880,[1] decided that the figure was that of a *signifer* or standard-bearer. It is possible, however, that the monument, which gives the statue a mixture of civil and military attire, com-memorates an officer wearing undress uniform, who, on the completion of his service, retired to Londinium.

A small monumental slab about 2 feet in height bears the representation, in a sunk panel, of a man wearing a toga that he is holding together with his right hand while by him stands a small child—apparently a boy. There being no in-scription it is impossible to determine the date of this simple little monument, but the toga would suggest an early period in view of the fact that the historic garment was going out of fashion by the end of the first century A.D. There can be no doubt that the cemeteries of Londinium were prolific in this simple type of memorial, for it is common in nearly all the Roman cities of the West, and their comparative rarity in London is doubtless due to the subsequent value of the stone for paving and building.

A sculptured figure discovered during excavations in Drury Lane and now in the London Museum shows the representa-tion of a man leaning, apparently in thought, against a sup-port with his head resting on his bent left arm, the elbow of which is supported by the right hand. The attitude is approximately that of the familiar statue of Shakespeare in Leicester Square. It has been suggested that this figure is Mithraic.

London has yielded more inscriptions and monuments than

[1] "On a bastion of London Wall," John Edward Price.

any other site[1] in Britain in spite of the almost universal indifference displayed towards these relics of a mighty past until

8¾ inches high.   4½ inches high.

TWO GOURD-SHAPED VESSELS DISCOVERED IN LONDON.

On the left: found 15 feet below the modern surface under the Phœnix Assurance Company's Office on the S.W. side of King William Street. On the right: formerly in the late Mr William Ransom's collection of Roman objects found in London and now in the Museum of Archaeology and Ethnology at Cambridge.

This type of vessel is still in use in Catalonia.

comparatively recent years. This fact may be added to those already cited as proving the pre-eminence of Londinium among the cities of Roman Britain.

[1] Even at Bath (Aquae Sulis), where, on account of its hot springs, so many went in search of health and died, the number of inscriptions does not reach that of London.

. A complete list is given in Appendix II, p. 253.

Opposite:

A RESTORATION OF A ROMAN MONUMENT, THE FRAGMENTS OF WHICH (DRAWN WITH SOLID LINES) WERE DISCOVERED IN A BASTION OF THE WALL IN CAMOMILE STREET IN 1876.

It has been suggested that the figure represents an officer or soldier in undress uniform. No trace of any inscription has been found.

Chapter XII

RELIGIOUS LIFE IN ROMAN LONDON

FROM the earliest years of its Romanisation Londinium must have possessed temples, for it was impossible for any town owned by Roman citizens to fail to erect structures to the worship of their gods. As the city grew in wealth the size and elaboration of its temples doubtless advanced with it, yet so slight is the archaeological material so far collected from the many excavations for building purposes in the last hundred years that no single site can be at all definitely located.

Epigraphy gives evidence for a shrine to the Mother Goddesses; a temple to the glory of an emperor or emperors; and a third, perhaps in Southwark, to Isis. Sculptured fragments add to these three evidence for there having been temples to Diana, the Mother Goddesses, Jupiter and Juno, a river god, Bonus Eventus, and Mithras. In addition a number of bronze statuettes have been found representing several members of the Romano-Hellenic pantheon or the worship of virtues, which was a notable and inspiring feature of the Roman state religion at its best. Besides these there are the usual types of figurines representing the *lares* and *penates* of the household, and finally there are portable altars. Here the brief archaeological list terminates, and until further discoveries are made it is only possible to review in detail the information concerning each, and from the result to form, if possible, some idea of the pagan religious organisation of Londinium.

The worship with regard to which the archaeological evidence is the least scanty is that of Deae Matres = the Mother Goddesses. This adoration of the Three Mothers was of great antiquity. Plutarch, who had religious antiquarian tendencies, says that it was Cretan in origin; in fact, traces of the worship of a mother goddess have been found at Knossos and in Asia Minor. In Gaul and Britain there was a development of the idea into the form of a trinity usually associated with the name of a people or tribe. There are, for example, dedications found in Gaul to the Matres Treveri. At Corstopitum, near Hadrian's Wall, a group has been unearthed; at Winchester Roach Smith mentions one to the Italian, German Gallic and British Mothers; at York there is an altar to the

united Mothers of Africa, Italy and Gaul; at Chester a dedication was found in 1938,[1] while at Lyons there is another to
the Augustan Mothers.

Two indications[2] of this worship have come to light in
London. The most important in size was found in Hart Street,
Crutched Friars, in 1837.[3] It is typical of the treatment of the
most precious relics of Roman London at that time that this
sculptured stone, when brought to light during the excavation
of a sewer, was for some time in the city stoneyard, not only
neglected, but in daily danger of being broken up.[4] Further,

THE MOTHER GODDESSES (DEAE MATRES) FOUND BENEATH HART STREET,
CRUTCHED FRIARS.

The adoration of the three mothers was of great antiquity and was widespread in the
western provinces of the Empire. (*Guildhall Museum.*)

although it lay among the obvious ruins of a Roman building,
no attempt was made to search for the missing portions of
the group or other objects connected with it. Beneath Hart
Street to-day, therefore, it may be inferred that the means of

[1] *J.R.S.*, XXIX. pt. 2, 1939, p. 225.
[2] Roach Smith mentions what he conceived to be a third in which the
three figures are standing, but they appear, from the illustration that he
gives in his *Illustrations of Roman London*, Pl. VI. fig. 1, to be so unlike
any other representations of the Mother Goddesses, being shown empty-
handed, that the identification is open to question.
[3] C. R. Smith, *Ill. R. Lond.*, p. 33.   [4] *Collectanea Antiqua*, vol. i. 138.

throwing further light on the question of this particular form of worship remains buried. It is at least probable that in this portion of Londinium there stood a temple of a once popular and widespread cult.

The second indication of this worship is in the form of an inscription on a small piece of moulded stone, $15\frac{1}{2}$ inches in length, found in Budge Row on the west side of the Walbrook. It is as follows: MATR[IBVS] VICINIA DE SVO RES-[TITVIT], which may be interpreted as "To the Mother Goddesses; the district[1] restored this shrine at its own expense." Unfortunately there is a little lack of precision in regard to the provenance in London of this important little piece of stone. The shrine may have been a small stone canopy supported on pillars in proportion.

A more purely Roman cult, that of the Glory of the Emperor (Numen Augusti), was diffused widely throughout the Empire, and evidence as to its prevalence in Londinium was found in June 1850 in Nicholas Lane when a piece of inscribed stone was also accidentally thrown up during the construction of a sewer. Concerning the circumstances of this important discovery Roach Smith says: "It was found at a depth of between 11 and 12 feet, lying close to a wall 2 feet in width. There was every reason to believe that other stones, having the remainder of the inscription, were not far from the one extricated; but it was impossible to induce either the contractor . . . or the 'City Authorities' to countenance the slightest search."[2] The stone was nearly 3 feet in length and evidently formed only a small part of the original dedicatory tablet. From this circumstance, and from the large size and good quality of the letters (6 inches high), it may be inferred that the structure to which it belonged was of considerable pretensions and importance. The position of its discovery suggests that the building stood in the very heart of the city. The letters on the portion of the dedication discovered were:

NVMC
PROV
BRITA

[1] See note on "VICINIA" on p. 258.
[2] *Illustrations of Roman London*, p. 29.

The stone, which seems to have been subsequently stolen from the Guildhall, was not broken, and therefore formed one of the component parts of a composite whole. A reasonable reconstruction of the three lines on the upper stones would read:

Numini Caesaris Provincia Britannia

—that is, "To the deity of the Emperor and the Province of Britain" or "Set up by the Province of Britain."

THE MOTHER GODDESSES SHOWN ON A PLAQUE OF BASE SILVER.
Found in Moorgate Street.   About 4 inches wide.
(*London Museum*.)

The finest relic of any religious cult so far discovered in London is the Mithraic relief found (without absolute certainty[1]) in Bond Court, Walbrook, in 1889, at a depth of 20 feet. Within a circle, adorned by the twelve signs of the zodiac, appears Mithras, with cloak flying out from his shoulders, slaying the bull, and attended by the two torch-

[1] The stone came into the possession of the late Mr William Ransom, but he was not present when it was brought to light. It is not, however, doubted that the general details of the discovery that are associated with this sculpture, and two others in marble representing a river god and Bona Fortuna, are correct.

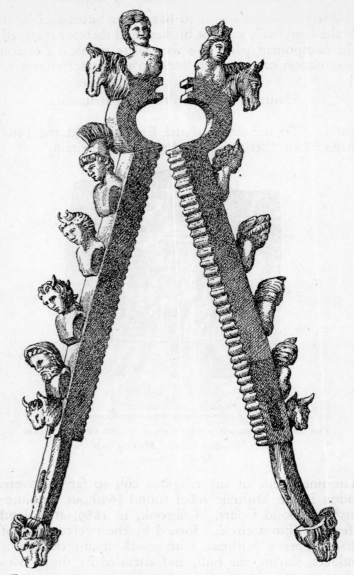

BRONZE FORCEPS USED IN THE CASTRATION OF THE PRIESTS OF CYBELE FOUND IN THE THAMES NEAR THE LINE OF THE ROMAN BRIDGE.

The busts represent: on top (left) Attis, (right) Cybele, and below left and right the planetary deities associated with the eight days of the Roman week. The lower end of the right-hand arm has been broken and carefully repaired.

A conjectural restoration of this instrument by Mr A. G. Francis, together with an article in which he gives his conclusions as to its use, was published in the *Proceedings of the Royal Society of Medicine*, XIX, 1926, p. 95.

(*British Museum.*)

bearers symbolising life and death, while beneath are the dog, the crab or scorpion, the serpent and basket. Without the circle, in the four corners of the slab, are shown the Sun in a four-horse chariot, the Moon in a chariot drawn by oxen, a bearded head and another, apparently a female, with flowing locks. The last two represent deities of the wind.

This sculpture was dedicated in fulfilment of a vow by Ulpius Silvanus, a retired soldier of Legio II. It is a mere coincidence that the badge of this legion, *i.e.* the Capricorn, appears in the circle of the signs of the zodiac. The name of the donor suggests a date in the second century.

Mithraism, with its high ideals of duty and self-sacrifice, was essentially the cult of the army, and seeing that Londinium, so far as is known, had no garrison, apart from the guards of honour for high officials, the question might be asked how a temple of this deity came to exist in the capital. The only answer is that there was not improbably a considerable element of retired military men who, after long and hard service in the frontier camps, were only too keen upon ending their days as pensioned veterans amid the attractions and comforts of Londinium. Mithraic temples were almost invariably subterranean, in imitation of the cave sanctuaries in Asia, where the cult originated. The making of underground shrines was also associated with the legend that Mithras chased the sacred bull into a cavern before he slew it. If the spot where this sculptured stone was found be correctly recorded, it is just possible that the Mithraeum to which it belonged was excavated in the slope down to the Walbrook.

The only clue to there having been a temple dedicated to Isis in the southern suburb is an inscription or graffito in cursive writing on a jug unearthed in Southwark. The wording is **LONDINI AD FANVM ISIDIS** = At London at the Temple of Isis. Although it may be argued that a vessel of this small character (it is illustrated facing page 209) might have been brought to Southwark from any part of the city, and is therefore not necessarily to be associated with the actual site of the temple, yet this suburb is eminently the place where one would expect to find the shrine of such a form of worship. The transpontine suburb would naturally have been the abode of temporary cosmopolitan residents, among whom Isis was

likely to find her most numerous votaries. Secondly, although
the cult had exalted ideals and also ascetic practices, it was for
long regarded with considerable suspicion by the Roman
Government as being associated with disreputable orgies. It
was again and again suppressed at Rome, and it would be
natural to find the Temple of Isis in the detached quarter that
retained until the Tudor period a somewhat undesirable character, playhouses, stews and the cheapest form of lodging
being the suburb's outstanding characteristics.

During the building of the present London Bridge a pair
of bronze forceps was dredged from the river-bed. Their
purpose was for many years the subject of conjecture only,

A Janus Head found
at St Thomas à
Watering in South
London.

but there is now no doubt that this instrument was used for the castration of the
priests of Cybele. A temple of triangular
form, dedicated to this deity, was discovered at Verulamium a few years ago.

Another discovery of a religious character made in Southwark was a double head
in stone resembling a Janus, but in this case
one face was male and the other female.
The male head had ram's horns and a
laurel wreath, and the goddess was wearing
a sphendone in her hair. The sculpture may
have represented (it has been lost) Jupiter
and Juno, or possibly a deified emperor and
empress. The horns seem to indicate the
combination of Zeus with Amen-Ra, or, as the Graeco-
Romans called him, Jupiter-Ammon. In that case, the twin
heads may be those of Hadrian and Vibia Sabina, who made a
tour up the Nile to Thebes in 130.

Despite the fact that most of the pagan cults disappeared
somewhat passively in face of the oncoming of Christianity,
including even Mithraism with its high ideals, yet the worship
of Isis survived, even in Italy, until well into the fifth century.

Ever since the days of Henry III. (*i.e.* 1220) a tradition has
been current that a temple of Diana stood on or near the site
of St Paul's Cathedral during the Roman period. Wren was a
sceptic[1] in regard to this idea, for he discovered nothing in
the course of his extensive excavations for the new cathedral

---

[1] *Parentalia,* pp. 265-7.

that would justify such a belief—at least for a Roman temple within the area of the cathedral site. The great architect's opinion, however, in no way invalidates the possibility of a temple dedicated to the huntress goddess in the immediate neighbourhood, and there is certain archaeological evidence worthy of some consideration. Summarised, it is as follows:—

1. A stone altar to Diana, $2\frac{1}{2}$ feet high, found 15 feet below the surface, and built into the foundations of Goldsmiths' Hall, in Foster Lane (N.E. of St Paul's), when the old hall was rebuilt in 1830.

2. In association with the altar above mentioned were masses of stonework so admirably cemented that they had the consistency of rock, and had to be broken up with the help of gunpowder. The thickness of these walls is given as 2 feet.

3. A bronze statuette of Diana, $2\frac{1}{2}$ inches high, was found between the Deanery of St Paul's and Blackfriars, *i.e.* S.W. of the cathedral.

4. On the south side of the cathedral, at the rebuilding after the Great Fire, "were found several Scalps of Oxen, and a large Quantity of Boars' Tusks, with divers earthen Vessels, especially Paterae of different shapes."

5. In the cathedral archives of the year 1220 a messuage on the south side of the cathedral is mentioned as "Domum que fuit Diane."

Taking the first two together, there is some ground for thinking that the altar may have been associated with the building whose walls were found close by. That the statuette was found so far away as between the Deanery and Blackfriars weakens its significance, but it is nevertheless the only small representation of Diana recorded among the discoveries made in London, and is certainly in the same quarter, but that the area connected with a single temple in a town such as Londinium should have extended from Foster Lane (behind the site of the old General Post Office) to the slope towards the Fleet River at Blackfriars is obviously untenable. It has been suggested that a link between the two sites is indicated by the fourth piece of evidence recording the discovery on the south side of the cathedral of what were taken to be the remains of sacrifices accompanied by paterae. But these remains may have a totally different significance from that which was ascribed to them.

The fifth fragment of evidence, by which the name of Diana is associated with a messuage on the south side of the cathedral as early as the thirteenth century, would perhaps be of value if it could be traced back to any record of the sixth or seventh century. Even the discovery of an early connection of the site with the name Diana might prove to be of no importance in view of the fact that it was not uncommon in medieval times. It might merely reveal that an early landowner had borne that name.

ALTAR TO DIANA.

Found on the site of Goldsmiths' Hall, in Foster Lane, to the north-east of St Paul's Cathedral.

Reviewing the evidence, one is compelled to admit that the only item carrying any weight is the stone altar found in association with very well-built walls a little to the north-east of the cathedral.

The worship of Diana does not appear to have been very popular in Britain, for apart from the shrine in Londinium, only one other locality, namely Newstead, near Melrose, has so far revealed any association with this goddess. It is possible that, like Isis, she was worshipped mainly by foreign elements, perhaps from central Italy or the Hellenic lands, where her cult was anciently very widespread.

At Londinium, as at Rome, adoration of the god of the river upon which the city so much depended would have been popular. It is therefore not at all surprising to find in London

ROMAN STATUARY IN STONE AND BRONZE FOUND IN LONDON.

1. Harpocrates with finger to mouth, indicating silence on the mysteries of religion (*British Museum*). 2. Hercules (*British Museum*). 3. Mars (*Guildhall*). 4. Figure in high relief, perhaps of Cautopates, who holds the inverted torch in Mithraic sculptures. Found in Drury Lane (*London Museum*). 5. A representation of Attis (or Atys), a mythical being prominent in the worship of the Phrygian goddess Cybele-Agdistis. At the beginning of spring a festival of several days was held in honour of Attis and Cybele. Found in Bevis Marks in 1849 (*British Museum*). 6. Ganymede. Bronze found in the Thames at London. Hebe was worshipped under the name of Ganymede and the Romans identified Hebe with Juventas, the personification of youthful manhood (*British Museum*).

FLAGON BELONGING TO THE TEMPLE
OF ISIS FOUND IN SOUTHWARK.

It bears the inscription "*Londini ad fanum Isidis*"
="At London at the Temple of Isis." 10 inches
high.

(*London Museum.*)

MEMORIAL TO A VETERAN OF THE SECOND LEGION "AUGUSTA."

He appears to have been closely associated with the Mithraic community. The sculpture shows in relief Mithras
slaying the bull, with the torch-bearers on either side, the whole surrounded by a circle bearing upon it the signs
of the Zodiac (see p. 205). Found in Walbrook.

(*London Museum.*)

a life-size statue in marble of a river deity. It must have been, judging from the head and part of the torso that remain,[1] quite a fine work of art, having distinctly Hellenic characteristics. The eyes show exceptional feeling, quite remote from the hard, almost staring expression of Roman busts of the fourth century. The discovery of this sculpture was made, it appears, in Bond Court, close to the Walbrook,[2] in the same place as the Mithraic slab, and a decapitated marble statue perhaps representing Bona Fortuna or, more probably, Bonus Eventus, for the figure appears to be male.

It may be noted that the discovery of the two figures in marble is not without significance, for, with a community the prosperity of which depended very largely on sea commerce, the erection of a fane to the deity of the Thames, in conjunction with Good Fortune, was precisely the idea that would occur to the average merchant. The quality of the sculptures shows them to have been importations, and this, in view of the fact that the mercantile fraternity would have possessed facilities for such acquisitions, lends colour to the idea.

The name of Lud connected with one of London's gates has been regarded as evidence of a survival in Roman times of one of the obscure Celtic deities of pre-Roman Britain, but it has still to be proved that the life of Roman London continued sufficiently unbroken through the Dark Ages to make possible the survival of a gate-name. Gomme, however, was very confident that the name Ludgate was associated with a Celtic deity. He was so convinced of this that he roundly asserted "that the name of Ludgate in modern London contains the god-name Lud is a fact, therefore, which takes us back to the Celtic Britons in London".[3] Sir John Rhys[4] decided after much research that Lud was a Celtic god of the waters and that the name of the god Belinus, also Celtic, has persisted in Billingsgate, east of the northern end of London Bridge.

This concludes the evidence for the existence of temples of the pagan deities in Londinium, and it is certainly very meagre, but, at the same time, in face of the wholesale de-

---

[1] London Museum.
[2] The provenance is not absolutely certain.
[3] *The Making of London*, p. 47.
[4] *Celtic Heathendom*, pp. 125-133.

14

struction of massive buildings that has undoubtedly taken place in the last fourteen centuries, this is not at all surprising. All Londinium's great structures have vanished from sight, apart from the foundations of the basilica and scattered portions of the defensive wall, but the fact that the base of a column, composed of red granite 5 feet 3 inches in diameter, has come to light, if it is not the base of a commemorative column, may be an indication of the scale of the more important edifices. It has been shown that there is some evidence pointing to temples in honour of an Emperor, to the Mother Goddesses, Mithras, Diana, and Isis, and it cannot be doubted that other Roman divinities, pre-eminently Jupiter, as well as

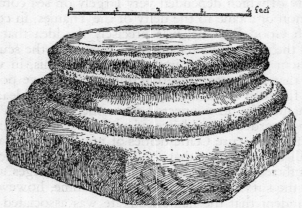

BASE OF A ROMAN COLUMN (ABOUT 40 FT. IN HEIGHT).
(See p. 191.)

Juno, Mars and Minerva, possessed fanes on a suitable scale in the greatest city of Roman Britain. Who can tell how many Roman columns that had been utilised in the construction of medieval churches and public buildings were calcined in the two devastations of London during the reign of Alfred; in the many known fires throughout the Middle Ages; and in the Great Fire of 1666, that swept away such a large proportion of the antiquities of the city?

The British Church, with which alone the Roman period of London is concerned, was the first Christian Church established in Britain (*i.e.* England and Wales) before St Augustine founded the English Church in 597. Unfortunately there is so little recorded about this early foundation that beyond the facts that there were British martyrs, that British bishops attended councils at Arles and elsewhere, and that the heresy of Pelagius spread widely in Britain in the fifth century, very little is known.

That the new faith did penetrate extensively in the province is supported by Tertullian, who, writing in c. 208, makes reference to there being places in Britain inaccessible to the Roman, yet subject to Christ. About thirty years later Origen refers in two passages to the British people having come under the influence of Christianity. Mr F. E. Warren,[1] dealing with the question of how this came about, suggests that, in the absence of precise information, the most probable supposition is that Christianity came through Gaul, between which country and Britain commercial intercourse was going on. He continues: "There may, too, have been individual Christians among the numerous Roman soldiers who were then stationed in Britain. The almost universally Latin, or at least non-Celtic names of such British martyrs, bishops and others as have been preserved point to a preponderating Roman rather than Celtic element in the personnel of the British Church; though against this inference it must also be remembered that, as in the cases of Patricius and Pelagius, the names known to us may be assumed Christian names superseding some earlier Celtic names of which, in most cases, no record has survived. Possibly the British Church consisted at first of converts to Christianity among the Roman invaders, and of such natives as came into immediate contact with them; and the native element only preponderated gradually when the Roman troops were withdrawn and when civilian Roman settlers would for their own safety leave the island as well."

For many centuries Bede's account of a British king named Lucius, who made an application to Pope Eleutherus in A.D. 156[2] for permission to be made a Christian, that his request was granted and that the king and nation were then converted to Christianity was accepted as a valuable piece of history. Stow linked the story with St Peter's Church in Cornhill. "There remaineth in this church," he writes, "a table whereon is written, I know not by what authority, but of a late hand, that King Lucius founded the same church to be an archbishop's

---

[1] *Dictionary of English Church History*, ed. S. L. Ollard, p. 70.
[2] Eleutherus did not become Pope until A.D. 177.

see metropolitan and chief church of his Kingdom, and that it so endured the space of four hundred years, unto the coming of Augustin the Monk."

The claim of the parish to precedence in the Whitsuntide processions having led to disturbances, a full-dress enquiry into the matter was made in 1399, and early in the reign of Henry V the Court of Aldermen laid it down that the claim of the parish of St Peter to be the oldest parish in the city had been fully proved to be a rightful one, it having been shown that this church was founded by King Lucius.

In spite of all this the story of a British King Lucius must be abandoned, for not many years ago Professor Harnack[1] drew attention to the extreme probability that Lucius was King of Birtha (confused with Britannia) in Edessa, a Mesopotamian realm, one of whose sovereigns was Lucius Aelius Septimus Megas Abgarus IX.

The antiquity of the site of St Peter's, Cornhill, nevertheless remains unchallenged, and now that the Roman foundations on which it stands are found to be associated with the Basilica, Dr Wheeler has suggested that it may occupy the site of what must have been the chapel of the governmental buildings, and so, when Christianity was adopted as the state religion, would very probably be the first place officially recognised as a Christian church.

No other site of any Christian church in Londinium has been located and, in addition, the testimony to the existence of Christianity in Londinium is so very slight that were there no literary evidence to establish its reality, one might almost be led to doubt altogether the prevalence of the new faith in the British capital. Slight as it may be, it is worth while to consider the archæological material that is at present available.

At St Etheldreda's Church, Ely Place, there can be seen a curiously archaic mortar-shaped font of limestone similar in form to the two unearthed in the cloister of Brecon Cathedral. It was found buried in the centre of the undercroft, and in that respect affords a parallel with those at Brecon. Of the St Etheldreda's font Sir Gilbert Scott said, "You may call the bowl British or Roman, for it is older than the Saxon period," and some support to this statement is provided by

[1] *Eng. Hist. Rev.*, xxii. pp. 767-70.

the fact that Roman bricks have been found on the site.[1] The position is on the crest of the western slope of the vale through which the little Fleet River flowed (and continues to flow, though out of sight), and is therefore well outside the walled area of the city; in other words, just where one would expect to find an Early Christian church before, or even after, the new faith had been officially recognised. It has already been mentioned that everything points towards the Christian Church in Britain having been without wealth, and such a condition would naturally militate against the acquisition of a site in the heart of the busy and crowded capital, where land could only be purchased at a high figure.

FONT AT ST ETHELDREDA'S CHURCH, ELY PLACE, HOLBORN.

Considered by Sir Gilbert Scott to be "older than the Saxon period." It is composed of a hard limestone (not granite) and may be an importation.

There are two small earthenware lamps in the Guildhall Museum bearing the Chi-Rho monogram conspicuously in the centre. They may have been imported, but their presence in Londinium might perhaps indicate a demand. At Battersea were found eight lamps of pewter bearing two types of Christian stamp, in conjunction with the late Gallo-Roman name of Syagrius. In Lothbury was discovered a silver pin with an ornamental head in the form of a flat disc, bearing upon it a representation of a helmeted Emperor gazing upwards at a cross in the heavens among stars. This can only represent the vision of Constantine, the cross being in place of the Chi-Rho. Other very uncertain indications are a bronze chain-bracelet[2] bearing upon it a cross in the form of two short pieces of tube intersecting one another, but its significance is doubtful; the central design of a mosaic pavement found on the site of the Bank of England consisting of a floriated cross; an enamelled

[1] The writer noted five Roman bricks in the forecourt of the church in June 1924. They had lately been dug up and were all incomplete, but averaged 1¼ to 1⅝ inches in thickness.

[2] In the British Museum.

plate, on which the ornamentation includes two winged beasts apparently drinking from a vase; and lastly, a funeral cist of lead found in Warwick Square (E.C.), bearing upon it a double-cross monogram. The stone sarcophagus found on the north side of Westminster Abbey has an inscription, of which

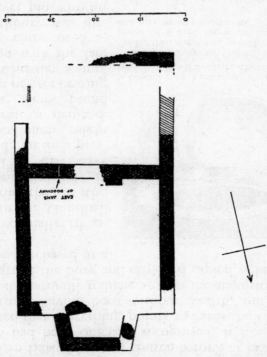

PLAN OF A BUILDING FOUND WITHIN THE AREA OF THE FORUM.

The structure had walls 3 ft. thick constructed of flanged tiles on a foundation of flint rubble. The site is at 17-19, Gracechurch Street.

REPRODUCED BY PERMISSION OF THE "JOURNAL OF ROMAN STUDIES."

the form is decidedly Christian, and may perhaps, in spite of the fine quality of the lettering, belong to a late epoch.

This is all the archaeological material so far discovered in London that bears any association with Christianity, and its total is so meagre and unsatisfying that there is scarcely any-thing to be deduced from it. In fact there is so little to discuss that one must be content with the historical facts that a Christian community in Londinium did exist, and that it was ruled by a bishop as early as the third century.

Chapter XIII

PRIVATE AND BUSINESS LIFE IN LONDINIUM

> "*quam pecuniam petisionis item scriptis solvere mihi debbit Cres- cens isve ad quem ea res per- tinebit* . . . . . . *ris primis* . . . . . . *ss* . . . . . . *t.*"

The earliest record of a business transaction preserved in London. It was part of a deed stating: "which money by the terms likewise of the claim shall be paid to me by Crescens or by the person concerned."

Found in Lothbury scratched with a stilus on part of a wooden tablet normally covered with wax for writing purposes.

(*London Museum.*)

LONDINIUM being to a remarkable extent the focus of all the activities of Britain, private life in the city reached its greatest development. Where wealth is amassed there must always be considerable increase of comfort and luxury, and that the capital possessed the means of satisfying the desire for display is unquestionable.

References to many of the buildings of the city have already been made, and from the numerous mosaic pavements and quantities of wall decoration brought to light, it is fairly clear that the interiors were adorned according to the class of the building, ornament in some cases reaching a high level. In view of the large percentage of tessellated pavements found in country houses, it is certain that all the better-class dwellings had, on their ground floors, this permanent form of decorative treatment, and that a considerable proportion of the apartments were warmed by hypocausts is proved by the discoveries that have been made.

Painted plaster covered the walls internally and sometimes externally as well, and in houses of the superior class there was sometimes a thin sheathing of marble. The homes of the artisan and the labourer were no doubt roughly built and poorly finished. Their materials may have been timber and roughcast, and much has been found in favour of thinking that thatch was commonly the roofing material.

There is ample evidence of the forms of illumination employed in Londinium, oil lamps of the usual earthenware type

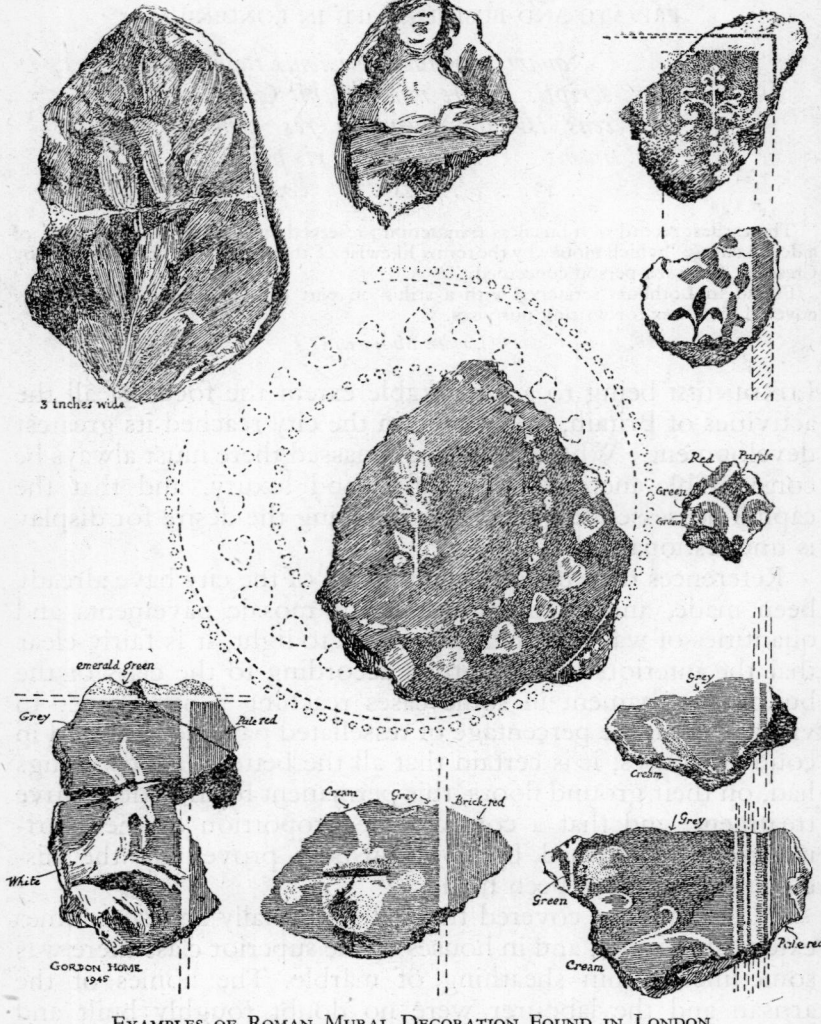

3 inches wide

emerald green
Grey
Pale red
White
GORDON HOME 1945

Cream **Grey** **Brick red**

Red **Purple**
Green
Green

Grey

Crebm

Grey
Green
Cream
Pale red

EXAMPLES OF ROMAN MURAL DECORATION FOUND IN LONDON.
That on the top left-hand corner, showing a design of leaves, was found on the site
of the Great Basilica.

of the Roman Empire as well as a few in bronze having been found. In addition, tallow candles (sebaceus) have come to light, and it is, of course, common knowledge that wax was used. A number of iron candlesticks in tripod form for holding small tapers have been unearthed recently, and from beneath the Bank of England[1] has come a pottery candlestick for a fair-sized candle. Of furniture no traces have survived. Every chair and table, every bed, couch, press and chest has vanished, but keys, hinges and hasp locks tell of the existence of the latter as well as the usual variety of boxes and cupboards with doors. Bronze bells of various sizes suggest internal communication and the calling of servants. That the interiors were possessed of many ornaments in bronze—perhaps gilded —is clear from the large number of small figures discovered. They range from little gnomes, of a couple of inches, to statuettes of fine workmanship, from 6 to 8 inches in height. Figurines in terra-cotta and pipeclay are common but less numerous, being more exposed to destructive influences. No doubt some of these small figures in all the different materials may have been designed for religious purposes. Certain of them were doubtless the household *lares* and *penates*. The *lar* was probably in its original idea the house or farm god, while the *penates* were the dual patrons of the household storeroom.

As in every other city that has yielded relics of its ancient civilisation, London possesses vast quantities of the pottery and a representative collection of its glass ware. From these it is abundantly clear that the dining-tables of the Roman period were provided with all the usual varieties of continental and home-made plates, dishes, cups, beakers, vases, carafes, and bowls, as well as pieces, the purpose of which may have been mainly ornamental. The red glazed ware of Gaul, variously known as "Samian" or "terra sigillata," was in very general use, and there is evidence that it was preserved with the greatest care after its manufacture had ceased, owing to the devastations wrought by the Alemanni and Franks in the third century. One small piece of this fine red ware that has come to light in recent years had been smashed into many pieces, and had afterwards been cemented together. The commonest form of repair was that of riveting with rather clumsy-looking

[1] 1928-34 excavations.

leaden clips. It is possible that the decorated forms of Samian pottery were always expensive, and on that account it was not unusual to repair them, even when the Gaulish makers were pouring so much of their output into the British market. Repairs have been found on quite early examples, including the type numbered *form 29*.

Relics of Londinium's nurseries have been found in the form of earthenware *tetinae* or feeding bottles.

Enough glass has been found to obtain a very good impression of the average type of vessel in use. Unfortunately a very large proportion has been broken, even when chance has brought it safely through the centuries, for the excavator's pick and spade reduces many articles of glass to splinters before their presence is known. There were graceful long-necked glass jugs with flat handles of various colours, particularly amber and blue, and broad shallow dishes, while bowls of blue, white and greenish glass, with what is called "pillar" ornament, are frequently found.

TWO TETINAE OR FEEDING BOTTLES
UNEARTHED IN LONDON.
The larger one was found at Smithfield.
Guildhall Museum.

Knives and spoons have been discovered in considerable numbers. In spite of the fact that it is commonly accepted that forks for table purposes were not used by the Romans, a few with two prongs have been found in the Roman levels of London.[1] These may have been used in the kitchen or for a variety of purposes apart from eating, for a small implement with two prongs is too useful not to have been invented by this time.

Very little has survived of the immense quantity of silver plate that must have been in use. A handled silver bowl and a graceful little jug, now in the British Museum, seem to be the only articles not in private collections. A very small object of gold in the form of a child, two-thirds of an inch in height, was found in Poultry in 1873. Doubtless it was a charm or part of a personal ornament.

[1] There are eight in the Guildhall Museum.

Of the food of the citizens of Londinium one can only gather information from the bones of animals and oyster shells. It is known that the Romano-British table was provided with a large variety of meat, poultry and game, and no doubt different types of bread were in demand, from the usual farm or household bread to the very light and porous *panis Parthicus* only to be seen on the tables of the rich. Hand-mills of volcanic stone from the Eifel, in the neighbourhood of Andernach on the Rhine, were imported into Britain in great quantities, and slave labour would grind the necessary quantity of flour for daily consumption. To what extent mills, the power for which was provided by animals, supplied household flour can only be guessed, but the large form of millstone has been discovered in London.

In 1928 one of the large hour-glass-shaped millstones was found at the corner of Princes Street and can be seen in the Guildhall Museum. It is the only one that has come to light complete and has also been preserved. Roach Smith[1] refers to many fragments of millstones having been found in various parts of the city and that they were "chiefly of two kinds; for turning with the hand, and for working with mules and asses." He adds that some of the latter had been of large size, but having been broken up for building purposes it had not been possible in any instance to reconstruct the fragments sufficiently to complete either of the two stones that formed a Roman mill.

In the kitchens were used great amphorae and all sizes of jugs, dishes, plates, bowls and mortaria. In the latter food of various sorts was worked up or pounded, and so thin are the bottoms through hard use that it is rare to find one not worn into a hole. In the large jars and amphorae were kept wine, oil, water, and other liquids. A ladle and strainers are among other culinary articles in the Guildhall Museum.

Apart from the statuettes and sculptured stones discovered in London, there are no indications of what fashions in clothing were followed, except in regard to footware. One monument seems to indicate that in early days, at any rate, some of the citizens liked to wear the toga. The effigy found in the Camomile Street bastion shows that the sleeved cloak or *paenula* was at one time undress uniform.

[1] *Illustrations of Roman London*, p. 147.

The types of leathern shoes and boots found in London vary considerably, and include a great many sandals, some of them of the best quality. All footware was entirely lacking in heels, and there was a tendency to perforate the leather in elaborate patterns. In some cases the uppers are merely cut to form loops for lacing, the rest of the sides being solid. Women's sandals were long and narrow with pointed toes, at least in one period; how far fashion changed the shape it is not easy to say, but there seems to have been a tendency to keep to this form during the four centuries with which this book is concerned.

SOLE OF A WOMAN'S SANDAL.
Found at the Bank of England.
(*Guildhall Museum.*)

In recent years it has chanced that excavations in the city have brought to light from deeply buried deposits considerable numbers of particularly well-preserved shoes and sandals.

The rebuilding of the Bank of England that has proceeded for some years within its unchanged outer walls has been remarkable in this direction. Literally hundreds of examples of the footwear of Londoners at this period have been recovered in as perfect a state of preservation as when last worn. Even the design impressed on the upper surface of leather of many of the sandals is unaffected by burial for some sixteen or seventeen centuries. One of these is illustrated here. It is ornamented with a long-tailed bird, a leaf design and a border enclosing a wavy line around which are small concentric circles that mark the positions of the nails holding together the layers of leather forming the sole. In some instances the owner of sandals has marked them with his or her initials.

The sandals were always shaped to fit the wearer's foot, including the toes, for it has been noticed that none are closely alike. Soles were usually composed of three thicknesses, though not infrequently of four or more. There are no signs of their having been sewn, the nails, carefully clenched on the inside, being regarded as the only method for securing the leather that made contact with the ground.

To secure the sandal to the foot a thong of leather attached to the sole passed between the great and second toes; it was then taken round the ankle and tied, the heel being fastened by the same strap. It was usual to cover the whole of the sole with nails, and not infrequently they are placed so as to make a decorative effect. It should be noted that in Diocletian's famous edict fixing the prices of all articles of commerce, mention is made of country *caligae*, and also military *caligae*, both without nails. Here is presented the most complete inversion of modern usage in which town-dwellers cannot tolerate the idea of a sole studded with large-headed projecting nails while the soldier and farm labourer accept them as a necessity.

The Roman shoe, like the sandal, had its sole covered with nails and the upper portion, in one piece much perforated, was sewn together at the heel. What names were applied to the different varieties of shoes it is not easy to state. In the pages of Aulus Gellius some space is devoted to the names given to shoes. He writes of *gallicae*, *crepidae* and *crepidulae* as those usually worn by civilians, and mentions that they belonged to the same class of shoe as the *soleae*, which were the simplest and most primitive kind, for they left the upper part of the foot nearly naked, being bound only with slender straps, in contrast to the *calcei* that fitted closely and covered the ankle.

A few years ago part of a Roman shoe so large that it would be suitable for a man of about 12 feet in height was dug from the slimy black mud of the Walbrook. The idea that it had belonged to a Romano-British giant being absurd, another reason for its manufacture must be sought. Mr Waddington made the attractive suggestion that it formed part of a bootmaker's sign, at one time a familiar feature of a street or byway of Roman London.

It is unfortunate that, up to the present time, with the exception of a head and shoulders on a sarcophagus, no sculpture portraying a contemporary woman has been found in London. There are small earthenware and bronze statuettes, for the most part representing deities or ideal figures, and can therefore hardly supply any information. Metal objects of personal adornment, however, are quite numerous. Those made of the precious metals have almost entirely disappeared. There is a silver armlet in the Guildhall Museum, and the small gold charm just mentioned. Bronze brooches have been found in large numbers, also hairpins of jet, bone, and bronze, the latter often possessing ornamental heads. Combs of box-wood and bone[1] are not uncommon, and bronze mirrors of the usual Roman type occur infrequently. Earrings, bracelets, armlets, rings for the fingers, in one case of gold and another of bronze inlaid with gold, have been brought to light in large numbers, also quantities of glass and earthenware beads.

Toilet articles are represented by numerous unguent and perfume bottles of glass, also by manicure sets, tweezers, strigils for use in the bath, earpicks, and other small implements and objects.

Writing materials are more abundant in Roman London than in any other site in Britain. Inkpots of bronze and earthenware (including Samian) are comparatively numerous, and quite recently one of glass has been found, while one at least seems to have been made for carrying on the person. A few pens have been found, and *styli* for writing on wax tablets are exceptionally numerous. The bed of the Walbrook during the summer of 1934 gave up hundreds of these little iron writing implements. They were singularly well preserved, their points as well as the edges, the spade-shaped opposite ends being still quite sharp. Wooden tablets for use with the *stylus* have also come to light, some of them in a remarkably good state of preservation, and the impression one gains from the quantities of these objects is that Londinium contained a great number of offices with their ample staffs.

Indications of the games played in Roman London afforded

[1] Mr Waddington writes: "All the combs that I have come across in circumstances which leave no doubt about their being Roman have been of boxwood and I am inclined to think that those of bone are all post-Roman."

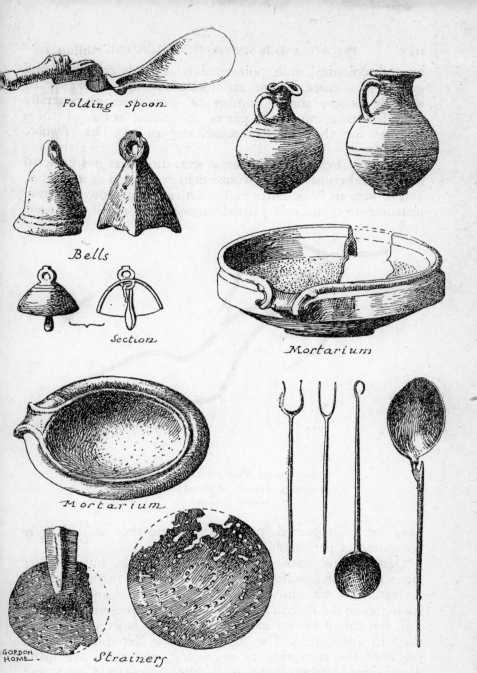

Folding spoon

Bells

Section

Mortarium

Mortarium

Strainers

GORDON HOME.

CULINARY OBJECTS FOUND IN LONDON.

The mortaria or mortars were used for the trituration of different foods, the inside surfaces being roughened by the insertion into the clay before baking of small fragments of crystalline stone.

(*Guildhall and British Museum.*)

by archaeological finds point mainly towards gambling and games of chance. There are numerous dice, *astragali* or knuckle bones, and a number of circular discs generally regarded as counters or pieces in games, some of them perhaps for the famous amusement called The Twelve Lines.

The only evidence of musical recreation that has hitherto been found consists of a bronze plate, regarded as a cymbal, and of various bone flutes and whistles. That more elaborate instruments of melody existed cannot be doubted, but none

SCOURGE OR WHIP FOUND IN LONDON.
It consists of strands of plaited bronze wire.
(*Guildhall Museum.*)

have been discovered, probably because they were largely composed of perishable materials.

Dancing and music are almost inseparable, but whether any stratum of Londinium's society indulged in this form of recreation is not known. One at least of the small bronze statuettes in the British Museum seems to represent a dancing girl, but this does not indicate that social dancing was practised to any extent. The Roman of the Republican period regarded the recreation as degrading, and there are many disparaging references to it in the pages of Cicero and other writers. The Roman Londoners may have viewed

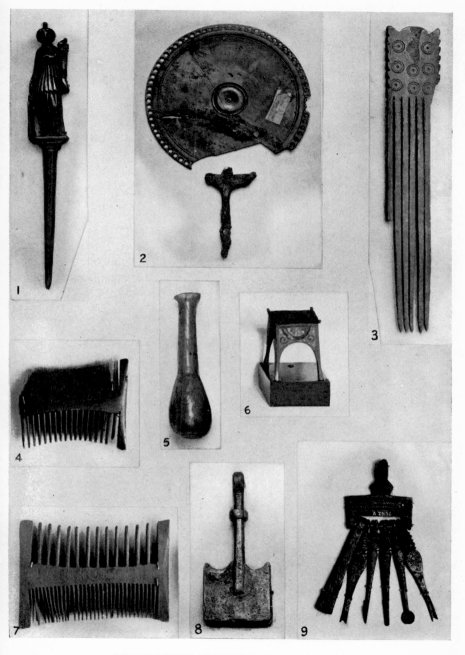

ROMAN TOILET ARTICLES FOUND IN LONDON.

1. Bone pin ornament with a figure of Bona Fortuna. 2. Bronze mirror found in Southwark. 3. Bone comb from Coleman Street. 4 and 7. Boxwood combs. 5. Glass scent or unguent bottle. 6. Bronze stand, perhaps for a scent bottle. 8. Bronze tweezers. 9. A set of manicure and other implements on a bronze clip.

(*British and Guildhall Museums.*)

ROMAN SHOES FOUND IN LONDON.

No Roman shoe possessed any raised heel. Above and below are leather open-work slippers or *carbatinæ*. On the left is the sole of a woman's shoe and on the right that of a child.

(*British Museum.*)

the matter in a different light, but evidence is entirely lacking.

The service of the household was naturally performed by slaves, not necessarily ill-treated, but without rights. Readers of Juvenal will remember the terrible picture in the "Legend of Bad Women," of the lady who amused herself by crucifying her husband's slaves, and perhaps the little twisted four-tailed scourge in the Guildhall Museum was the property of one of those cruel mistresses lashed in verse by the great poet.

In what may be termed the middle-class houses of the city and suburbs there would be rather less amusement and fewer slaves. A great deal of the woollen cloth required for the household was doubtless woven by the mistress, her daughters, and her maids. Of this home industry, from which the young unmarried woman of to-day derives her honourable title of spinster, many traces have survived in the form of spindles of bone and wood, spindle whorls of almost every material, and finally carding combs.

Needles and bodkins, generally of bronze or bone, that are found in great numbers, reveal that the women of Londinium resembled those of all ages in their love of sewing and kindred tasks.

Every household would possess certain ordinary tools, such as pincers, chisels, hammers, choppers, gimlets, and awls. These have been found in abundance, and one of the more recent additions to the Guildhall collection is that of a claw-ended hammer exactly resembling a present-day type.

The provision of household supplies necessitated the usual daily round of shopping and marketing, and the equipment of Londinium's stores is well represented. Bronze scales of various sizes, from a tiny pair for carrying in a pouch, to one suitable for average sales in a shop, have been unearthed, together with steelyards and various weights.

It is well known that Roman surgical skill employed a large variety of specialised implements. They are slightly represented in London, and include lancets, spatulae, and a silver-plated object—the use of which cannot be determined.

When eyes were giving trouble it was possible to go to at

least one druggist who specialised as an oculist. His name was
Caius Silvius Tetricus, and among the forms of relief he offered
to sufferers were an ointment for roughness of the eyelids and
a lotion "for attacks of bleariness." It has been suggested that

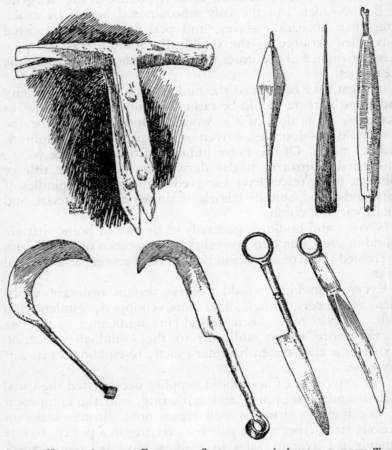

A CLAW HAMMER (FOUND IN FENCHURCH STREET IN 1925), AWLS, AND OTHER TOOLS,
PRUNING HOOKS, AND KNIVES WITH RINGS FOR SUSPENSION.

All found in London and now in the Guildhall Museum.

eye defects were caused in the Roman period through the
heated air in the baths.

C. Silvius Tetricus has succeeded in preserving his name
through having used a little tablet of green soap-stone

2 inches square by $\frac{3}{8}$ of an inch thick.[1] On each of its four edges he had had engraved backwards in clear capital letters his name and the purpose of one of his drugs. If he used an inking pad he could have employed the tablet after the manner of a rubber stamp to print labels for his medicaments, while he could, if required, make impressions on wax tablets or any of his salves of sufficient solidity.

A TILE-MAKER'S COMPLAINT AGAINST A FELLOW WORKMAN.

This Roman tile found in London has a graffito traced upon it reading "Austalis dibus xiii vagatur sibi cotidim" [=Au(gu)stalis is going off by himself every day for these thirteen days].

A slight clue to the date when this earliest-known London oculist and at the same time earliest-known tradesman of the city was dispensing his salves and ointments has been suggested by his unusual third name, but the fact that the Emperor Tetricus was recognised in Britain in 268 is hardly firm enough ground for dating the little stamp to the early years of the fourth century.

[1] Guildhall Museum.

This short survey of the domestic life of the capital of
Roman Britain, based upon the objects that have been preserved throughout fifteen destructive centuries deep down
beneath the present surface of the city, can only give an imperfect impression of the many-sided activities of the cosmopolitan population of one of the great cities of the Western
Empire. If one considers the small proportion of objects in
common use to-day that will be in existence fifteen centuries
hence, it will be easy to understand how little of that which
makes up the furnishing and appearance of domesticity to-day
will survive. Of the Roman period of London there have
vanished all woven materials, all furniture, all wooden articles,
with a few trifling exceptions, and all paper. Enough colour
in wall painting, mosaics, and personal ornaments has come
down to the present day, however, to give one the feeling of
a life in which there was no lack of brilliant contrasts and
gaiety.

Among all the many relics of Roman London that have
come to light, there is one which stands out from them all in
bringing before the eyes in one of the most imperishable forms
the permanence of certain qualities in human nature. This is
a sentence, scribbled on a bonding tile before it was baked, in
which a workman grumbles at the slackness of a fellow-
labourer. "Austalis," he complains, "is going off by himself every day for these thirteen days."[1]   It is always interesting to study the surface of tiles and bricks, for they tell
of the dogs, cows and other animals that walked over the soft
clay as it rested on the ground drying before being fired. In
Reading Museum there is preserved in this manner the
evidence from Silchester of the form of a child's foot in
Romano-British times.

The tendency of those who do not realise that every age is
essentially modern and not at all disposed to regard itself as
ancient is to forget that the human equation plays its all-
pervading part in every period of social development, and
they therefore fail to realise that conditions of life to-day are
in their essentials as they were between the first and the fifth
centuries of this era. Human nature has changed very little
since that epoch. Alter the architecture to the Roman style,
think of the costume as it varied throughout those centuries,

[1] See list of inscriptions in Appendix II, p. 266.

replace modern political affairs with those of the great Empire, modify the menus of the dining-table, above all eliminate the mechanical contrivances of recent years, and imagine the result upon people who are to some extent of the same stock as modern Londoners. Then the filling in of the picture becomes a task of the greatest simplicity, for one has only to imagine the daily affairs of domestic, business, and public life as experienced to-day, with such modifications as a certain callousness in regard to human life and a different standard of general morality.

APPENDIX I

DISCOVERIES MADE IN THE ROMAN LEVELS OF LONDON BETWEEN 1926 AND 1938 RECORDED IN THE GUILDHALL MUSEUM REPORTS

1926.

MILES LANE AND ARTHUR STREET NEAR UPPER THAMES STREET. A substantial wall of heavy timber construction between Miles Lane and Arthur Street running parallel with Upper Thames Street some 80 feet to the north of it. It had the appearance of a riverside construction of the first century A.D.

15 CORNHILL: "BIRCH'S." A length of a Roman wall some 4 feet thick was found under this site.

AT THE JUNCTION OF BREAD STREET AND CANNON STREET. At a depth of 15 feet the sculptured capital of a Roman pilaster was found.

ST MARTIN'S LE GRAND. On the completion of the excavations at St Martin's le Grand the conclusions arrived at after a thorough investigation of the site in 1914 were confirmed, viz. that the numerous rubbish pits covering the site of the G.P.O. revealed a chronological sequence from south to north. At the extreme south-west corner of the site there was found a Roman burial of the first century A.D.

1928.

LOMBARD COURT. In the earlier part of the year there was brought to light in Lombard Court much Roman pottery, confirming the opinion that the first Roman settlement was in that quarter of the city.

MIDLAND BANK, PRINCES STREET. An extensive excavation on the line of Walbrook revealed heavy timbering of the banks of the stream and yielded considerable quantities of pottery and leather as well as a few Roman coins. The pottery mainly of late first to middle third century, but it included one fragment of a Samian "crater"—a form usually associated with the period just preceding the Roman era in Britain. Among the coarse wares were found two examples of the pre-

Roman type known as "pedestal urns."[1] A Roman millstone was also found here.

1929.

NATIONAL PROVINCIAL BANK, PRINCES STREET AND MANSION HOUSE STREET. There was found in February a structure consisting of 9-inch piles on the top of which baulks 12 inches by 12 inches rested horizontally. These timbers lay nearly in a N.E. to S.W. direction at a depth of 28 feet below the existing street level. An iron chisel similar in form to the modern type was found driven into one of these piles, and the same site gave up a large stone adze of Neolithic or Early Bronze Age about 2000 B.C.

3-6 KING STREET, CHEAPSIDE: "ATLAS" OFFICES. On this site were found considerable quantities of Roman ware bearing the names of potters of such early date as to suggest that this site to the west of Walbrook was occupied before Boudicca's forces destroyed the town in A.D. 60. The early potters' names were AQUITANUS, BASSUS, CELADUS, FIRMO and LICINUS. Other pottery and potters' stamps of dates perhaps a century later were abundant, but there was little attributable to the third and fourth centuries. Exactly below the party wall separating Nos. 2 and 3 King Street were found the remains of a substantial Roman wall.

75-69 COLEMAN STREET AND 55-61 MOORGATE. Between these streets was excavated an extensive site. The presence of black mud and numerous traces of piling and camp-sheathing indicate that there was an open stream here in Roman times. Its relation to the Walbrook situated some 120 yards to the east is not clear. Nearly all the pottery discovered was of the second century, earlier forms being quite rare, a fact suggesting that the extension of the Roman town northwards was a gradual one.

51-54 GRACECHURCH STREET WITH TALBOT COURT. The pottery found on this site was remarkably early. It included the stamp of the potter BALBUS, who was one of the first of the Gaulish makers of Samian ware.[2] The

---

[1] See p. 24.   [2] Pre-Flavian, Tiberius-Claudius.

only other example of his manufactures discovered in London is in the British Museum.

20-27 FISH STREET HILL AND 43-45 KING WILLIAM STREET. In this area between King William Street and Fish Street Hill just to the north of Thames Street was found an eastward continuation of the vast structure of oaken beams noted in previous years beneath the sites of the present King William Street House and Imrie House. Some of the baulks of timber were as large as 26 by 18 inches, but in no case was it possible to ascertain their extreme length. They formed part of a great embankment scheme constructed along the line where the gravel slope merges into alluvial mud. In the filling between the great timbers was found pottery bearing the names of makers who were producing as early as the reign of Tiberius (A.D. 14-37), but the latest pieces in a similar position suggest that this great engineering work was completed about A.D. 75. In the highest part of the filling, and just above that of the uppermost timbers, many tons of oyster shells had been used as ballast. This deposit was in places as much as 8 feet thick. About 4 feet above the timbering were the footings of a wall still standing several feet high and composed of ragstone, chalk and cement with a few bonding tiles. It was 3 feet in thickness and ran north and south along the Fish Street front of the site. The impression gained was that it dated from about the same time as the construction of the timber sub-structure. Piled against the masonry wall on its western side, and extending over practically the whole area, was a stratum of burnt material. It consisted mainly of a substance similar to red brick-dust interspersed with fragments of charcoal and contained innumerable sherds of Samian crockery burnt to every shade between the original scarlet and a glossy jet black. It would seem that the débris from a conflagration, involving a large area densely built over with houses of wattle-and-daub, had been dumped here, on what was doubtless in Roman times the river-bank. The forms, decorations and numerous potters' stamps on the fragments leave no doubt that this fire must have occurred in the latter part of Hadrian's reign about A.D. 130.

1930.

FISH STREET HILL. Throughout the year the excavation of the site of Regis House was continued. The area is bounded by King William Street, Arthur Street East and Fish Street Hill. Further evidence was forthcoming of the construction of the Roman embankment and of a great fire in the second century A.D. mentioned in the 1929 report. Several walls of Roman date were found in the northern part, and the lower portion of a limestone column was brought to light. It was similar to those discovered at Silchester, Wroxeter and elsewhere that formed parts of buildings facing the more important thoroughfares of those towns.

52 CORNHILL. Beneath this site immediately to the west of the church of St Peter were found massive walls 6 feet thick running east and west. It was discovered that these linked up with those of a similar nature to the east under Leadenhall Market, surveyed by Mr Henry Hodge in 1881-3, and others recorded ten years later under 50 Cornhill adjoining the scene of these (1930) excavations to the west. From this it was found possible to reconstruct the plan of the Roman building that stood on the site, now accepted as being the governmental head-quarters of Londinium. Mr G. C. Dunning's drawings recently exhibited at a meeting of the Society of Antiquaries show a basilica about 500 feet in length standing athwart the present Gracechurch Street from Whittington Avenue on the east to the church of St Michael-on-Cornhill to the west. Pottery found in rubbish pits, covered in before or at the time of the building of the walls beneath 52 Cornhill, suggests that the great edifice was erected at the end of the first century A.D. (See p. 180.)

70-73 CHEAPSIDE. Until 1930 a portion of this site was occupied by a building that was popularly known as "The Old Mansion House." Some 20 feet below the modern surface oaken piles and camp-sheathing have been found from which it appears that a small tributary of the Walbrook existed here in Roman times. Much of the Samian pottery discovered is of a sufficiently early date to suggest that this area was occupied at the beginning of the Roman occupation. The potter's stamps include those of BILICATUS and LICINUS,[1] both of whom were producing some twenty years before the Claudian invasion.

6 LOTHBURY. On this site (Royal Bank of Canada) was discovered in 1927 a corner of a Roman tessellated pavement. Further operations have revealed more of this pavement, but it was found that it had been damaged by piles that had been driven through it, perhaps as long ago as the fifteenth century, when it had already been buried many feet below the present surface. The design of the pavement shows a cable pattern in red, white and black surrounding the main area filled with inch squares of red, white and grey tile. Pottery fragments found below confirmed the opinion formed three years before that the pavement was made in about A.D. 125.

CHURCH OF ALL HALLOWS, BARKING. Two walls of Roman date have been discovered during excavations under the chancel. Their direction was north and south and they appeared to form the sites of a long and narrow room, for they were only 9 feet apart. The trench for their chalk foundations was dug in soil that already contained sherds of pottery belonging to the first and second centuries. These walls may therefore be assigned to a period a good deal later than most of the Roman structures in London to which so far it has been possible to give a date. In 1928 two Roman pavements of small tesserae were brought to light under the tower and the west end of the nave. It is possible that these pavements were, with the walls, part of a single house.

10-12 LITTLE TRINITY LANE. This site adjoins the Painter-Stainers' Hall which forms its northern boundary, and extends along the whole width between Little

---

[1] La Graufesenque potters. Bilicatus, Tiberius-Claudius; Licinus, Tiberius-Nero.

Trinity and Huggin Lanes, and here were discovered in the latter part of 1929 and the beginning of 1930 the remains of two large Roman buildings. Across the middle of the site from west to east ran a wall 5 feet thick, and parallel with it, 10 feet to the south, was another 2 feet thick. Where they pass beneath the roadway of Huggin Lane these walls almost reach the surface. The thicker one was penetrated by an arched culvert formed of voussoir tiles 17 inches long, 7 inches wide and 3 inches thick at the large end. A third Roman wall parallel with the others was found under the southern wall of the Painter-Stainers' Hall. Its foundations were, however, at a considerably higher level, and it is unlikely that it formed a part of the same building. From this difference in levels it would seem that the slope towards Upper Thames Street was more pronounced in Roman times than it is to-day. Owing to the fact that very little pottery was found on this site, and even this was not well placed for the purpose of establishing dates, it was not found possible to determine the age of the walls.

BLOSSOM'S INN YARD. The irregularly-shaped area known by this name, lying to the west of Lawrence Lane and north of Trump Street, was excavated during this year, and though nothing notable in the way of structural remains were found, it formed a veritable mine of objects illustrating the history of London from the first century to the eighteenth. There was Roman pottery of such an early date—*e.g.* fragments with the stamps of the potters AMANDUS, BILICATUS, INGENUUS and SENICIO[1]—as to suggest that the very first settlement of the Romans must have extended at least thus far to the west of Walbrook. Roman pottery of about the middle of the second century was particularly plentiful. Altogether there were over a hundred fragments with legible names stamped upon them. The third and fourth centuries, too, relics of which are generally so strangely rare in London, were well repre-

---

[1] All La Graufesenque potters. Amandus and Ingenuus, Tiberius-Nero; Bilicatus and Senicio, Tiberius-Claudius.

sented in numerous pieces of the red-coated earthenware, decorated either with impressed devices or in
white pigment, characteristic of the potteries of the New
Forest and other parts of the country in the fourth
century.

1931.

GREAT PRESCOTT STREET. A Roman burial dating to
the early second century was found in January on the
north side of the street where building operations had
been in progress for the premises of the Co-operative
Wholesale Society Ltd. The ashes were contained in a
jar that was found within the body of a large globular
amphora. It closely resembled the grave group now in
the crypt at Guildhall that was discovered in Great
Alie Street only about 100 yards to the north.

During the following months other burials were found
on this site. All of them were inhumations and were
probably at least a century later in date. These finds are
further evidence of there having been an extensive cemetery in this area outside the town wall to the east of
Minories and south of Aldgate High Street. The district
is known as Goodman's Fields, where a number of
burials have been disclosed at various times.

MANSELL STREET, also in this area, gave up one or
more Roman incineration burials during the year on
the site of the railway goods depot on the western side
of Mansell Street opposite the end of Great Alie Street.

64-66 CHEAPSIDE. These buildings were demolished
during the year and the site excavated. The objects
found belonged to two very widely separated periods—
the Roman and the late Stuart, with scarcely anything
of the twelve intervening centuries. The early part of
the Roman period, as is so usual in London, was much
better represented than the third and fourth centuries.
Among the score of potters' names was that of BILI-
CATUS, and its presence here gives support to the suggestion put forward in reference to the pottery found
in 1930 in Blossom's Inn Yard, that the Roman settlement must have already extended well to the westward
of the Walbrook stream when the place was sacked by

the followers of Boudicca in A.D. 60, the activities of
the potter just mentioned having seemed to cease about
ten years before that disaster.

129-130 UPPER THAMES STREET. This site adjoining
the first arch of London Bridge on the north side of
the street was deeply excavated during the first half of
the year. No trace was found here of the massively
constructed timber embanking works which have in
recent years been traced running parallel with the line
of Thames Street at a distance of 80 feet to the north of
it, and extending from Arthur Street on the west to
Fish Street Hill. It had been considered likely that this
great wooden structure forming a formidable embankment was built about A.D. 75 and the finds made on this
fresh site tend to confirm this dating. The nature of the
soil in which the objects scattered over the site were
found and the fact that they had not been buried in pits,
but broadcast over the area, suggest that they were
rubbish thrown from the bank into the river. Amongst
the finds was a coin of Vespasian, well worn, as though
it had been long in circulation before being lost, but
no coin of an earlier date was encountered. This may
be taken as typical of the finds as a whole; they belong
mainly to the last quarter of the first century and to the
succeeding centuries.

Among the potters' stamps on Samian ware some
120 legible specimens were collected, amongst which
there were, it is true, examples of those of AQUI-
TANUS, INGENUUS, MASCULUS and SENICIO,[1] whose
vessels would, in the ordinary course of events, be
more likely to be broken and thrown away before
than after A.D. 75. The other sherds bore names which
showed that they were probably deposited here after
that date. Among the many small objects found were
an oculist's stamp and a circular brooch in bronze
and enamel of a second century type. There were a pair
of bronze tweezers, pins, needles, spoons, ear-picks,
iron styli and a key. Remains of leather sandals were

---

[1] All La Graufesenque potters. Aquitanus, late Tiberius-Nero;
Masculus, Claudius-early Vespasian.

well preserved in the damp soil, and so were wooden objects, including several spindles and portions of two ladles.

67 LOMBARD STREET. This corner site (Glyn, Mills and Co.'s Bank), bounded by Lombard Street on the south and Birchin Lane on the east, was in this year completely excavated down to the London clay. It had been hoped that the operations would confirm and amplify the plan made in 1785 showing the walls of adjacent buildings that had been partially uncovered when a sewer was laid. A sketch plan of these discoveries was published in *Archaeologia*, Vol. 8, 1787. Unfortunately it was found that previous excavations had obliterated nearly all structural remains of early date. The one Roman wall brought to light was a substantial one 4 feet thick running parallel with Birchin Lane and 11 feet within the building line. There was no wall, however, in the 1787 plan that could be brought into relation with it. Good examples of both early and late Roman pottery were found on the site.

143-149 FENCHURCH STREET AND 18-20 CULLUM STREET. This large site of irregular shape has added little to the knowledge of the lay-out of the Roman city. It has, on the other hand, furnished a large quantity of interesting objects for study.

A Roman well was discovered early in the digging operations. It went deep into the gravel, was rectangular and lined with wooden staves. The contents included a large accumulation of broken jugs, two of which were almost complete. These were all of a late first to early second century date, and therefore about contemporary with the great basilica that stood only some 120 yards away to the north-east.

The well contained only a single fragment of Samian ware. Upon it was the stamp of M. CRESTIO,[1] whose output was selling from about A.D. 80 to 110. There was, however, evidence that the site was occupied some thirty years earlier than this, for there were found in addition a thick-walled mortarium of a type that

[1] La Graufesenque potter, Domitian-Trajan.

does not seem to have persisted beyond the days of Claudius, and also sherds bearing the stamps of BILI-CATUS, ARDACUS and INGENUUS.

1932.

BOW CHURCH, CHEAPSIDE. A large crack having appeared in the south wall of Wren's church, excavations were made at the beginning of the year with the object of underpinning. It was then found that Wren's wall was built with its outer face touching a presumably pre-existing wall of imposing dimensions, 4 feet thick, and composed of ragstone, chalk and rubble set in a hard cement. It was found only just beneath the pavement of the alley that bounds the church on this side and was excavated to its base, where at a depth of 16 feet it rested upon a layer of burnt material. The adjoining soil contained pottery and tiles of Roman date, but the wall was not coeval, as it contains fragments of bricks that are certainly of a much later date. It does not appear to be a part of the earlier church, since it lies outside the limit of the present building, which itself extends some 11 feet further in this direction (south) than does the Norman crypt. The discovery of this wall was made by Mr E. S. Underwood, F.R.I.B.A., the surveyor of the church.

ST MICHAEL'S HOUSE, ST MICHAEL'S ALLEY. Most of this site was excavated in connection with the rebuilding and enlargement of Barclay's Bank, and a wall of Roman date nearly 5 feet in thickness was found running north and south. It was built with courses of bonding tiles and had its foundation in gravel. Near it was a quantity of painted wall plaster. The position of this massive wall in relation to the great basilica, the western end of which would be about 80 feet to the north, suggests that it belongs to an imposing building that stood on the western side of the great open quadrangle of the forum. Buried beneath the soil, it still stood, in places, to a height of well over 10 feet.

BARTHOLOMEW LANE. The site fronting this lane, between Capel Court and Lothbury, has been entirely cleared and excavated to a great depth for new offices for the Alliance Assurance Company.

The building that has been demolished was erected only about seventy years ago and had deep basements that went far down into the Roman level, so that there was little left for this final excavation. One or two deposits of Roman pottery of the first century A.D. were found, and these were probably the bottoms of rubbish pits, the upper parts of which were cleared away when the previous foundations were made. Among the few objects discovered was one of considerable rarity in London, namely a Roman altar. It was of oolitic lime-stone, probably from a quarry in the west of England. The die is square in section and it is not inscribed. This altar has been given to the Guildhall Museum, where it is at present the only object of its class and the third so far found in the city.

15-18 LIME STREET INCLUDING PEWTERERS' HALL. The excavation of this site furnished the most important archaeological discovery of the year, no less than the fixing of the position of one of the streets of Roman London.

Pits sunk in the north-west corner of the site exposed a mass of road material at a depth of 16 feet below the present pavement level and extended to a further depth of 8 feet. The street was composed of layer upon layer of gravel, showing that it had been continually in use for many years, perhaps as many as three centuries.

Fragments of pottery were found actually beneath the lowest stratum of roadmaking material. Among these was a piece of "bead rim pot," a class of vessel that was in use in the south-east Belgic parts of Britain in the century before the Roman conquest by Claudius, but which remained in use until nearly, if not quite, the end of the first century A.D. With it were found fragments of more distinctively Roman wares. These included part of a Samian bowl with decoration of the Claudius-Nero period (c. A.D. 45-65); there were found also two fragments of the same glazed red ware which bore stamped upon them the names of their makers.

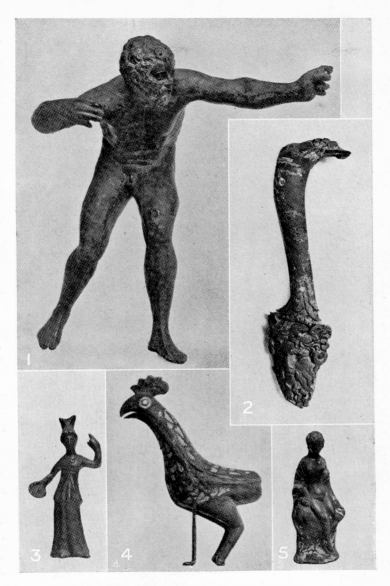

BRONZE OBJECTS FOUND IN ROMAN LONDON.

1. The statuette of an archer (the bow is lost) was found in Queen Street in 1842 at a depth of more than 12 ft. Like the head of a river god and the Bonus Eventus illustrated on p. 80, it stands apart from the average level of Romano-British art. The poise of the figure and the expression of concentration in the face—the eyes are of silver—is on the level of Mediterranean culture (*British Museum*). 2. Bronze handle of a jug adorned with a bearded head of extremely fine workmanship. It may represent a marine god. Winged monsters are enmeshed in the hair. Found in Threadneedle Street (*London Museum*). 3. Small bronze statuette of Minerva (*Guildhall Museum*). 4. Bronze cock inlaid with champlevé enamel, considered to be probably of British workmanship. Found at a Royal Exchange site (*British Museum*). 5. Pipeclay figure of Leda and the Swan (*Guildhall Museum*).

EXAMPLES OF RED-GLAZED WARE IMPORTED FROM GAUL, KNOWN AS SAMIAN OR TERRA SIGILLATA, FOUND IN LONDON.

1. Mortarium with lion-faced spout from a Central-Gaulish pottery at Lezoux Auvergne, Dragendorff (form 45), late 2nd century A.D. 2. A bowl found in St. Mildred's Court, also from Lezoux, classified as Dragendorff (form 37), A.D. 100–130. 3. Rutenian bowl from a South Gaulish pottery at La Graufesenque, *circa* A.D. 40–60 (form 29), found in Gracechurch Street. 4. Early type of Rutenian cylindrical bowl (form 30). 5. Rutenian bowl (form 29), *circa* A.D. 50.

These potters were PERRUS, who worked at Banassac in South Gaul from the time of Claudius to that of Nero, and PONTUS, whose kilns were at La Graufesenque, in the same part of Gaul, but whose wares do not seem to have been on the market much, if at all, before A.D. 70.

From these datable finds, therefore, it would seem that the making of this street was a part of the great rebuilding and town-planning scheme that replaced the doubtless haphazard planning of the town burnt by Boudicca in A.D. 60. Recent research favours the idea that this Roman city, planned as it probably continued four centuries or longer, came into being at the same time as its great basilica in the seventies or eighties of the first century A.D.

The roadway was more than 30 feet wide, but its western edge was just beyond the limits of the present operations. The section exposed was 40 to 50 yards south of the basilica, the eastern end of which would have come right up to it. Continued southwards it would follow the line of Philpot and Botolph Lanes to the point where the Roman bridge probably stood; continued northwards it would meet the Roman wall at Bishopsgate. If this is eventually proved to be correct it would mean that a section of the main north and south thoroughfare of the city has been discovered. This accords approximately with previously-held ideas except that in hypothetical reconstructions of the street plan of Londinium the main street from the bridge has been shown going straight up to the basilica and not skirting its eastern end as this one does.

If the street did follow the line suggested here, which can only be decided by the result of future excavations, it would have the advantage of giving a straight and uninterrupted thoroughfare from the bridgehead to the northern gate, thus avoiding two right-angled turnings to get past the 500-foot long basilica and the forum in front of it, as suggested in the plan in the volume devoted to Roman London published in 1928 by the Royal Commission on Historical Monuments.

16

32-35 JEWRY STREET. The most important addition to
the archaeology of London made during this year
resulted from excavations made at this site.

Here, for the first time, occurred a deposit of
pottery actually beneath the foundations of the Roman
city wall where it crossed the course of a small and
hitherto unrecorded stream. This pottery all proved to
be Roman wares of the first century A.D., none of it
attributable to a date later than that of the emperor
Domitian. There seems to be no reasonable doubt that
the latest of this pottery must provide the date of the
building of this part of the wall, for an open stream was
dammed and a culvert made to carry the water beneath
the wall, the stream bed being filled with the customary
foundation deposit of clay and flints. It is reasonable
to suppose that as long as the stream remained open
potsherds would be deposited in it. There was an
abundance of fragments dating from the first years of
the Roman occupation up to a period which may be put
somewhere between A.D. 75 and 85, the series then
ending abruptly. The dating of one portion of the
Roman wall is the dating of the whole, for the wall was
evidently, with the exception of the river front and the
bastions, all built to one design and at one time.

The channel of the culvert was rectangular in section,
15 inches wide and 9 inches high, the top of the opening
being some 6 inches below the bottom of the plinth.
Its line of penetration was at an angle of 50° with that
of the wall, the point where it entered the western side
of the wall being thus a couple of feet or so to the north
of its exit. As stated above, the pottery sealed in the
bed of this stream dates the wall at A.D. 75-85.

The Roman ditch outside the wall could also be
traced at this point. It was not V-shaped here, but had
a flat bottom 5 feet wide, as at New Broad Street. The
foundation of the wall did not penetrate below the
stratum of brick-earth, but the ditch went down rather
more than a foot into the gravel which underlies it.
The inner lip of the ditch was some 12 feet from the
wall, and there was evidence at one spot that the inter-

vening space, the "berm," had been surfaced with gravel. The depth of the ditch was 8 feet and its width at the top must have been about 10 feet, but the outer lip had been obliterated by the later town ditch, the black filling of which occupied the whole eastern portion of the site.

BANK OF ENGLAND. The most interesting discovery made so far is that of a tessellated pavement of Roman date. This was at a depth of 20 feet below the roadway of Princes Street. It formed the floor of a large room in what was probably a house of some importance. The decorated portion was a square of just under 8 feet.

The pavement has been raised and will probably be relaid in one of the floors of the Bank of England. It was laid on a raft of concrete about 8 inches thick and rested on the damp black alluvial soil on the edge of the Walbrook. All the pottery and other objects that lay actually below the pavement, and were thus sealed by it, were carefully collected. Among them were fortunately a considerable number of fragments of figured Samian ware that through recent research can now be dated within very narrow limits. The latest of them belonged to the reign of Trajan or the early years of Hadrian, so that the pavement was probably laid some time about A.D. 115.

Some 60 feet to the south of this another paved area was encountered comprising portions of three rooms. The paving here was all of 1 inch tesserae without decoration. This second pavement appeared to be of the same date as the other. The fact that it is at a level 8 feet above the decorated one is easily accounted for by the fact that it is further from the stream whose banks rose somewhat steeply at this point.

LOMBARD STREET—IN FRONT OF ALL HALLOWS CHURCH. There was found beneath the footway on the north side of the street in front of All Hallows Church a Roman wall 4 feet in thickness. It was built of ragstone and brick of the usual Roman type. The wall is the continuation westwards of that which was recorded when Barclay's Bank at the corner of Gracechurch Street was rebuilt in 1927 and was thought likely to be the southern wall of the Forum. Nothing was found that threw any light on the date of its construction; the masonry is, however, of much the same character as that of the basilica itself, that is late first century A.D.

69-73 CANNON STREET. This site is on the north side of the street, between Tower Royal and Queen Street. An interesting feature of the excavation was the presence of a red layer of burnt material at the Roman level. This contained Samian sherds contorted and half fused by heat. It was a notable fact that this pottery was of the same date as that found in the burnt débris forming a dump on the site of Regis House, Fish Street Hill, in 1929 and seems to be further evidence of a disastrous conflagration that destroyed a great part of the Roman town somewhere about A.D. 130. Mr Lambert noted some years ago a great quantity of burnt pottery of this date in King William Street, and it is interesting to observe that the collection of sherds from the site of the National Safe Deposit building, presented to the museum by Mr Harcourt Smith, contained a number of pieces of figured Samian discoloured by fire of just this period, and that quite a considerable number of similarly damaged pieces have appeared on the Bank of England site in course of the prolonged digging there.

OLD JEWRY CHAMBERS. Three brooches of Roman date, one of iron and two of bronze, found here.

1934.

BANK OF ENGLAND. In February a second tessellated pavement was discovered to the east of the one noted in last year's Report, so close to it that there can be little doubt that it was a part of the same building. It was a square with sides of 4½ feet and, like the other pavement, was carefully taken up to be relaid in the reconstructed portion of the Bank of England. Two wells of Roman date were also found. They were lined with wooden wine-barrels, one of which had staves 6 feet in length. Two of these staves were stamped with the name CALVISI in letters more than an inch in height.

A notable feature of the concluding stages of the excavation of this site, on the course of the Walbrook, was the very large amount of Roman leather found. This consists mainly of shoes and sandals which, considering their age, are in a remarkable state of preservation. In addition there were large quantities of pottery and many tools and other interesting objects of iron, including several hundreds of stili.

OLD JEWRY CHAMBERS. The pits sunk on this site did not reveal the plan of buildings of early date, though evidence of continuous occupation was supplied by numerous small finds, including three brooches of Roman date, a fragment of an earthenware vessel of the ninth century and leather of the fourteenth.

83-87 GRACECHURCH STREET. This site occupies a large area immediately to the south of Leadenhall Market. The foundations of the great basilica lie beneath the market and extend westward beyond the church of St Peter-in-Cornhill. This Gracechurch Street site should, by analogy with other Roman town sites, correspond with the forum or large open market square. A Roman wall of some importance had, however, been recorded in 1908 running north and south, 30 feet east of the Gracechurch Street frontage. It was $3\frac{1}{2}$ feet thick, was 21 feet from the surface and stood 5 feet high. Operations this year have revealed the presence of a wall parallel with this just beneath the street frontage and another running east and west along the southern limit of the site. These would seem to be of about the same date as the basilica itself (late first century A.D.) and must have formed parts of a building of some importance. When the other walls found later to the north and east are taken into consideration it seems that from the time of the erection of the basilica the area in question was not entirely open.

17 GRACECHURCH STREET. This site on the western side of the street is providing confirmation of the same

theory. Several walls show that there were buildings here, too, just to the south of the western half of the basilica. As excavation proceeds it may be possible to recover the plans of some of them.

19-21 BIRCHIN LANE. Excavations have been begun on the site of Messrs Williams, Deacon's Bank, which lies only a few yards west of the last named. Although the work has not yet proceeded very far, a piece of Roman road metalling has been encountered, similar in construction to that found beneath Pewterers' Hall in 1932, and it is hoped that further digging will make it possible to determine the width and direction of the street concerned.

LONDON WALL. A Post Office excavation in June in the roadway, to the west of Copthall Avenue, opposite to No. 50 London Wall, encountered the wall of the Roman city still standing to a height of 10 feet. It was found 3 feet below the present street level, and a tunnel, the bottom of which was at a depth of 12 feet below street level, was cut right through it. This boring extended from below the lowest bonding course (of three tiles) to above the second bonding course (of two tiles). The Roman ground level would therefore be about a foot below the excavation made.

1935.

HOUNDSDITCH AND BEVIS MARKS. Several excavations this year have exposed the remains of the Roman town wall. At 28-30 Houndsditch, immediately west of the corner of Duke Street and Bevis Marks, nothing but the footings remained, but a few yards further west, at 19 Bevis Marks, the wall was found running across the site for some 25 feet in excellent condition from the foundations up to the first bonding course, about 3 feet in height from the original ground level. The work in progress necessitated its destruction, but before it was demolished, in November, an excellent photograph of its northern face was obtained, showing the footings, plinth and four courses of masonry. To the north of it the medieval town ditch had obliterated all traces of the earlier Roman one.

TOWER HILL. In December the Tower Hill Improvements Council decided to make an excavation in the cellar of No. 19 Tower Hill with the idea of exposing the inner face of the Roman wall. To the surprise of all concerned, the operation revealed the presence of a rectangular chamber with inner dimensions of 11 feet by 6 feet. This had been constructed apparently at the same time as the city wall itself and of similar materials; the town wall forming indeed the chamber's eastern wall.

It was then proposed to carry the excavation further with a view to determining the nature and purpose of the building, nothing similar having been recorded along the whole course of the wall.

TRINITY PLACE, MINORIES. By far the most interesting archaeological discovery of the year was made by the London Passenger Transport Board at Trinity Place, Minories. Here, during the work for the construction of an electric sub-station, workmen encountered not only the original Roman town wall, but also a small remnant of one of the bastions (No. 2 on the plan) still in its original position. These bastions were semicircular or horseshoe-shaped towers built up at intervals against the outside of the wall at a period long subsequent—perhaps two hundred years—to the building of the wall itself. In their construction was used material from former buildings which had either fallen into decay or been demolished for the purpose. One of the stones forming the base of this bastion was seen to be a large squared block, bearing on its exposed face (which measured 5 feet by 1½ feet) an inscription cut in letters 3 inches high:

PROC · PROVINC · BRIT ·
IVLIA · INDI · FILIA · PACATA · I
VXOR

A heap of stones, evidently part of this bastion, was found a few feet from this spot in 1852, and among them was one bearing the beginning of a funerary inscription from the tomb of someone named CLASSICIANUS. It was

suggested at the time that this might possibly be the
Classicianus who, according to Tacitus, was appointed
Procurator of Britain after the rebellion of Boudicca in
A.D. 60. This idea was rejected as unlikely by the
scholars of that period. A comparison of the lettering,
the size and nature of the stone of the two fragments
soon showed that they were parts of the same monument.

The newly discovered stone has accordingly been
presented by the London Passenger Transport Board
to the British Museum, where, with the portion found
eighty-three years before, it has made the finest and
earliest example of an important Roman inscription
hitherto found in this country. It is probable that
originally there were two more lines of lettering, occu-
pying a space about a foot deep, between the old and
the new portions, and if so these would no doubt have
recorded the previous appointments held by the
procurator.[1]

A stretch of the Roman town wall encountered
during the same operations in the Crescent, Minories,
has been preserved by the L.P.T.B., and will be available for inspection.

17 GRACECHURCH STREET. At the beginning of this
year, the remains of a large Roman building were
found on this site. In the south-west corner of one
chamber (which had a diagonal measurement of 40 feet)
the walls were still standing to a height of 2 feet. A
peculiar feature of the walling was that it was constructed, not of the ordinary bricks, but of roofing tiles.
They were laid flat, the flanged edges giving just the
appearance of a wall of bricks of the normal Roman
type, about 2 inches thick. There were other rooms of
smaller size both to the north and south of the large
one. What the purpose of this building was is open to
conjecture, but its position, in front of the western end
of the great basilica, taken in conjunction with the
position of the remains found in 1934 on the other side
of Gracechurch Street, proves that there was not here,

[1] See in Appendix list of Roman inscriptions found in London, p. 254.

as in most Roman towns, an entirely open forum in front of the administrative headquarters.

19-21 BIRCHIN LANE. This site was excavated in the first half of the year, in preparation for the rebuilding of Williams, Deacon's Bank. An interesting find was a small area of Roman road metalling. Unfortunately there was not enough of it to show in what direction the road ran, though it seemed probable that it might be part of a north to south street, just to the west of the great basilica, thus corresponding with the street found beneath Pewterers' Hall, Lime Street, in 1932.

Here also occurred a considerable deposit of pottery of the second century A.D. that had been discoloured by fire, affording further evidence of the extent of the great conflagration which appears to have destroyed a very large area of the city about A.D. 130.

SPITAL SQUARE. On the north side of this square a large area was excavated on the site where the Wholesale Co-operative Society Ltd. was erecting new premises. Foundation arches and the footing of medieval walls were found. It appeared that in Roman times there was a cemetery here, for a number of burials were discovered both cremated and inhumed.

1936.

TOWER HILL. The excavation mentioned in last year's Report as being then in progress was continued by the Tower Hill Improvements Committee, and the base of the city wall was exposed on both sides of 20 Tower Hill, a narrow building erected actually on the foundations of the Roman wall. Here pottery of the early second century was found close beside the wall at the original ground level and also in earth piled against the inner face of the wall to form a ramp. If this ramp was piled, as is the opinion of some investigators, as soon as the wall was put up, it would give A.D. 120-150 as the period in which the wall and ramp were built.

COPTHALL CLOSE AND GREAT SWAN ALLEY. A large site here, touching Moorgate at No. 24 on the west and extending eastwards almost to Copthall Avenue, was deeply excavated during the year. Towards the eastern

end of the site were unearthed large quantities of
"wasters" from a Roman potter's kiln. This was a find
of great interest, for although the kilns themselves were
not found, it is evident that they must have been, if not
on the site itself, certainly on one of the adjoining plots.
No site of a Roman potter's kiln has been found in the
city for many years, the only other one recorded being
that found beneath the north-west part of St Paul's
Cathedral, discovered by Sir Christopher Wren when,
in 1672, he was digging the foundations for the present
structure.

The excavation showed that the gravel on the site in
question sloped rapidly down to the bed of the Walbrook, the course of which here followed more or less
closely the line of the thoroughfare now known as
Copthall Avenue. It would seem, then, that the potters
made a practice of tipping their rubbish down the bank
of the stream which formed the eastern limit of their
holding.

The remains of the spoilt pots recovered comprised
those of shouldered jars of grey ware, open pans with
reeded horizontal rim, and platters with upright walls.
In addition to these quite coarse and unpretentious
wares, there were two classes of crockery of some distinction. The first was mica-dusted, that is to say that
the vessels were liberally sprinkled with powdered mica
before firing. When this was fixed by the heat of the
kiln the surface of the finished article received a metallic
lustre, so that it had the appearance of having been made
of gold. Ware of this kind has often come to light in
this part of England, in deposits of the first and second
centuries A.D., but the fact that it was manufactured in
this country had not previously been established. This
last remark also applies to the second kind of "fancy"
ware made at the Moorgate kilns. This is a grey ware
of thin fabric, the outside of which was given a jet-like
black polish by the application of bitumen. It was
decorated with incised designs, mainly consisting of
arrangements of concentric circles connected with
parallel straight lines. The forms most favoured were
bowls (hemispherical in imitation of the Samian

varieties known as "Dragendorff 37," or carinated like "Dragendorff 29") and pedestalled vases with narrow necks. It was, up to the time of this discovery, generally supposed that this ware was imported from beyond the Channel.

All these damaged pots are of forms that were in vogue in the latter half of the first century A.D. and might be dated *c.* 80-90. As the site of their discovery is well within the area of the walled city, it may be wondered whether the absence of crockery of later fashions may not be accounted for by a compulsory removal of the industry to a site outside the town when the city, surrounded by its new-built wall, became conscious of its dignity.

1937.

ROOD LANE. On a site adjacent to the north wall of the church of St Margaret Pattens, Roman walls and traces of *opus signinum* flooring were found in the north-east corner of the area.

16 ST DUNSTAN'S HILL. Excavation still in progress has revealed the presence of several Roman walls. Further digging may disclose enough of their plan to enable an opinion to be formed as to their relationship to the building of which the well-known hypocaust beneath the Coal Exchange forms a part. This is distant from the newly-found walls some 80 feet to the west.

LOMBARD STREET. Excavations in July for a new sewer beneath this thoroughfare uncovered a piece of Roman walling running at right angles to the street, a few feet west of Nicholas Lane. It stood $7\frac{1}{2}$ feet high and had five courses of bonding tiles. Possibly this wall aligns with a similar one found at the time of the rebuilding of Glyn, Mills and Co's Bank, within its area. A fortnight later another wall was encountered opposite the end of Clement's Lane. This one ran in the direction of the line of the street. Like the other it was about 3 feet thick. Although only the lower portion of the masonry remained a photograph of it was obtained.

JOINERS' HALL BUILDINGS. A pit sunk here on a site bounded on one side by Greenwich Street was remarkable for producing an object of unusual character, namely a Roman ink-well of glass, the first recorded instance of a glass one from the soil of London.

1938.

6 THE CRESCENT, MINORIES. "Toc H" has rendered a service to London archaeology by excavating and leaving open to view the portion of the Roman town wall which forms its western boundary. The outer surface of the wall, which is that exposed, is here in an excellent state of preservation, from the ironstone plinth that marks the ground level at the time of its construction up to the second course of bonding tiles, that is about 6 feet, and above this the inner core of ragstone rubble remains in places as high again.

1-5 QUEEN STREET AND 67-69 CHEAPSIDE. Excavation here has brought to light a certain number of scattered Roman objects—pottery, leather, coins and querns; but more interesting was the recognition of a quantity of road-metalling material as forming part of the roadway that in Roman times corresponded with the present Cheapside. The same street had been noted by Sir Christopher Wren as crossing the site of Bow Church some 60 yards further west.

ALDGATE HIGH STREET. Excavations made in connection with the extension of the Underground Railway Station, Aldgate East, exposed interesting sections of this ancient thoroughfare outside the city gate. The lowest layers, resting on virgin clay, at a depth of 10 feet below the present street level, were undoubtedly Roman.

APPENDIX II

GREEK AND ROMAN INSCRIPTIONS FOUND IN LONDON
[Ligatured letters are shown with a bracket below]

1. GREEK

. . . ΩΝΙΑ ΜΑΡΤΙΑ
ΛΙ·Ι ΤΩΑΝΔΡΙ

[?Ant]onia to Martialis her husband.

21¾ in. × 15½ in. × 3½ in. On marble tombstone with relief of a gladiator. Found in ruins of a house in Islington and rediscovered in Tottenham Court Road. *C.I.L.* VII. p. 21. *Illustrated facing p.* 129.

(*Guildhall Museum.*)

ΔΕΞΙΕ ΔΙοΤΙΜοΥ
ΧΡΗϹΤΕ ΧΑΙΡΕ

Jnl. Rom. Studies, Vol. XVI.
pt. 2, p. 244.

The suggested interpretation of this half-obliterated inscription is: "Good Dexios, son of Diotimos, farewell."

24 in. × 14 in. On a marble tombstone showing, in low relief, a mourning woman seated on a draped stool with her feet on a footstool and in front of her a boy (nude) representing the deceased. Found in Drury Lane. Very considerable doubt has been felt as to whether this is genuinely Romano-British.

Illustrated facing title-page. (*London Museum.*)

. . . . . ΟϹ
. . . Τ · ΘΥ
. Ϲ ΧΑΙΡΕ

Beneath a relief of a half-draped male figure standing with staff in left hand. The only words legible suggest ". . . son of . . . tios; good . . ., farewell."

Originally found at Islington (see drawing in British Museum by Archer, dated 1850), afterwards rediscovered in Lamb's Conduit Street.

Illustrated facing title-page. (*British Museum.*)

2. A PROCURATOR OF BRITAIN

DIS
[M]ANIBVS
[C·IVL·C·F·F]AB·ALPINI·CLASSICIANI·

(central portion not yet found)

PROC·PROVINC·BRIT[ANN]
IVLIA·INDI·FILIA·PACATA·I[NDIANA]¹
VXOR

"To the Divine Shades Gaius Julius Alpinus Classicianus, of the Fabian tribe, son of Gaius . . . and Procurator of Britain, (this monument was set up by) his wife Julia Pacata Indiana, daughter of (Julius) Indus."

The upper portion of this inscription, together with a "bolster" belonging to the top of the altar-shaped tomb to which it belonged, was found in 1852 in the remains of a bastion of the Roman wall at the back of Trinity Place, Tower Hill. This is Bastion No. 2 on the plan in this book and also in that of the Roman London volume of the Royal Commission on Historical Monuments.

In June 1935, when excavations were being made for a new sub-station of the L.P.T.B. at the same place, a stone 5 feet long, 1 foot 6 inches high and 2 feet wide was discovered. It bore the three lines that conclude the Classicianus inscription; those giving earlier information concerning his career have yet to be discovered, but the recent "find" establishes the fact that these stones are parts of the monument of the procurator of Britain mentioned by Tacitus.

Illustrated facing p. 65.   (*British Museum.*)

---

¹ The restoration of this inscription in the British Museum gives the penultimate word as "infelix." E. B. Birley (*Antiquaries' Journal*, XVI, 208) and also Ian A. Richmond favour, as a second cognomen, "Indiana."

3. SOLDIERS OF THE ROMAN LEGIONS IN BRITAIN

LEGIO II AUGUSTA

Stationed at Caerleon in South Wales, *c.* 74, probably until removed to Richborough, *c.* 293.

VLPI	EMERI	
VS	TVS·LEG	
SILVA	II·AVG	Ulpius Silvanus, veteran of
NVS	VOTVM	the Second Augustan Legion,
	SOLVIT	paid his vow; made at Arausio
. . . .		(Orange in Provence).
FAC	ARAV	
TVS	SIONE	

Whether "made at Arausio" refers to the vow or to the stone has been much discussed. Prof. R. G. Collingwood's note in R.C.H.M. *Rom. Lond.*, p. 170, is as follows: "*Factus* has been taken to mean 'made a veteran,' *i.e.* discharged; but we should perhaps expect *missus* in that sense, and *factus* may mean rather 'initiated' into some grade of the Mithraic community. That it was the sculpture which was made at Orange is not likely."

Sandstone slab, 22 in. × 17 in. On Mithraic monument found (?) in Bond Court, Walbrook, in 1889.

Illustrated facing p. 209.   (*London Museum.*)

D·M	D[is] M[anibus]
VIVIO MARCI	Vivio Marci-
ANO♭ LEG II	ano Leg[ionis] II
AVG IANVARIA	Aug[ustae] Januaria
MARTINA CONIVNX	Martina conjunx
PIENTISSIMA POSV	pientissima posu-
IT·MEMORIAM	it memoriam.

"To the Divine Shades Vivius Marcianus of the Second 'Augustan' Legion; Januaria Martina, his most devoted wife, raised this memorial."

What appears to be a leaf stop between the words MARCIANO and LEG has in the past been mistaken for an abbreviation of *militi*.

Inscription above full-length relief of a Roman soldier. Found in Ludgate Hill at the time of the rebuilding of St Martin's Church by Wren, in 1669.

(*Now in the Ashmolean Museum, Oxford.*)

[Dis Mani] BVS . . . . ER·L[ucii] F[ilius] G[al(eria)]
CELSV[s]·SPEC[ulator] LEG(ionis) [IIÀ]VG(ustae)
AN[to]N(ius) DARDANVS·CV[r(ator)] RVBRIVS
PVDENS . . . . PROBIS·SPEC(ulator) LEG . . . .

"To the Divine Shades . . . Valerius (?) Celsus, of the Galerian tribe, son of Lucius, *speculator* in the Second 'Augustan' Legion; [set up by] Antonius Dardanus, *Curator*, Rubrius Pudens, and . . . . Probus, *speculator* in the same legion, [his heirs] . . . ."

Found in Playhouse Yard, Blackfriars, near Apothecaries' Hall, in 1843.

(*British Museum.*)

LEGIO VI VICTRIX

Stationed at York from about A.D. 122 to an uncertain date, perhaps 410.

D·M	D[is] M[anibus] Fl[avius]
FL·AGRICOLA·MIL·	AGRICOLA MIL[es] LEG
LEG·VI·VICT·V·AN·	[ionis] VI·VICT[ricis] V[ixit]
XLII·D·X·ALBIA·	AN[nos] XLII D[ies] X · AL-
FAVSTINA CONIVGI	BIA FAUSTINA CONJUGI
INCONPARABILI·	INCONPARABILI F[acien-
·F·C·	dum] C[uravit]

"To the Divine Shades Flavius Agricola, soldier of the Sixth Legion, 'Victorious,' lived 42 years and 10 days; Albia Faustina had [this stone] made for her matchless husband."

ROMAN MEMORIAL STONES FOUND IN LONDON.

1. One of the "bolsters" or terminal ornaments on the monument to Classicianus, Procurator of Britain. It can be seen end-on in the illustration facing p. 65 (*British Museum*). 2. Tombstone to Aulus Alfiditus Olussa, aged 70 (see List of Inscriptions in Appendix). Found on Tower Hill (*British Museum*). 3. Part of a tombstone of a private of the XXth Legion (*British Museum*). 4. Part of a roofing tile marked TPFC. 5. Part of a memorial slab to a Roman centurion aged 57. Found in Bishopsgate in 1922 (*London Museum*).

PART OF A TESSELLATED PAVEMENT FOUND AT 37, FENCHURCH STREET IN 1857.
In the panel formed by a guilloche and plain border is a peacock and vase.
(*British Museum.*)

ROMAN WRITING MATERIALS FOUND IN LONDON.

Above are two of the usual type of wooden writing tablets, the recessed surfaces of which were covered with a thin layer of wax for writing upon with a bronze stylus. They were tied together through holes in the rims so that when closed the waxed surfaces were protected. Two bronze styli, of which large numbers have been discovered in London, are on either side of the tablets. The broad end was used for smoothing out words that required to be erased. The earthenware inkpot on the right is of the type most frequently found in London. The other three are of bronze and are not common. Three pens are shown with the inkpots.
(*Guildhall Museum.*)

On slab 15 in. × 12 in. Found in Goodman's Fields (south of Aldgate High Street) in 1787.

(*Society of Antiquaries, Burlington House.*)

LEGIO XX VALERIA VICTRIX

Stationed at Chester from A.D. 71 to an uncertain date in the fourth century.

D[is] M[anibus] IVL[ius] VALENS, MIL[es] LEG[ionis] XX V[aleriae], AN[norum] XL, H[ic] S[itus] E[st]; C[uram] A[gente] FLAVIO ATTIO HER[ede].

"To the Divine Shades Julius Valens, soldier of the Twentieth 'Valerian Victorious' Legion, aged 40; here he lies; set up by his heir Flavius Attius."

The Twentieth Legion became the permanent garrison at Chester soon after A.D. 71 and the memorial probably dates from late in the first century.

It was found in 1776 in Church Lane, Whitechapel; was at the Old Bailey in 1784 and has since been lost. *C.I.L.*, VII. 27. C. Roach Smith, *Coll. Antiq.*, p. 134, pl. 46.

[Sat]VRNI[no mil(iti)] LEG(ionis) XX [V(aleriae) V(ictricis) C·ACI[lius] M . . .

"[To the Divine Shades] . . . Saturninus, a soldier of the Twentieth 'Valerian Victorious' Legion, [set up by] Gaius Acilius M . . . . . ."

14 in. × 12 in. Fragment of a tombstone found at Pentonville in 1842 on the eastern side of Maiden Lane, near Battle Bridge (King's Cross). *C.I.L.*, VII. 26.

Illustrated facing p. 256.   (*British Museum.*)

The number of the Legion is illegible.

[D(is)] M[anibus]
[Sempro]NIO·SEMPRO[niano]
[Cen]TVRIONI·LEG[ionis]
[. . . . Vi]xit ANNOS·LI·
[et fratrib]VS SEMPRONIIS
. . . . . . .ET·SECVNDO
[liber]TI EIVS
[patronis bene me]REN
[tibus pos]V[e]RVNT

"To the Divine Shades Sempronius Sempronianus, Centurion of the . . .th Legion, aged 51, and his brothers Sempronius . . . and Sempronius Secundus; erected by his freemen to their deserving patrons."

Found in 1922 in the southern end of Bishopsgate. Much defaced on the left.

Illustrated facing p. 256.   (*London Museum.*)

---

4. REFERENCES TO TEMPLES

NVM[ini] C[aesaris] . . .   "To the deity of the Emperor and the Province of Britain . . ." or perhaps "set up by the Province of Britain."
PROV[incia] . . . .
BRITA[nnia] . . .

Length "between 2 and 3 ft."—C. Roach Smith, *Illus. of R. Lond.*, p. 30.

Found in Nicholas Lane, Cannon Street, in 1850. It had disappeared from the Guildhall Museum by 1859. *C.I.L.*, VII. 22.

MATR[ibus]   "To the Mother Goddesses;
VICINIA·DE SVO·RES[titvit]   the district restored this shrine at its own expense."

It is possible that Vicinia is here a proper name and, if so, the interpretation would be changed to Vicinia's having restored the shrine at her own expense.

On moulded white marble 15½ in. long by 4½ in. high.

The figures of the three Mother Goddesses seated closely side by side with baskets of fruit on their laps may have occupied a small canopied shrine supported by pillars. Found in Budge Row, near Walbrook, in 1855.

(*Guildhall Museum.*)

LONDINI
AD FANVM ISIDIS

"At London at the Temple of Isis."

Graffito on an earthenware flagon. Found in Southwark. *See illustration facing p. 209.*

(*London Museum.*)

---

5. TO MEN

M
AVR ▲ EVCARPo
FIL ▲ PIENTISSIMO
VIXIT ▲ ANN ▲ XV
M ▲ VI ▲ AVR·EVC
ARPIA · MA ▲ POSSVIT

"To Marcus Aurelius Eucarpus, my most devoted son; aged fifteen years and six months; set up by his mother Aurelia Eucarpia."

Small marble tablet 12 in. × 9 in. Found in Moorgate Street in 1911. *Ephem. Epigr.*, IX. 1371.

(*London Museum.*)

A·ALFID·PoMP
OLVSSA EX TES
TAMENTO·HER
POS·ANNOR·LXX
Na·ATHENI
H   S   EST

"Aulus Alfidius Olussa of the Pomptine tribe; set up by his heir in accordance with his will; aged seventy; born at Athens; he lies here."

In the fifth line the TH in ligature is doubtful. Na(ve) or Na(varchus) are possible alternatives with the name of a ship following. Mommsen's rendering was as given above. Probably dates about the end of the first century.

Found on Tower Hill in 1852. *C.I.L.*, VII. 29.

(British Museum.)

Illustrated facing p. 256.

DIS	DIS MANIB[us] T·LICINI ASCANI;
MANIB	V[ivus] S[ibi] F[ecit]
T·LICINI	"To the Divine Shades Titus Licinius
ASCANI	Ascanius; he made this for himself when
V·S·F	alive."

On a base for a statue found at the Ordnance Office on Tower Hill in 1777.

In *C.I.L.* VII. 32 it is recorded as lost, but in *Ephem. Epigr.*, IX. p. 515, it is given as rediscovered. It seems to have been lost a second time.

MEMORIAE · VALERI · AMAN
DINI · VALERI · SVPERVEN
TOR·ET·MARCELLVS·PATRI·FECER

"In memory of Valerius Amandinus, made by Valerius Superventor and Valerius Marcellus for their father."

Illustrated facing p. 196.

On the side of a stone sarcophagus that seems to have been re-used for a post-Roman burial. Found in 1869 in churchyard north-west of north transept of Westminster Abbey.

(Now in entrance to Chapter House of Westminster Abbey.)

6. TO WOMEN

D · M
GRATA DAGO
BITI FIL AN XL
SOLINVS CON
IVGI KAR F C

D[is] M[anibus]
GRATA DAGOBITI
FIL[ia] AN[norum] XL;
SOLINUS CONJUGI
KAR[issimae] F[aciendum]
C[uravit]

"To the Divine Shades Grata, daughter of Dagobitus, aged 40; erected by Solinus to his dearest wife."

A small slab 12½ in. × 11½ in. Second century. Found in London Wall, opposite Finsbury Circus, in 1837. *C.I.L.*, VII. 31.

(Guildhall Museum.)

[DIS MANIBVS]
. . . . ET·MEMORIΛ[E]
(? T]VLLIAE·NVMIDI[AE]
[PIE]NTISSIME FEMIN[AE]
. . . . IS RELIQVA CAV . . .

"To the Divine Shades and in memory of Tullia Numidia . . . a most devoted woman. . . "

From a rough pencil note made by Prof. Haverfield in 1889-90. The stone was found in Castle Street and placed in the Guildhall Museum. It is now lost. *Ephem. Epigr.* VII. 819, where it is noted as of late date.

D · M
CL ·MARTI
NAE·AN·XIX
ANENCLE
TVS
PROVINC
CONIVGI
PIENTISSIMAE
H · S · E

D[is] M[anibus]
CL[audiae] MARTINAE,
AN[norum] XIX;
ANENCLETUS
PROVINC[ialis]
CONJUGI
PIENTISSIMAE;
H[ic] S[ita] E[st].

"To the Divine Shades Claudia Martina, aged nineteen; set up by Anencletus, slave of the provincial authorities, to his most devoted wife; she lies here."

On one face of a hexagonal column, 3 feet 11 inches high. Found in Ludgate Hill near the London Coffee House, by St Martin's Church, in 1806.

(*Guildhall Museum.*)

. . . .
CARISSIMA[E] . . .
SVA[E]MERITUS EIVS

The name in the first line has become illegible; what follows was rendered by Prof. Collingwood ". . . to his dearest . . . for her deserts." He thought that the first line probably contained a man's name and the word *fil(iae)* daughter.

On a sculptured sarcophagus found at Clapton in 1867. *See illustration facing p.* 192.

(*Guildhall Museum.*)

----

7. ON A MOSAIC PAVEMENT

WUNANI
NIIISTGNATIVS
IMNTESSEL STRAT
SEMDSTD

There is little that can be interpreted from this. The third line appears to contain [pav]IM[e]NT[um] TESSEL [atum] STRAT[um].

An inscription on a tessellated pavement of which all traces are now lost. It was found in 1887 between Pudding Lane and Botolph Lane at a depth of 12 feet. The name Egnatius is associated with the laying of a tessellated pavement. If the last three letters could be taken as S.P.D. they might convey the giving of the pavement at someone's own expense. The materials for this inscription are based on fragments of the pavement from which a sketch was made by Henry Hodge.

8. FRAGMENTARY

DIS   "To the Divine Shades"
MANIB[vs]

Letters about 2 in. high.

(Guildhall Museum.)

M
LIV
TVS
VI·ANL
CA·SERT
··· NNAC

Fragment of a tombstone found in Houndsditch; placed in Guildhall Museum and since lost. *Ephem. Epigr.*, VII. 822.

[D·M]   "To the Divine Shades
AVI[DIV]   Avidius Antiochus, aged
[A]NTIO[CHVS]   seventy years [or more]."
[ANNO]R[VM]LXX

Fragment 12 in. × 8 in. Found in Castle Street Bastion in 1884.

(Guildhall Museum.)

CANDIDI

Stone 1 ft. 11 in. × 5 in. From Houndsditch. *(Lost.)*

IVI   LV on small cake of lead,
. . . .   possibly a seal.
S   Found near Walbrook in
DO   *(Lost.)*   1902.

·P·M·
HELLE

On a fragment of marble. The inscription of at least three lines contains a proper name that might have been Hellenicus.

(*British Museum.*)

IVL
S
D

Fragment found in Castle Street, 18 in. by 18 in.

Ephem. Epigr. VII. 821.

(*Guildhall Museum.*)

TIIRT
IVS = Tertius.

On a bone counter unearthed in 1940 in 1, Lombard Street. Other counters have been found with the single word "PRIMVS."

(*Guildhall Museum.*)

On a miniature representation in bronze of the prow of a ship. In niello-retrograde

AMMILLA AVG FELIX

This perhaps has reference to a victory won by a warship bearing the name Ammilla.

Ephem. Epigr., IX. 1319.

(*British Museum.*)

[Dis]MA[nibus]
PRIM
VIX[it Annos]

"In memory of Prim . . ., aged . . . years."

Purbeck marble 7 in. × 6 in. Found in Cloak Lane in 1846.

(*British Museum.*)

[B]ENEM[ERENTI]
E·FI[LIVS or LIA]
(age)XVI

Fragment of a tombstone 7 in. × 6 in. Found in London Wall. *C.I.L.*, VII. 346.

(*British Museum.*)

SVP

On fragment of marble. Found on Tower Hill, in buttress or bastion of the Wall of London.   (*Lost.*)

9. MAKERS' STAMPS

EX OFFE
HONORINI

"From the workshop of Honorinus."

The second E in the first line has been read as I, also L.

On a silver ingot. Found at the Tower of London in 1777 with coins of Arcadius and Honorius.

Illustrated on p. 103.   (*British Museum.*)

Chi-Rho monogram and
$$\left\{ \begin{array}{l} \text{SYAGЯ} \\ \text{SYAG} \\ \text{SYAGЯI} \end{array} \right\}$$
Various forms of makers' stamps.
(*British Museum.*)

also two stamps with Chi Rho monogram
$$\left\{ \begin{array}{l} \text{SYAƆ} \\ \text{ЯIVS} \end{array} \right\}$$
(*Yorkshire Museum, York.*)

Stamped on six pewter cakes. Found in the Thames at Battersea.

Stamped on roofing tiles:

Complete
$$\left\{ \begin{array}{l} \boxed{\text{PP BR}} \\ \boxed{\text{TP·FC}} \\ \boxed{\text{P·PR·BR}} \end{array} \right.$$

(*British and Guildhall Museums.*)

For an interpretation of these letters see p. 268.

Incomplete
$$\left\{ \begin{array}{l} \text{PBR·LON} \\ \text{P BRRI·LO} \\ \text{P·BR·LON·} \\ \text{PPBR·LON·} \\ \text{P·PR·BR ...} \end{array} \right.$$

Recorded by Roach Smith.
(*Illust. Rom. Lon.*, p. 31.)

Complete   PP·BR·LON   (*In Ransom Collection now*
          PRR^T LON   *dispersed and is in part at*
                         Museum of Archaeology and
                         Ethnology at Cambridge.)

Other forms are RP·BR·LON, PR·BR·LON, P·P·BRI·LON, P.BRI.SAN.

Mommsen suggested that the abbreviations stood for P(ublicani) P(rovinciae) BRI(tanniae) LON(dinienses). Prof. R. G. Collingwood was not at first inclined to accept *publicani* nor *procuratores*, preferring *portitores* = the officers of the *portoria*, a suggestion made by Mr G. H. Stevenson.[1] Later, after the discovery of a stamped tablet, he inclined to *procuratores* (see p. 268).

On a tile in the London Museum is stamped in three lines: [?r]OMVLI . . . [?p]OMP[ei] . . . TCR . . .

---

10. GRAFFITI FOUND IN LONDON

AVSTALIS   "Austalis   (= Augustalis)
DIBVS XIII   is going off by himself every
VAGATVR SIB[I]   day for these 13 days."
COTIDIM

                         The numeral is indistinct, causing a little uncertainty between VIII and XIII.

On a bonding tile. Found in Warwick Lane, Newgate Street.

Illustrated on p. 227.   (*Guildhall Museum.*)

On Samian ware:
                (*Guildhall Museum.*)

(1) ALIIXANDIIR   (7) OPTATVS
(2) ANI RECINI   (8) M PIIT OPTA
(3) L·AE·FESTI   (9) VAR
(4) Q BIIRA   (10) GAI SVM PECVLIARIS
(5) IVL SI . . .   "I belong to Gaius."
(6) MVM

[1] R.C.H.M., *Rom. Lond.*, p. 176.

On Samian ware—*continued:*

A date on an amphora in the British Museum:

M VIIS VINI (=7½ measures of wine) *Ephem. Epigr.* IX. 1350.

V[A]PRILIIS (=V kal. apriles)

(London Museum.)

(11)	AIIL (Aelius)	(15)	MANIAN
(12)	FIILIX	(16)	SIIVII
(13)	T FLAVI MATVNI	(17)	TVLLI
(14)	INAT	(18)	VIA

(19) FELICVLA *C.I.L.* 1338. 8.

(20) AVNIIV^R MARTIIALIS

(21) PIITRON (Petronius)
  C.I.L. 1338 21.

(22) PAVLLVS *C.I.L.* 1338. 20.

(23) [VE]RIICVN[D]V
  C.I.L. 1338. 29.

(24) IVAIA

(25) IX

In 1914 there were found on the site of the old General Post Office barrel staves stamped T.C.PACATI and in 1933 and 1934 staves lining wells in the Bank of England area bore the names CALVISI. L.E.FL., L.E.PL., L.M.F., MLL.

11. ON AN OCULIST'S STAMP OF STONE

Incised on the four edges of a tablet of steatite or soapstone 2 in. square and ⅜ in. thick for impressing on cakes of ointment of four varieties.

(a) C SILVI TETRICI EVODES
  AD ASPRITVDINES

"Caius Silvius Tetricus's scented ointment for granulations."

(b) C SILVI TETRICI PENICILL
  AD IMPET LIPPITVDIN

"Caius Silvius Tetricus's salve (? applied with a swab) for an attack of inflammation (or onset of blepharitis)."

(c) C SILV[I TET]RICI DIAMI
  [SVS] AD D[IATH]ES ET CICAT

"Caius Silvius Tetricus's salve (of a particular kind) for diseases and sores (or scars) in the eyes (or against affections and scars)."

(d)   C SILVI TETRICI BIPROSO
         PVM AD IM . . .
         "Caius Silvius Tetricus's" (the next
         word is unknown, but probably im-
         plies use in two different ways).

Found near London Bridge.   *J.R.S.*, XXII. 1932, 227, 17.
        Antiquaries' Journal, XII. 1932 (with errors in transcription), 437 *f.*
          (*Guildhall Museum.*)

An oculist's inscription on the bottom of a Samian vessel.

"L. Iul. Senis crocod. ad aspr."

"Lucius Julius Senex's ointment for roughness [of the
eyes]."   *See note on p. 272.*   (*British Museum.*)

STAMP ON STATIONERY OF PROVINCIAL PROCURATOR'S OFFICE.

On the back of a wooden writing tablet 6 by 4⅛ in. is a
branded circle 2½ in. in diameter enclosing in circular form the
words DEDERVNT PROC AVG and in the remaining space
BRIT PROV. Professor R. G. Collingwood interpreted this
stamp as "Issued by the imperial procurators of the Province
of Britain." This tablet is therefore an example of the official
stationery of the financial department of the government of
Britain. Collingwood regarded the fact that the tablet bore
no writing on its face that it was not in use when lost and was
therefore an item of the stock of writing materials held by the
central finance office in London. This he regarded as a
confirmation of the P. PR. BR tile stamps (see p. 265) as being
procuratorial and lending support to the suggestion that
London superseded Colchester as the seat of the provincial
government soon after Boudicca's rebellion.

---

12. A SOLEMN CURSE

On a roughly-cut piece of lead, 4½ in. by 3 in.

The writing is incised on both sides of the metal and
there is a hole in the centre suggesting that the curse was
nailed to a wall. The repetition on both sides of the plate
seems to convey the idea of making sure of the continuance
of the curse if the exposed side were defaced.

Outside.	*Inside.*
T[ITVS] · EGNATIVS	T[ITVS] EGNATIVS
TYRANVS · DEFIC[T]VS	TYRANVS DEFICTVS
EST ET	EST ET
P[VBLIVS] CICEREIVS FELIX	P CICEREIVS FELIX
DEFICTVS E[S]T	

"Titus Egnatius Tyranus is hereby solemnly cursed; like-wise Publius Cicereius Felix."

Found in Princes Street.   (*London Museum.*)

The three other Roman curses that have been recorded in Britain were found at Bath, Lydney and Caerleon.

13. BUSINESS MEMORANDA (GRAFFITI)

In cursive script scratched on fragments of wooden tablets normally used in the Roman period for messages written with a stilus on a wax surface. These three graffiti were all found in Lothbury right in the hub of the financial area of modern London.

> *em optimum maximum et per ge*
> *nium imp*[eratoris] *Domitiani c*[a]*esaris aug*[usti] *Ge-*
> *rmanici et per deos patrios s . .*
> *. . . . . et . . . . mer . .*

". . . . by Jupiter Best and Greatest and by the Genius of the Emperor Domitian Caesar Augustus, Conqueror of Germany, and by the Gods of our fathers . . ."

The very great interest of this oath or promise is the date, A.D. 84-96, it gives within the limits of Domitian's reign, thus revealing the style of cursive writing at the period.

> *quam pecuniam petisionis item*
> *scriptis solvere mihi debebit Cres-*
> *cens isve ad quem ea res per-*
> *tinebit . . . . ris primis*
> *. . . . . ss . . . t*

"which money by the terms likewise of the claim shall be paid to me by Crescens or by the person concerned . . ."

This little fragment of a document is evidently part of a deed relating to a debt or a sale or purchase, and it is with little doubt the earliest record of this description that London possesses.

. . . .
. . . . . . *rem vendidisse* . . . .
ex taberna sua . . . .
. . . .*m navem faci-*
endam et permissionem dedisse
. . . . *clavi faciendi*

It is not easy to make a reconstruction of these disjointed groups of words. There can be little doubt, however, that it refers to a sale from a shop and to the granting of permission in some way connected with the building of a ship and the making of a rudder.

(*London Museum.*)

D M
ONESIMO · VIX · AN · XIII
DOMITIVS · ELAINVS · PATER
FILIO B · M

Stated to have been found in Basing Lane in 1852, but there is no authentic record of its discovery. It resembles a number of other small inscriptions brought to England from the Continent in recent times. It is wholly unlike any British work and probably comes from Rome.

(*Guildhall Museum Catalogue*, p. 105.)

The inscription that Archer thought he saw on the back of the altar to Diana now preserved in Goldsmith's Hall has been found to be an error. The altar seems to have never borne any inscription.

---

14. POTTERS' STAMPS ON SAMIAN WARE

For a list of these see: London Museum Catalogues, No. 3, "*London in Roman Times.*" Appendix I, pp. 160-188.

Royal Commission on Historical Monuments, London, Vol. III, "*Roman London.*" Appendix III, p. 179.

"*Illustrations of Roman London,*" C. Roach Smith, pp. 102-108.

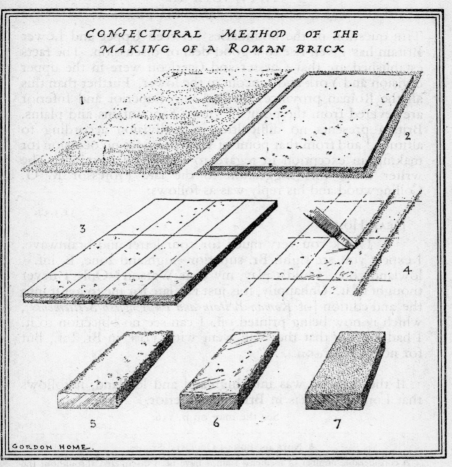

CONJECTURAL METHOD OF THE MAKING OF A ROMAN BRICK

1
2
3
4
5
6
7

GORDON HOME.

The under surface of a Roman brick is always rough, indicating that the wet clay was spread out on a surface of sand (1). It would appear that a layer of clay about 1⅝ inches in thickness was placed upon a flat sanded space (2), where, while still soft, it was exposed to the weather (marks of raindrops have been noticed) and the passage of dogs, cows and human beings. It was then cut up into the sizes required (3 and 4). The knife lifted the clay a little on all four sides and required smoothing off with knife or trowel (5 and 6). No. 7 shows the finished brick turned upside down to show the granular under surface.

It is not suggested that Roman bricks were always made in this manner, but the evidence provided by large numbers that have been examined point to this method having been common in Britain.

APPENDIX III

WAS LONDINIUM IN BRITANNIA INFERIOR?

THE question of the boundaries between Upper and Lower Britain has given rise to a good deal of discussion. The facts established are that Chester and Caerleon were in the upper division and York and Lincoln in the lower. Further than this all the Roman provinces divided into Superior and Inferior are severed from the point of view of mountains and plains. Britain presents no difficulties in a division according to altitude,[1] and from that point of view provides no occasion for making an exception in regard to the island province. The writer made this suggestion to the late Professor R. G. Collingwood and his reply was as follows:

31.3.37.

DEAR HOME,

Thank you very much for your letter and brainwave. I expect you are right: Br. superior = highland zone, B. inf. = lowland zone. Child's play, my dear Watson! Only I never thought of it. Unhappily, it is just too late for me to get it into the 2nd edition [of *Roman Britain and the English Settlements*], which is now being printed off. I can see no objection to it. I had *assumed* that the Wall went with York in Br. Inf., but for no good reason. . . ."

If the division was into highland and lowland, it follows that Londinium was in Britannia Inferior.

[1] See the map on p. 136.

A NOTE ON ROMAN OCULISTS' STAMPS.

A considerable number of medicine stamps have been discovered throughout the Roman Empire, and the curious fact is that they are all concerned with drugs for the cure or relief of diseases of the eye. Those found in London certainly conform to this rule. It would therefore appear that ophthalmic troubles were remarkably widespread in the provinces of the great empire, and that these little stone stamps were peculiar to the oculist's business or had come to be used by doctors solely for eye medicines.

Roman writers, including Celsus, Galen, Aetius and others, make many references to the oculists at Rome and reveal how closely were diseases of the eye studied by the practitioners of that age. Galen alone has left formulae for more than two hundred of the ancient collyria or salves.

In his lengthy essay on *Ancient Roman Medicine Stamps*,[1] Sir James Y. Simpson discusses the many obscure words that appear on the tablets. *Lippitudo* is considered by high medical authority to be catarrhal conjunctivitis and *Penicillum* was the name applied to a fine sponge for introducing soothing washes and for cleansing the eyes.

[1] *Archaeological Essays*, Vol. II, Ed. John Stuart, 1872.

APPENDIX IV

CHRONOLOGY OF BRITAIN AND OF LONDINIUM

PART I., 55 B.C.–A.D. 43.—FROM JULIUS CAESAR'S RAID TO THE ROMAN CONQUEST

PART II., A.D. 43–457.—TO THE LAST DEFINITE MENTION OF LONDINIUM AS A ROMAN CITY.

NOTE.—Emperors whose names are marked * died violent deaths, either in battle or by assassination. For a Roman Emperor, during the period 46 B.C.–A.D. 476, to die a natural death was the exception and not the rule.

PART I.—CÆSAR TO CLAUDIUS

DATE B.C.	EUROPEAN EVENTS.	BRITISH EVENTS.
55 B.C.		Caesar makes reconnaissance raid into Britain.
54		Caesar invades Britain, defeats Cassivellaunus and imposes tribute.
52	Commius, King of Gallic Atrebates, defeated by Caesar	
51	Caesar completes conquest of Gaul. Commius expelled	Commius settles with the British Atrebates and founds a kingdom in Britain.
46	*C. JULIUS CAESAR, 1st Roman Emperor	
44	Murder of Caesar	
		Three Kingdoms—
		(1) Cassivellaunus (Catuvellauni, etc.)
		(2) Commius (Atrebates, Cantii, etc.).
		(3) ? (Trinovantes, etc.).
35 ?		Tasciovanus, King of the Catuvellauni.
34	Octavianus was at this time, according to Dio, considering the question of invading Britain	
31	Defeat and death of Antonius C. Julius Caesar Octavianus-AUGUSTUS, 2nd Roman Emperor	
27-6		Augustus in Gaul for British expedition.
		Tasciovanus and other kings probably enter into direct relation with Rome.
		Commutation of tribute into customs duties on British overseas trade.
20 ?		Tasciovanus conquers the sons of Commius.
15		About this time Dubnovellaunus was possibly the last independent King of the Trinovantes.
10 c.		Tasciovanus introduces coinage in three metals on Roman model.
5		Cunobelinus ("Cymbeline"), son of Tasciovanus, King of Southern
5 B.C.-	B.C.	Britain.

PART I.—CÆSAR TO CLAUDIUS—*Continued.*

DATE A.D.	EUROPEAN EVENTS.	BRITISH EVENTS.
A.D. 14	A.D.	Rapid increase in wealth and prosperity. Commerce, and especially valuable exports, noted by Strabo.
A.D. 14	TIBERIUS (I.) Claudius Nero Caesar	Britons render assistance to wrecked Roman warships.
A.D. 21	Revolt of Florus and Sacrovir in Gaul	
A.D. 37	Death of Tiberius	
	* GAIUS Caesar "CALIGULA"	
A.D. 40	Caligula, receiving Adminius, announces "submission" of Britain	Family troubles in court of Cunobelinus. His son Adminius rebels and flees to Rome.
A.D. 41	* Tiberius CLAUDIUS I Nero Drusus Germanicus Caesar	? Death of Cunobelinus. Caratacus and Togodubnus, Kings of South Britain.
A.D. 43	Claudius determines to subjugate Britain	

PART II.—ROMAN PERIOD, A.D. 43-457

DATE A.D.	ROMAN EMPERORS.	LEGATES OR GOVERNORS OF BRITAIN.	EVENTS.
43	Tiberius CLAUDIUS I Nero Drusus Germanicus Caesar	Aulus Plautius	Invasion of Britain and conquest of South-East. *Battle at the bridge of Londinium.* Death of King Togodubnus.
47		Publius Ostorius Scapula	c. 48. Uriconium founded as base of XIVth and XXth legions.
49			Defeat of Brigantes.
50			Defeat and capture of King Caratacus.
51-2		Aulus Didius Gallus	
54	* L. Domitius Ahenobarbus Claudius Drusus NERO		
58		Dec. Veranius Nepos	*Growing commercial importance of Londinium.*
59		C. Suetonius Paulinus [Catus Decianus Imperial Procurator]	
60			Decianus Catus flees to Gaul during Boudicca's revolt. Great British rising under Boudicca. *Destruction of Camulodunum, Verulamium, and Londinium.* Defeat and death of Boudicca. Polycletus sent to enquire into the state of Britain.
		[Julius Classicianus, Imperial Procurator] His monument, found in a bastion of the Roman wall of London, is now in the British Museum	

DATE A.D.	ROMAN EMPERORS.	LEGATES OR GOVERNORS OF BRITAIN.	EVENTS.
66	(NERO)	[? Augustanus, Imperial Procurator, may have succeeded Classicianus during the decade of the Boudiccan rebellion]	
61		P. Petronius Turpilianus	*Restoration of Londinium. Period of peaceful economy and organisation.*
63		M. Trebellius Maximus	
68 *	Serv. Sulpicius GALBA		
69 *	M. Salvius OTHO	M. Vettius Bolanus	
*	Aulus VITELLIUS		
	Titus Flavius VESPASIANUS		70 c., Legio XIV recalled from Britain.
71		Q. Petillius Cerealis	Cerealis brings to Britain Legio II Adjutrix and attacks Brigantes.
74		Sextus Julius Frontinus	
74-7			Frontinus conquers Wales.
77 or 78		Gnaeus Julius AGRICOLA	Several strong forts built.
78			Subjection of Brigantes.
79	TITUS Flavius Vespasianus II.		
79-84			Agricola's campaigns in North. Rapid Romanisation of Southern Britain.
81 *	Titus Flavius DOMITIANUS		
84-85		L. (?) Sallustius Lucullus. (Executed by Domitian for allowing lances of a new pattern to be called Lucullean.)	Domitianus reduces garrison of Britain from 4 Legions to 3. Revolt of Brigantes under King Arviragus.
87		Cornelius Fuscus	
90 c.		... Metilius Nepos	
95 c.		C. Salvius Bassus (?)	
96	M. Cocceius NERVA		
98	M. Ulpius Nerva TRAJANUS I.	T. Avidius Quietus (Friend of the Younger Pliny.)	
101 c.- 103		L. Neratius Marcellus, brother of the jurist Neratius Priscus. T. Pomponius Mammilianus Rufus Antistianus	
117	P. Aeilus Trajanus HADRIANUS	Funisulanus Vettonianus (between 103 and 109).	
118		Q. Pompeius Falco	
119			Destruction of Legio IX by Brigantes. Replaced by Legio VI, "Victrix."
120-1		? Statue of Hadrian erected in London	Emperor Hadrian in Britain.

PART II.—ROMAN PERIOD, A.D. 43–457—*Continued.*

DATE A.D.	ROMAN EMPERORS.	LEGATES OR GOVERNORS OF BRITAIN.	EVENTS.
122 c. 124 125	(HADRIAN)	A. Platorius Nepos	Building of Wall of Hadrian.
120- 130			*A great part of Londinium destroyed by fire. J.R.S., vol. XXVI, pt. 2, p. 255.*
126 130		M. Appius Bradua Sextus Julius Severus	Building of first town-wall of London c. 100-130.
117- 138 c.		... Licinius Priscus	
135		P. Mummius Sisenna (*Clas. Rev.* Feb., 1928, XLII., pp. 11-14).	
138	Titus Aurelius ANTONINUS I. "Pius"		
139		Q. Lollius Urbicus. *Inscription discovered at Corstopitum (Corbridge). J.R.S., vol. XXVI, pt. 2, p. 264.*	Building of Turf Wall between Clyde and Forth.
146 158 160 161	M. Aurelius ANTONINUS II. (M. Annius Verus) L. Aelius Verus ANTONINUS III.	Cn. Papirius Aelianus Cn. Julius Verus M. Statius Priscus Licinius Italicus	Last revolt of Brigantes. Final subjection of Brigantes.
162		Sextus Calpurnius Agricola (161-162)	War on Northern Frontier.
165	GREAT PLAGUE IN VARIOUS PARTS OF ROMAN EMPIRE.		
167		L. Ulpius Marcellus (1st Term)	
170 175		C. Julius... ... Calvius Rufus Antistius Adventus	
180 * 184 c.	L. Aurelius COMMODUS ANTONINUS IV.	L. Ulpius Marcellus (2nd Term) P. Helvius Pertinax	Caledonians invade Britain. Defeated by Marcellus. Abandonment of Turf Wall of Pius.
186 c. 190 c. 192 * 193 *	P. Helvius PERTINAX C. Didius JULIANUS I. L. Septimius SEVERUS I.	Dec. Clodius Albinus	Conclusion of war. Britain proclaims Albinus Augustus. Severus acknowledges him as Caesar.
197		[Albinus Caesar] L. Virius Lupus	Severus defeats and kills Albinus. Britain divided into two provinces=Upper and Lower. *Londinium probably in Lower Britain.* Lupus buys off Caledonian invasion.
200 c.		(Deputy ?) M. Antius Crescens Calpurnianus	

PART II.—ROMAN PERIOD, A.D. 43–457—*Continued.*

DATE A.D.	ROMAN EMPERORS.	LEGATES OR GOVERNORS OF BRITAIN.	EVENTS.
204-8c.	(SEVERUS I)	. . . Pollenius Auspex	
205		L. Alfenius Senecio	
206 c.			Caledonians invade Britain and break Wall of Hadrian.
208			Senecio sends for help.
209			Arrival of Severus and his sons. Antoninus accompanies him to North. *Geta left to administer South Britain, presumably at Londinium.*
211 *	M. Aurelius Bassianus ANTONINUS V. "CARACALLUS"	. . . Marcus (?) Marcellus	Caracallus abandons territory north of Wall of Hadrian and outposts.
*	P. Septimius Geta ANTONINUS VI.		
213		M. Julius Martius	
216		. . . dianus	
217 *	M. Opelius MACRINUS		
218 *	L. Opelius Diadumenianus ANTONINUS VII.	. . . Modius Julius	
*	M. Aurelius ANTONINUS VIII. "Elagabalus"		
219		Tib. Claudius Paullinus	
221		Marius Valerianus	
222 *	M. Aurelius SEVERUS II. Alexander		
	L. Julius Aurelius Uranius ANTONINUS IX.		
225		Claudius Xenophon	
227		. . . Maximus	
		. . . Claudius Apellinus (?)	
230		Valerius Crescens Fulvianus	
235 *	Gaius Julius Valerius MAXIMINUS I.		
237		. . . ccianus	
238 *	M. Clodius MAXIMUS I. Pupienus	Nonius Philippus	
*	Dec. Junius BALBINUS		
*	M. Antonius GORDIANUS I.		
*	M. Antonius GORDIANUS II.		
*	M. Antonius GORDIANUS III.		
239 c.		Egnatius Lucilianus	
241 c.		Maecilius Fuscus	
242		Nonius Philippus	
244 *	M. Julius PHILIPPUS I.	?? Tib. Claudius Quintianus	
*	M. Julius PHILIPPUS II.	?? M. Didius Provincialis	

PART II.—ROMAN PERIOD, A.D. 43–457—*Continued.*

DATE A.D.	ROMAN EMPERORS.	LEGATES OR GOVERNORS OF BRITAIN.	EVENTS.
249 *	C. Messius Quintus DECIUS TRAJANUS II.		
250	HERENNIUS ETRUS-CUS		? *Martyrdom of Augulus, Bishop of Londinium.* (6th Century Martyrologia of Pseudo-Hieronymus.)
250-1			Persecution of Decius. Martyrdom of St Alban may have occurred then.
251 *	HOSTILIANUS		
*	C. Vibius Trebonianus GALLUS I.		
253	AEMILIANUS P. Licinius VALERIANUS I.	Titus Flavius Postumius Varus (before 271)	Between 253 and 268 occurred the destruction of the chief potteries in East and Central Gaul, whence Terra Sigillata or Samian ware had been imported into Britain in great quantities.
*	P. Licinius Egnatius GALLIENUS (SALONINUS)	Cornelius Rufilianus	
255	"The Thirty Tyrants"—local emperors in various parts of Empire. They are not to be regarded generally as usurpers, much less tyrants in a discreditable sense. Only those who exercised authority in the West are here noted.		
257-60		Octavius Sabinus (? between 259 and 268)	Persecution of Valerian in which martyrdom of St Alban may have occurred.

GREAT PLAGUE IN ROMAN EMPIRE.

258	M. Cassianius Latinius POSTUMUS (Gaul)		Recognised in Britain.
259 c.		T. (?) Desticius Juba	Probably the last Legatus Augusti pro-Praetore.
265	M. Piavonius VICTORINUS LAELIANUS ⎫ Gaul, Rhine, Britain and Spain		Victorinus coins found in Britain. Laelianus coins found in Britain.
268	MARIUS VICTORIA TETRICUS ⎬ C. Pius Esuvius ⎭		Marius coins found in Britain. Tetricus coins found in Britain.
	M. Aurelius CLAUDIUS II., "Gothicus" M. Aurelius Claudius QUINTILLUS		
270 *	L. Domitius Valerius AURELIANUS		

DATE A.D.	ROMAN EMPERORS.	LEGATES OR GOVERNORS OF BRITAIN.	EVENTS.
275 * *	M. Claudius TACITUS M. Annius FLORIANUS		
276 *	M. Aurelius Valerius PROBUS		
277	Bonosus (son of British schoolmaster) and **Proculus** (Gaul), usurpers on Rhine defeated by Probus	"The Nameless Usurper"	The Nameless Usurper killed by general of Probus. Probus settles Vandal and Burgundian prisoners of war in Britain.
282	M. Aurelius CARUS	Carinus (*Hist. Aug. Scrip.*, p. 372)	SAXONS TROUBLE BRITISH COASTS.
283 * *	M . A u r e l i u s NUMERIANUS M. Aurelius CARINUS		Carinus assumes title of *Britannicus Maximus*, presumably for victory over Saxons.
284 *	C. Aurelius Valerius DIOCLETIANUS "Jovius"		
285 *	M. Aurelius Valerius MAXIMIANUS" Herculeus" (colleague)		*Carausius Maus(onius)* appointed *Comes Litoris Saxonici* (Admiral of Britain).
286		*M. Aurelius Valerius CARAUSIUS Augustus	Carausius defeats Maximianus.
288			Carausius recognised as Augustus of Britain by Diocletianus and Maximianus *Mint established at Londinium*, also at Camulodunum, etc.
292	Flavius Valerius CONSTANTIUS I. "C h l o r u s," Caesar (Junior Emperor) of the West C. GALERIUS MAXIMIANUS II., Caesar of the East		
293 296		*ALLECTUS	Allectus murders Carausius. London mint ceased to strike gold and silver with the exception of the issues of Magnus Maximus (383-388). Defeat and death of Allectus. *Londinium entered by routed army and relieved by Constantius.*
303			? *Bastions added to town-wall of Londinium.* Persecution of Christians. Martyrdom of St Albanus may have occurred, but

PART II.—ROMAN PERIOD, A.D. 43–457—*Continued.*

DATE A.D.	ROMAN EMPERORS.	LEGATES OR GOVERNORS OF BRITAIN.	EVENTS.
			more likely in either the persecutions of Decius or Valerianus.
305	Constantius succeeds Maximianus Galerius succeeds Diocletian		
306	**Flavius Valerius CONSTANTINUS I.,** Caesar of the Gauls		Picts invade the North. Defeated by Constantius. Death of Constantius at Eboracum (York).
*	M. Aurelius Valerius **MAXENTIUS** Caesar of Italy and Africa		
307 *	**Flavius Valerius SEVERUS III.**		Constantine gains victories over Picts and Irish, and apparently annexes territory in the north.
*	C. Galerius Valerius **MAXIMINUS DAIA** Caesar of the East		
*	Flavius Galerius Valerius Licinianus **LICINIUS** Augustus of Illyricum		
311		? Octavius Sabinus	Death of Galerius.
312	Constantinus I., Emperor of the West		Defeat of Maxentius by Constantine.
314			Synod of Arelate. *Restitutus, Bishop of Londinium, present with Eborius, Bishop of York, and Adelfius, Bishop of Lincoln.*
323	**CONSTANTINUS I., (THE GREAT)** sole Emperor		Defeat and death of Licinius.
330			Consecration of Constantinople. *Mint at Londinium closed about this time. Londinium renamed Augusta between 337 and 368.*
337 *	**Flavius Julius CONSTANTINUS II.** (West) **Flavius Julius CONSTANS I.** (West)	Pacatianus vicarius in 13th year of Constantinus I (the Great) (*Theodosian Code*)	337. Death of Constantinus I. the Great.
*	**Flavius Julius CONSTANTINUS II.** (East)		
340 *c.*			Death of Constantinus II.
342-343		Gratianus	BRITAIN INVADED BY IRISH (?), WHO ARE DEFEATED BY CONSTANS I. IN A MID-WINTER EXPEDITION.
345			British bishops present at the Council of Sardica.

DATE A.D.	ROMAN EMPERORS.	LEGATES OR GOVERNORS OF BRITAIN.	EVENTS.
			The martyrdom wrongly ascribed to St Jerome makes reference to Augulus, Bishop of London, presumably in the fourth century.
350	* MAGNENTIUS (Briton)		Magnentius kills Constans I.
	* DECENTIUS (Brother) Usurpers		
	* VETRANIO		
	* NEPOTIANUS		
353	CONSTANTIUS II., sole Emperor	Martinus	Constantius II. defeats usurpers. Death of Magnentius. Political inquisition in Britain conducted by Paulus "Catena." Suicide of Martinus.
355	* Flavius Claudius JULIANUS IV.,Caesar of West	Alypius	
359			At least three British bishops at the Council of Ariminum.
360			PICTS AND IRISH THREATEN BRITAIN. *Julianus sends Magister Equitum Lupicinus to Londinium Augusta.*
361	JULIANUS IV., sole Emperor		
362			Drought in Britain.
363	Flavius JOVIANUS		Death of Julianus in Mesopotamia.
364	Flavius VALENTINIANUS I. (West)		PICTS, IRISH, "SAXONS," ATECOTTI AND FRANKS THREATEN BRITAIN.
	* Flavius VALENS (East)		
368			COLLAPSE OF DEFENCE. FULLOFAUDES, *Dux Britanniarum,* AND NECTARIDUS, *Comes Litoris Saxonici,* DEFEATED AND PROVINCE OVERRUN.
		Count Theodosius Civilis, Civil Governor	Valentinianus despatches as specialGovernor-General the *Comes* Theodosius the Elder. *Londinium besieged, but relieved by Theodosius.* Valentinus (a native of Pannonia living in Britain) plans rebellion; his plot discovered and he is executed by order of Theodosius.

PART II.—ROMAN PERIOD, A.D. 43-457—*Continued.*

DATE A.D.	ROMAN EMPERORS.	LEGATES OR GOVERNORS OF BRITAIN.	EVENTS.
369			THEODOSIUS THE ELDER DEFEATS INVADERS, reorganises province and probably establishes definite protectorate over region north of Hadrian's Wall (Valentia ?).
374			Drought in Britain.
375 *	Flavius GRATIANUS (West)		
*	Flavius VALENTINIANUS II. (West)		Soon after 376 Theodosius the Elder put to death by order of Valens.
378	Flavius THEODOSIUS I. (East) [son of Theodosius the Elder]		Defeat and death of Valens at Battle of Adrianople.
380		Magnus Clemens Maximus, Count of Britain (?)	
383 *	Magnus Clemens MAXIMUS III. (West)		Defeat and death of Gratianus.
*	Flavius VICTOR (son)		*Londinium Mint reopened 383-387.*
			Maximus defeats Picts.
388			Theodosius I. defeats Maximus at Aquileia and he is beheaded.
			The mint at Londinium, probably working down to this date for gold and silver. There is no evidence that it was ever reopened.
390 c.			PICTS, IRISH, ETC., RENEW ATTACKS UPON BRITAIN. (Army probably weakened by withdrawals to civil wars.)
392 *	Flavius EUGENIUS(West)		Eugenius kills Valentinianus II.
			IRISH OVERRUN WALES.
			Flavius Stilicho, *Magister Militum* of the West.
394	THEODOSIUS I., Emperor of East and West	Chrysanthus, son of Marcianus — Vicarius of Britain. [He was afterwards Bishop of the Church of Novantians at Constantinople. — *Socrates (Eusebius)*, Bk. VII., ch. xii.]	Theodosius I. kills Eugenius.
395	Flavius ARCADIUS (East)		
	Flavius HONORIUS (West)		
397-8			REORGANISATION OF BRITISH DEFENCES BY STILICHO.

PART II.—ROMAN PERIOD, A.D. 43–457—*Continued.*

DATE A.D.	ROMAN EMPERORS.	LEGATES OR GOVERNORS OF BRITAIN.	EVENTS.
401			Italy threatened by Alaric the Visigoth. Legio XX. (?) leaves Britain for defence of Italy.
402-3			Defeat of Alaric.
405			Stilicho annihilates fresh horde of Teutonic invaders of Italy.
406			Alans, Sueves, Vandals, Alemanni and Burgundians overrun Gaul.
407			Britons rise in revolt against Honorius and Stilicho on account of danger of Gaul.
		Marcus, Emperor Gratianus, Emperor Constantinus, Emperor	
*	Flavius Claudius CONSTANTINUS III. (Britain and Gaul)		Constantinus goes to aid of Gaul and withdraws troops from Britain.
408	Flavius THEODOSIUS II. (East)		Death of Arcadius.
409			SAXONS INVADE BRITAIN.
410	Local usurpers in Gaul		BRITONS disown Constantine III., raise fresh forces, and DEFEAT INVADERS. ACTION SANCTIONED BY HONORIUS. ALARIC SACKS ROME. PROBABLE DATE OF THE EVACUATION OF BRITAIN BY CONSIDERABLE PART OF ROMAN GARRISON.
411			Constantine III. overthrown by Count Constantius.
415 ?			RENEWED BARBARIAN ATTACKS ON BRITAIN.
417			Constantius sends back troops to Britain (according to Gildas, a legion) and invaders are defeated.
420 c.			Fastidius, Bishop of London (*Gennadius of Marseilles.* 490 *Catal. Script. Eccles.*).
421	Flavius CONSTANTIUS III. (West with Honorius)		
422			Death of Constantius III.
423 *	JOHANNES I. (West)		Death of Honorius and usurpation of throne by Johannes the Primicerius.
424			Johannes threatened by Eastern Emperor. Troops possibly called from Britain for his defence.

About this time last edition of *Notitia Dignitatum.* Britain a diocese with five provinces. *Treasury at Londinium.*

PART II.—ROMAN PERIOD, A.D. 43–457—*Continued.*

DATE A.D.	ROMAN EMPERORS.	LEGATES OR GOVERNORS OF BRITAIN.	EVENTS.
425 *	Flavius Placidus VALENTINIANUS III. (West)		RENEWED BARBARIAN ATTACKS ON BRITAIN. Revolt in Gaul.
426-7			Revolt in Gaul suppressed by Aetius.
428			Aetius defeats Franks in Northern Gaul. Reinforcements sent to Britain.
429			DEFEAT OF INVADERS. St Germanus in Britain. He visits Verulam, probably London also. The "Alleluia" Victory. Vandals invade Africa.
434			English invade Ireland. Britain probably too well defended.
439			Drought in Britain.
440			Vandals attack Sicily. Troops withdrawn from Britain to defend Italy.
442			ENGLISH, ETC., INVADE BRITAIN.
445 c.			Famine in Britain.
446			Romano-Britons appeal for aid without result. ROMANO-BRITONS RALLY AND DEFEAT INVADERS.
447		Elafius, Last Vicarius?	St Germanus again in Britain. Rise of Vortigern.
450	Flavius MARCIANUS (East)		
451			Attila invades Gaul and is repulsed by Aetius. Britons enlist English and Jutish mercenaries under Hengist and Horsa.
454 ?			PLAGUE RAVAGES BRITAIN.
455 *	Petronius MAXIMUS V. (West)		VANDALS SACK ROME.
? *	M. Maecilius AVITUS (West)		English mercenaries revolt and invade Kent. English defeated by Vortimer, son of Vortigern. Hengist entraps and massacres British notabilities.
457	Flavius LEO I. (East)		Britons defeated at the river Cray in Kent. *Remains of army take refuge in Londinium.*
*	Flavius Julius Velerius MAJORIANUS (West)	Augulus, Bishop of London. (Is mentioned in a martyrology not later than A.D. 630 on a fifth-century foundation.)	*Last glimpse of Londinium as a Romano-British city.* *No further mention until about* A.D. 600.

BIBLIOGRAPHY

Classical Sources.

Caesar. *The Gallic War*. Trans. H. J. Edwards, C.B. Loeb Series or text with notes by T. Rice Holmes. 1914.

Tacitus, *c*. A.D. 55-120. *de Vita Agricolae*. Edited by Furneaux, rev. by J. G. C. Anderson, with contributions by F. Haverfield. 1922. *Annals*, ed. Furneaux and others. Vol. ii. 1907.

Suetonius. *de Vita Caesarum*. Eng. trans. J. C. Rolfe, Ph.D. Loeb Series.

Ptolemy the Geographer, *c*. A.D. 100-151.

Cassius Dio, *c*. A.D. 150-235. *Historia Romana*. On basis of the version of Herbert Baldwin Porter, Ph.D., English trans. by Ernest Cary, Ph.D. Loeb Series.

Strabo, the Geography of. English trans. Horace Leonard Jones, A.M., Ph.D. 1917. Loeb Series.

Eumenius, *c*. A.D. 260-311. Panegyric to Constantius Chlorus.

The Council of Arles.

Ammianus Marcellinus, *c*. A.D. 325-390. *Historiae*.

Zosimus. *Historia Nova*. Ed. Mendelssohn. 1887.

The Notitia Dignitatum.

St Jerome. Not later than A.D. 630 on a fifth-century foundation.

Stephen of Byzantium. Early sixth century (probably).

The Antonine Itinerary. Possibly early third century. Seven of the routes in Britain begin or end with Londinium.

Anonymous Ravennas, or the Ravenna Geographer. Seventh century, but built on earlier sources.

Corpus Inscriptionum Latinarum, Vol. VII. 1873. Edited by E. Hubner. Also Supplements, edited by Hubner in Vols. III and IV of the periodical *Ephemeris Epigraphica*. Further supplements of a more scholarly character by Professor F. Haverfield appeared in Vols. VII and IX. This brought the knowledge of Romano-British epigraphy down to 1913, when there followed a gap of eight years. Since 1921 there have been published annually in the *Journal of Roman Studies* full reports on newly discovered as well as re-deciphered inscriptions. A new *corpus* of Romano-British inscriptions was prepared by the late Professor Collingwood; it will be completed and published when circumstances permit.

Post-Classical Sources.

John Stow. There are slight references to Roman sites in London in his works. *Survey of London*, 1598. Best modern edition. C. L. Kingsford. 1908.

William Camden. *Britannia*, 1586.

Dr John Woodward. *An Account of Some Roman Urns* . . . 1713.

Sir William Dugdale. *History of Imbanking and Drayning*. 1662.

John Stype. Enlarged edition of Stow's *Survey*. 1720.

William Stukeley. *Itinerarium Curiosum*. 1724.

William Maitland. *History of London*. 1739.

David Hughson. *London and its Neighbourhood*. 1805.

Thomas Allen. *History and Antiquities of London, Westminster and Southwark*. 1827.

James P. Malcolm. *Londinium Redivivum.* 1802-7.

Charles Knight. *London.* 1841-4.

Alfred John Kempe, 1785(?)-1846. Contributions to *Archaeologia* and the *Gentleman's Magazine* from 1816. Inspired Charles Roach Smith to active interest in the archaeology of Roman London.

Charles Roach Smith, F.S.A., 1807-1890, who may be called the pioneer of the study of the archaeology of Roman London. He devoted all his spare time from his work as a wholesale chemist to the watching of excavations in the city and to the exploration of Roman sites in England and France. His collection of Roman objects is now in the British Museum. *Illustrations of Roman London,* 1859, *Collectanea Antiqua.* 7 vols. 1848.

Sir William Tite. *A Descriptive Catalogue of the Antiquities found in the Excavations at the New Royal Exchange.* 1848.

General Pitt-Rivers in the *Anthropological Review,* 1867, recorded the excavation of the pile structures of the Walbrook.

J. E. Price. *The Roman Tessellated Pavement found in Bucklersbury.* 1870. *A Bastion of London Wall.* 1880.

Dr Philip Norman and Francis W. Reader, articles in *Archaeologia* and *Journal of the Royal Archaeological Institute,* particularly on the town-wall of London.

Frank Lambert. Papers contributed to *Archaeologia* when he was at the Guildhall Museum.

Victoria County History of London. Vol. I. The chapter on the Roman period of the City contributed by Reginald A. Smith, F. W. Reader and H. B. Walters. 1908.

Professor F. Haverfield. *The Romanisation of Roman Britain* and various articles.

Professor W. R. Lethaby. *Londinium: Architecture and the Crafts.* 1923.

William Page. *London: Its Origin and Early Development.* 1923.

Royal Commission on Historical Monuments. London. Vol. III. *Roman London.* 1928.

Professor R. G. Collingwood. *The Archaeology of Roman Britain.* 1930.

Professor R. G. Collingwood and J. N. L. Myres. *Roman Britain and the English Settlements.* 1936.

Journal of Roman Studies. The annual reports under heading "Roman Britain in 19..." by Professor R. G. Collingwood and Miss M. V. Taylor (now anonymous). Contributions by various writers.

London Museum Guide, 1930. *Roman London,* with introduction by Dr R. E. Mortimer Wheeler.

Catalogue of the Collection of London Antiquities in the Guildhall Museum.

F. Cottrill. *London Wall through Eighteen Centuries.* Chapter II. The Roman Wall of London.

Sir Charles Oman, *England before the Norman Conquest.*

Thomas Morgan, *Romano-British Mosaic Pavements.* 1886. Pp. 155-198.

T. Rice Holmes. *Ancient Britain.*

MUSEUMS AND PRIVATE COLLECTIONS IN WHICH ROMAN OBJECTS FOUND IN LONDON ARE PRESERVED

<u>London.</u>

Guildhall Museum, City of London, E.C.

London Museum, Lancaster House, St James's, S.W.1.

British Museum, Bloomsbury, W.C.

Bethnal Green Museum, Bethnal Green, E.

Goldsmiths' Hall, Foster Lane, E.C.

Westminster Abbey, entrance to Chapter House.

St Bartholomew's Hospital, Smithfield, E.C.

St Saviour's, Southwark. (Pottery in glass table case in west end of nave.)

Phoenix Assurance Company's offices in King William Street, E.C. (Pottery in glazed wall case.)

Guardian Assurance Company's offices in King William Street, E.C.

Overseas Bank, Gracechurch Street, E.C.

Atlas Assurance Co. Ltd., 92, Cheapside, E.C.

St. Paul's Cathedral. In the library.

Society of Antiquaries, Burlington House, Piccadilly, W. (Tombstone.)

<u>Cambridge.</u> Museum of Archaeology and Ethnology.

<u>Oxford.</u> Ashmolean Museum. (Inscribed relief of a Roman soldier; see *infra*, pp. 255-256.)

<u>Caerleon Museum.</u> Near Newport, Mon. (Bronze figure.)

<u>York.</u> The Yorkshire Museum. (Pewter cakes; see p. 265.)

WHERE THE TOWN-WALL OF ROMAN LONDON CAN BE SEEN

1. Nos. 15 and 16, America Square. A short length of the wall part of 65 ft. found in 1908.
2. Adjoining Cripplegate Church. A long length of the wall, an angle bastion (No. 12) and two hollow ones of the regular type (Nos. 13 and 14).
3. General Post Office Yard in Giltspur Street. A bastion (No. 19) at the angle north of Newgate.
4. Central Criminal Court. A small part of the wall.
5. Near Trinity Square, Tower Hill. In Barber's Bonded Warehouse. A considerable length of the wall visible on its interior face up to the full height in the Middle Ages with the parapet walk.

ABBREVIATIONS

Amm. Marc. Ammianus Marcellinus.
C.I.L. Corpus Inscriptionum Latinarum.
Ephem. Epigr. Ephemeris Epigraphica.
J.R.S. Journal of Roman Studies.
Lond. Mus. Cat. London Museum Catalogue.
R.C.H.M. Royal Commission on Historical Monuments.

INDEX

DATE DUE
